*Advance Legal Industry Praise for*

# THE INJURY CASE PLAYBOOK

A good playbook should be accessible and easy to understand. Jim lays out the basics so the new personal injury lawyer will have a foundation to handle his or her first PI case. I wish I had all this information in one place when I started out.

-Michael Neff, Author of *Premises Liability: A Guide to Success* and *Advanced Premises Liability: A Guide through Trial.*

Jim has made an important contribution to help aspiring personal injury lawyers develop their craft. I'm grateful for his willingness to share lessons and practices, to give the next generation of budding trial lawyers a firm footing to start their own journeys. People are bombarded daily by flashy nonsense about personal injury law on the web, TV, and billboards. In contrast, it's encouraging to read *The Injury Case Playbook,* as Jim freely shares the drive and skills that really make a good plaintiff lawyer.

-Alan Hamilton, Founder of Shiver & Hamilton, LLC

*The Injury Case Playbook* shows you the basics of each type of case, what to look for, what to avoid, and each step along the way that will guide you from the beginning of a case to the end. This book will drastically shorten the learning curve for those that want to know how to approach injury cases. It is the perfect primer for anyone who is thinking of following Jim's footsteps to start taking on injury cases or for the non-attorney wanting to understand the anatomy of an injury or wrongful death case.

-Michael Goldberg, Founder of Fried Goldberg, L.L.C and Author of *Understanding Motor Carrier Claims , 5th Edition*

As a divorce and family law attorney inexperienced in personal injury law, this book answers the question "where do I start?" If you're looking to break into personal injury law, this book is a must read: Jim gives a roadmap of injury law that would take years for an attorney to learn on his or her own.

-Aaron Thomas, Founder of Aaron Thomas Law and *Prenups.com*

# THE INJURY
## CASE PLAYBOOK

Elsie,

Getting a good injury case signed up can uncomfortably feel like winning the lottery. You meet wonderful people in a terrible situation after 1 second has changed their life. With the right case + the right defendant(s), you can change that family's outlook for generations to come.

I hope you try lawyering again for some injured folks who need you. This will get you started.

...And thank you for always being a resource for whatever!!

# THE INJURY CASE PLAYBOOK

## A Start to Finish Guide to Winning Your Injury Case

JAMES L. PAISLEY

with Alex Martinez

BOOKLOGIX®
Alpharetta, GA



ISBN: 978-1-6653-0253-1 – Paperback
eISBN: 978-1-6653-0254-8 – eBook



Printed in the United States of America 0 9 2 1 2 1

∞This paper meets the requirements of ANSI/NISO Z39.48-1992 (Permanence of Paper)

# TABLE OF CONTENTS

# FOREWORD BY MICHAEL GOLDBERG

When I first met Jim Paisley over 10 years ago, he was a successful criminal defense lawyer who was considering giving up his criminal practice to start a personal injury practice. Although he loved it, he was burned out on representing criminal clients and the grind of the daily emotions that go into those cases. But he had no experience with representing victims of accidents for personal injury claims. The thing I remember about Jim was that he knew he did not know all the answers but was smart enough to know what questions to ask, who to ask, and had the wisdom to really listen to the responses. I remember encouraging him to have a plan, put it into writing and follow it, and he could not help but be successful in his new endeavor.

Over the years, I have checked in with Jim to see how he was progressing, and we have even worked serious cases together. This book details some of his bumps and missteps along the way. It wasn't always easy. But steadily he built a successful personal injury practice, and before long, he found himself as one of the top personal injury lawyers in the state of Georgia.

Given Jim's success, it didn't surprise me when I learned that Jim had decided to write a book outlining how he handles the intricacies of each personal injury case. *The Injury Case Playbook* contains all the practical knowledge from his years of practice and from being in the trenches teaching himself the right way to practice law, not only as a profession but also as a business. Jim knows how important the details are in each stage of the case. His book shows you the basics of each type of case, what to look for, what to avoid, and each step along the way that will guide you from the beginning of a case to the end. This book will drastically shorten the learning curve for those that want to know how to approach injury cases. It is the perfect primer for anyone who is thinking of following Jim's footsteps to start taking on injury cases or for the non-attorney wanting to understand the anatomy of an injury or wrongful death case.

Congratulations Jim, you made it. I am proud of you for what you have accomplished. But I am even prouder of you for writing this book to help show other people the way.

Michael Goldberg
Author of *Understanding Motor Carrier Claims*
Founder of Fried Goldberg, L.L.C.

PREFACE

# A Roadmap to Georgia Personal Injury Law ... and Disclaimer

Whether you are a lawyer, my client, an injured layperson, a family member of an injured person, or their caregiver, it is important that you don't simply read this book and then presume you're an expert in Georgia personal injury law. That is not the purpose of sharing this book with you. The more I learn, the more I realize there is so much more to learn. This book is meant to be a guide, a crash course in where you can begin. It is just a tip of the iceberg of injury law. In the forthcoming pages, you will find an outline, a guide, the basics, and something anyone can pick up at any moment in their pre-litigation matter to better understand the basics of injury law. The material is based on Georgia law, and shouldn't be used as a guide for other states, although I suspect much of the processes and dealings with stingy insurance claim valuations are similar. Like any trade, the rules of the road are constantly changing. Thus, always check and double check the information contained herein to ensure it remains accurate and updated.

I wish I had access to a book like this when I started my personal injury practice. Instead, much of my first couple years were a series of trials, and lots of errors. Most of my Plaintiff's injury colleagues have worked for insurance companies and or big Plaintiff's law firms. Although I have since done some defense work, I had to learn all of this on my own, through my mentor and former business partner, Jason Ferguson, and many of my friends in the Georgia Trial Lawyers Association (GTLA).

Having said all this, nothing in this book is intended to be construed as legal advice or meant to substitute otherwise sound advice from seasoned and experienced lawyers. Each and every injury case is unique, so it is crucial to seek out and retain competent counsel's advice for the facts and law that are specific to your case. In other words, don't do anything stupid that will ruin you or your client's case, cost you or your clients money, or something worse. When in doubt, partner up with a lawyer that knows what they are doing. That decision is worth its weight in gold.

# CHAPTER 1
# My Path to Injury Law

How did I get into personal injury? While not entirely relevant to your practice, it is a common story we are seeing from more and more lawyers these days. I was making a good living practicing criminal defense, DUIs, and traffic law all over Georgia. I made more money than I could have ever imagined doing so, especially considering I grew up in a house with a single mom working relentlessly to support her five children. I loved working hard for people to resolve their criminal matters. I generally loved all of my clients as well. Even so, it wasn't a sustainable practice. The margins and volume were too small to scale.

When I was hustling traffic citations, I would handle 600+ a year, all by myself. In the metro Atlanta area, there are 45 traffic jurisdictions and collectively, still nobody knows them better than me. I was burned out after driving 30,000 miles a year visiting as many as six different courthouses in one day. So what was next?

I explored divorce law CLEs, but I had no real interest in handling divorces. I came from a broken family and my mother and father had both experienced multiple divorces. I had seen enough divorce to last a lifetime. I considered other areas of law as well, but in the end, none truly inspired me to give up a successful and thriving practice. But as fate would have it, the decision to make a change would soon come in the form of an injured young man looking to help his girlfriend with a speeding ticket.

Ryan was my first injury client. He hobbled into my office in 2012, walking with a distinct limp. 18 years old and he otherwise looked healthy. This kind young man was bringing me a copy of his girlfriend's speeding ticket so I could represent her and ensure she didn't lose her license. After convincing Ryan his girlfriend's case was in good hands, I asked him what happened to his leg. He told me how he was a passenger in a friend's car and after speeding through a stop sign, his friend lost control of the car and crashed into an oak tree. The accident broke Ryan's femur, and the corresponding surgery left him with a rod in his leg and a long road of recovery. He had lost his scholarship due to the injury. After telling me this, he insisted his family had no interest in hiring a lawyer because "the insurance company was handling everything." Instinctively, alarms were sounding in my head.

I asked Ryan if he would need future surgeries. I asked him how long he would be limping? Or if he was expected to make a 100% recovery? He didn't know those answers. Ryan was a good kid. After speaking with him for just a few minutes, I felt like I'd known him forever. He felt the same way about me, and he trusted me. I told Ryan if he were my brother, I'd drag him into a lawyer's office and force him to hire a personal injury lawyer. I suggested he call his mom and dad and set up an appointment with me to discuss what could be done. Ryan limped out of the office. I was left with one question screaming in the back of my head? What will I tell the parents when I have no clue on how to handle an injury case??!!

Weeks before that fateful meeting with Ryan, I'd just met a personal injury attorney named Tony Kalka. He was a speaker at attorney Michael Goldberg's first CLE titled "Secrets to a Successful Plaintiff's Injury Practice." We struck up a conversation, and Tony asked me where I was sending my injury cases. I mentioned the name of a lawyer that nobody had heard of. He wondered whether I was getting a co-counsel attorneys fee for making the connection and working the case with that lawyer. Tony instantly became a friend and bought me a beer. He explained that in the industry, it's best if the most competent attorneys are getting the right cases to ensure high levels of success and justice for those injured.

The Georgia Bar essentially encourages referrals to competent lawyers because it's the best practice for the clients. The alternative would be for incompetent injury lawyers to handle and then screw up potentially great cases where injured people deserve real justice. Tony suggested that I refer my personal injury cases to his firm. I could maintain my successful criminal practice, gradually transition into injury work, and learn from one of the best young trial lawyers in Georgia.

Now, back to Ryan's case. I called Tony and arranged an appointment at his office with Ryan and his parents. The meeting went great. We needed more information about the case to determine its value, but we were off to a good start. We didn't yet know the limits of the liability coverage, but Ryan's parents had five cars, each with uninsured motorist (UM) coverage limits of $25,000 per person/$50,000 per incident under State Farm. Tony pointed out that those policies stack and Ryan actually had $125,000 in UM coverage (more on UM stackable coverage in Chapter 9).

Ryan's mom was clearly overwhelmed by all the insurance bills, hospital bills, collector calls, adjuster calls, and all the expenses that went into treating her injured child. Tony had some swagger and effortlessly expressed that she shouldn't worry about the bills, and he would take these challenges off her shoulders. I remember Ryan's mom saying, "Meeting you guys has been the answer to my prayers."

After that meeting, I instantly fell in love with personal injury law. I could help people, offer them tangible benefits, get to know their families, fight for them, win for them, and hopefully make a good living along the way. Resolving Ryan's case offered me further motivation to forge ahead in this area of law. We recovered the maximum policy limits for liability and underinsured motorist coverage for Ryan's broken leg. It was a very good settlement, and everyone was happy.

But most important, we were able to help Ryan make an outstanding recovery, and even get his scholarship back. I had earned a co-counsel fee for working the case with Tony and ensured that I connected a wonderful family with a great lawyer. From that moment forward, I was hooked. I immediately overhauled my website to reflect personal injury representation and began the long (and sometimes painful process) of leaving criminal law.

In the coming months and years, I quickly learned that injury work was not always that glorious but offered wonderful opportunities to make a difference in the lives of those that have been injured by the negligence of another person. The cards were dealt, and I kept at it by learning as much as I could. But that wasn't always easy. I would have done anything for a step-by-step guide to teach me how to handle an injury case, from start to finish. So, years later and armed with a great deal of experience, I decided to write this book. This book is a sweeping guide to handling injury cases. It takes you, the reader, through the important steps you should consider from start to finish. Together, we will journey through evaluating a new injury case, avoiding the common pitfalls, maximizing the channels of recovery, minimizing medical bills for your clients, helping inured clients in the most desperate and unimaginable circumstances, and implementing the processes that create the best attorney-client experience. After reading this book, I am confident you will feel armed with the ability to serve your clients and your law firm at a high level.

Read on....

## CHAPTER 2

# Building an Injury Practice

Why practice personal injury?

I wrestle with this question at least once every few months. There is certainly no shortage of injury lawyers in practice. You can't go a quarter mile in Atlanta without seeing a flashy billboard advertisement for a local personal injury lawyer, glorifying the settlement they got for their latest client. Injury lawyer commercials only seem to cease when the next election cycle comes around. Whether in print or digital form, most injury lawyer ads are blatantly offensive. Injury lawyers are a dime a dozen, and here I am, showing you what to expect in an injury case.

I strongly believe that there is always room for one more good lawyer. I get calls every week from injured victims who are unhappy with their current representation. They never get a call back from their current lawyers; they can only talk to an assistant or a case manager; or even worse, multiple voicemails and emails have passed without a response. I've learned that just doing a good job for clients, calling them back, and being present for them immediately puts me ahead of 80 percent of the competition. Even if I wrote the most detailed playbook and guide on winning injury cases, only two percent of readers will follow through.

I also think there is power in numbers. Where some injury practices might hate competition, having more lawyers holding insurance companies accountable means that those insurance companies have increased pressure—and financial interest—in treating people fairly.

## Genuine Care for People is a Must

Should you even be representing injured victims? This entire chapter is based on the premise of integrity and genuine empathy as a prerequisite for any rainmaking capabilities. There is no greater honor than being invited into a family's home after a tragic loss or a catastrophic injury because they trust you to help start the healing process. To put it plainly: if a lawyer does not genuinely feel connected to people when they are hurting, then perhaps they should pursue another career path. Once a client entrusts me with their case, they become very much like a family member (though of course, it goes without saying that we maintain a very professional relationship). By the time we resolve their case through settlement or verdict, we know one another well.

I have found that most lawyers that go into personal injury for the money end up hating it in the end. It can be exhausting to wrestle with client questions, managing treatment, written discovery, or bickering with insurance adjusters and opposing counsel every day. If I was simply after the money, I'd burn out quickly (and I have seen it happen to many other lawyers). I can't fake empathy, credibility, or authenticity with clients. They can smell the salesman from a mile away. If we are authentic, caring, and compassionate, we have everything we need to be effective at landing injury clients.

## Previous Clients and Building Bridges

I leveraged my former law practice to catapult the success of my new personal injury practice in the early 2010s. I did great work for my clients in law, and as a result, they trusted me first and foremost to manage their injury cases. My firm does everything we can to stay connected. We keep track of former client's birthdays. We send them cards, put them on our newsletter list, and let them know if it's been a while and we want to know how they are. My good friend, Aaron Thomas, who practices family law in Atlanta, has an amazing discipline: he completes GAS ("Give a Sh*t") calls twice a week. He calls two former clients every week just to say hello and check on them. Lawyers who do not truly love their practice won't take this extra step. The result is anything but phony: clients recognize genuine interest and personal investment.

When I started my personal injury practice, just about all my cases came from previous or current clients. One former client (I'll call him Paul) had hired me years earlier for a speeding ticket in Gwinnett County. I was successful in getting his citation reduced so it didn't appear on his driving record. Most importantly, I was always reachable: he knew that I cared enough to respond to calls or texts at any time of day.

Two years later, Paul called me because his wife, Mandy, had been in a terrible accident and she was in the ICU unit. She had gotten caught in an 18-wheeler's blind spot on I-85 in Atlanta. The truck driver bumped the rear quarter panel of her SUV, sending her into the concrete median wall. She had suffered a traumatic brain injury and her brain was bleeding, causing paralysis on one side of her body. Fortunately, Mandy made a miraculous recovery and had full function after months of rehab care. We settled her case with the trucking company for a very sizeable (but confidential) amount.

As lawyers, we never know where our next BIG case will come from. Exceptional lawyers are always building bridges—never tearing them down. Calling clients back and treating everyone with dignity, no matter what, is critical. When former clients trust their lawyer, and know how to get in touch with them, that lawyer will be their first call for any legal issue.

## Networking with Lawyers

There are infinite bar associations and lawyer's clubs that anyone can join. Establish connections with lawyers in a variety of practice areas, both in your locality and nationally. I have been referred cases from lawyers in California and Washington simply from conversations at national conferences. Remember: the next big case can come from anywhere. Even networking with other personal injury lawyers is important. There are so many nuanced specialties within the practice of personal injury (some of which are mentioned in the next chapter), which certainly makes a case for creating as many personal connections as possible.

Three years prior to writing this, my law partner and I had split up. It was amicable and through our partnership we formed a friendship that will last a lifetime. We maintained our close friendship, and to this day he introduces me to attorneys all over southern Georgia. One such was introduction was to a prominent criminal defense attorney. Months later, that same lawyer called me with a referral for a potential client. This injured client had caught on fire in his friend's garage. Unbeknownst to him, his reckless buddy placed a commercial-grade propane heater placed within 18 inches of him. He had suffered third-degree burns over 20 percent of his body. Luckily the homeowner had a million-dollar insurance policy, and we settled that case three months later for the full policy limits. The referring attorney and I handled the case together and we split the attorney's fee down the middle. Attorneys are a great referral source to build any law practice.

## Networking with Other Professions

Consider joining local business associations or even a B2B referral group. Some examples include Powercore, Provisors, or BNI. These are business networking groups that have one of each type of profession. They might include a chiropractor, a real estate agent, different types of attorneys, and a travel agent. Each group contains a different mix of professionals, but the underlying idea is that nobody competes with each other. These groups are designed to bring referrals that will open business prospects and referral sources. I was a part of Powercore for nine years and made good money and helped a lot of people because of those connections made.

Katie is a client I recently represented. I met her through Powercore. One day after a meeting, she asked me for an opinion on her case. Unfortunately, she was represented by another attorney. I told her to patch things up with her lawyer, have a meeting with him, and ask the right questions. She kept coming back to me because her claim wasn't being managed properly. Worse, her lawyer would go weeks or months without returning her calls. I told her I could not advise her if she was represented by someone else. An hour later, she copied me on an email firing her lawyer, and I took off running with her case. Four months later, we attained a maximum policy limit settlement of $150,000.

Katie had referred me cases before that, and I handled those cases with great results. She saw how efficient and responsive I was with my clients. She knew she needed that type of attention in her case. It paid off for all of us. In fact, she still sends me great cases to this day. Interestingly, Katie runs a digital marketing business for lawyers—so to have someone that knows so many injury lawyers and still sends cases to me was an absolute honor.

In addition to networking with professionals, it is crucial to network in your personal life as well. Joining a neighborhood association, the PTA, the school board, or anything that empowers you to give back to your local community can unlock many doors. Coaching your kid's basketball team opens all kinds of opportunities to meet people. Church, temple, or any religious community is another great place to build that community and give back while getting to know people. Having a mom who tells all her friends at brunch that her child is a successful injury lawyer is also helpful. Make sure everyone you know is aware that you are a personal injury and wrongful death lawyer.

## Modify Your Website to Reflect Personal Injury

Putting a personal injury page on your current website goes along with being vocal about your practice specialty. (In this case, injury and wrongful death claims.) If you love your current practice and you want to add injury work to build value for you and your clients, add a personal injury section to your website.

One mother called me the day after Christmas, because her son had a speeding ticket, and he was in danger of losing his license. I suggested he take a defensive driving class. She said there was no way he could take defensive driving because he was barely getting around in a walker after suffering a horrific injury in a car accident two months prior. I told her I would do the ticket case at no charge, and that I wanted to hear more about her son's injury case. It was then that she told me that's why she had called in the first place: she was looking for a lawyer that could handle both cases. I had just recently added the personal injury page to my ticket website. Adding that page to my website allowed me to get my first big injury case and we settled it pre-litigation for the maximum policy limits of $1.3 million.

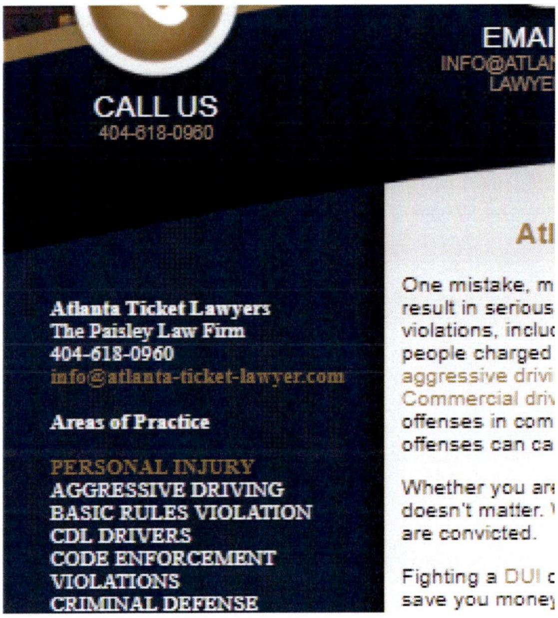


*Personal Injury practice area added to my old firm's website*

## Online Presence – SEO, PPC, Video, and Social Media

It is necessary to have an online presence to generate injury cases. Even if you can't compete or outspend the big firms, you need the web presence to validate who you are. People will be referred to you, and they will turn to Google and see what they can find on you. They will see reviews, legal directory ratings, and everything on your website. Have professional photographs taken and hire someone to put the website together. I've used Scorpion, First Draft Marketing, and Lawlytics, and they are all very effective at what they do—but the latter is more affordable and fits the content dropping blitzkrieg that I enjoy.

In general, I would advise against spending a penny on any of this without also maximizing all the other forms of originating cases mentioned above. The costs per acquisition are infinitely cheaper than trying to compete with big law firms. Different companies will have different strategies that can be brilliant. From my personal experience speaking with numerous online marketing gurus, a combined approach of social media, blogging, video presence, SEO content with backlinks, and PPC together can be utilized to generate online leads.

The most important aspect of generating business is being a good lawyer that treats people well. If you start with that, your business will grow.

## Law Firm Management and Consulting

Anyone I know who is successful has a coach of some sorts. Many of my colleagues have someone who keeps their practice focused and accountable. The good law firms are helping people, making a living, and protecting their own health and sanity to grow their firm to its ideal state. I've used several consultants for different avenues of direction I've needed. Here are just some of the resources I know of in the industry:

**Wildly Successful** – Nermin Jasani / President. Nermin gives you personalized no-nonsense consulting based on hard numbers and easily quantifies what resources need to be put where for success. **nermin@highlandoakgroup.com**, 770-235-1988.

**3a Law Management** – Alavaro Arauz is the owner of his consulting firm and is in almost 20 states. He guides lawyers in marketing and operations strategies that measure results and hold you constantly accountable. Alvaro has been a guest on my podcast in the past, and he said something that stuck with me. He suggested imagining what you would want your ideal firm to look like at its optimal state, and then work backwards from there at each stage of your journey to map out a path to build your machine. **3a@3alawmanagement.com**, 678-360-3211.

**How to Manage a Small Law Firm** – Rjon Robins is a lawyer and started this business after his wife was very sick and was forced to find a better way to balance law and his personal life. He offers real business consulting for small law firms. Everyone I know that is a part of his community loves the program and the coaches. **info@howtomanageasmalllawfirm.com**, 888-765-7460.

**Crisp Video Group** – Michael Mogill started his video company and grew it beyond comprehension. His wife and partner, Jessica, is a former Big 5 business consultant. They use their own growth strategies for coaching and mentoring law firms to grow and scale. Their business coaching programs now dwarf their vibrant video marketing business. I highly recommend Michael Mogill's podcast: *The Game Changing Attorney Podcast*. **connect@contact.crispvideo.com**, 404-267-9240.

## Remember, Sign the Case up Fast

If there is value for the client in a case, you need to move quickly to sign it up. I've heard this said more than once over the years: "Never let the sun set on a great case." If you wait on signing a case, there are too many ways you can lose it. Most notably, there are disgraceful law firms that have "runners" that will openly solicit potential clients in person or over the phone to get a case signed up. It's a crime in Georgia to openly solicit potential clients. This still has had little effect on deterring runners from slithering around hospitals, making grand promises of huge paydays, and calling people at their most vulnerable moments. Good lawyers that play by the rules have a duty to protect the public from a case getting in the wrong hands.

At my firm, we will either go to a client's home or hospital room the day they call us. If that doesn't make sense, we will get the case signed using an e-signature application, such as DocuSign. I have been burned before by not getting a case signed up fast enough and it hurts. Remember, never let the sun set on a good case.

The truth is, no matter what anyone will tell you, is that it takes time and great effort to build anything that matters. The same is true when it comes to your injury practice. Rome was not built in a day, and no successful injury practice was either. One step at a time is the attitude you should take to remain patient but constantly find yourself moving in the right direction. Now, we turn our attention to the clients, their injuries, and how they should proceed if and when they are injured in an accident or through the negligence of another.

## CHAPTER 3

# Assisting Clients After an Injury

I live in Grant Park. It's a beautiful neighborhood with a village-type feel, resting just east of Downtown Atlanta. For ten years I lived on Boulevard, which is a very busy street that leads directly to Zoo Atlanta. On any perfect spring day in Atlanta, the neighborhood is packed with local patrons and tourists. Recently, while working in my home office I heard a crash so loud I almost fell out of my chair. Without a second thought I ran out of the house, expecting something terrible, and it was certainly an ugly car wreck. 18-month-old twin girls were being driven to the zoo by their nanny when a car pulled out in front of them. The front end of the nanny's Ford Explorer was torn apart, with at least two airbags deployed. I ran up to the car as the nanny was sobbing, reaching into the back seat for the twin infants. I grabbed one of the girls, and the nanny snatched up the other. I begged her to get off the busy street and sit on my front porch.

The nanny instantly complained of her lower back amidst a waterfall of tears. She was freaking out, not making any sense, and trying to call the twins' mother, who was 45 minutes away. I cannot imagine what it was like to receive that call. The babies were hysterical. I ran inside and poured the girls some apple juice and gave them some of my own kids' toys to keep them busy until their mother arrived. Thankfully, the twins were okay; the nanny was escorted to the hospital by Grady EMS in an ambulance.

Unless you have witnessed it or experienced it personally, it is impossible to understand just how hectic, disorienting, and frantic the moments after a car wreck are. This is true even for the days and weeks to follow—even refusing an ambulance carries a mountain of paperwork. There is no foresight that can help anyone prepare for the emotional impact of a wreck. As a courtesy, I took several pictures of both vehicles involved and texted them to the mother. I also sent my statement of events, which included my memory of hearing the Defendant's admissions. I did not have the heart to tell the mother I was an injury lawyer—but even if I did, I likely couldn't represent her, as I was a possible witness in her case.

I dare any reader to google, "what to do after being injured." One might as well search for "best injury lawyer." This topic has been written about by nearly every injury law firm in existence, but I believe that my experiences from the past decade can add significant value to the conversation—and continue that conversation in a new, engaging way. Let's look at the immediate steps that a person must take once they have been injured.

## Seeking Medical Treatment

Our healthcare system does not always make it easy to seek medical treatment. Aside from the cost and finding an in-network provider, seeing a doctor is time consuming: patients wait forever, and the hassle of going back and forth with insurance can quickly become unbearable. Quite a few people have called me in the hours and days following their injury to ask me "What should I do?" My first question is always whether they are hurt. If they say they are hurt, I tell them to visit a doctor immediately. It seems simple, but I certainly understand why many people don't take this step.

Anyone injured should first go see a doctor. If for nothing else, they must establish a baseline of medical care. Some states have such strict laws that if a victim doesn't see a physician in the first couple days following an accident, they have effectively waived their right to make an injury claim. I suggest seeing a doctor immediately, but ideally, a client should see one within the first 48 hours after an accident or injury.

## Taking Pictures

Pictures and video are invaluable to a case. I use pictures everywhere, including within the body of my demands. We encourage clients to capture pictures of their injuries, their car, the scene of the injury, the Defendant's car, the clothes they were wearing, scars after surgery, etc. Some surgeons even take photos or video during surgery. This would be a great tool to show pain and suffering in a demand, at mediation, or at trial.

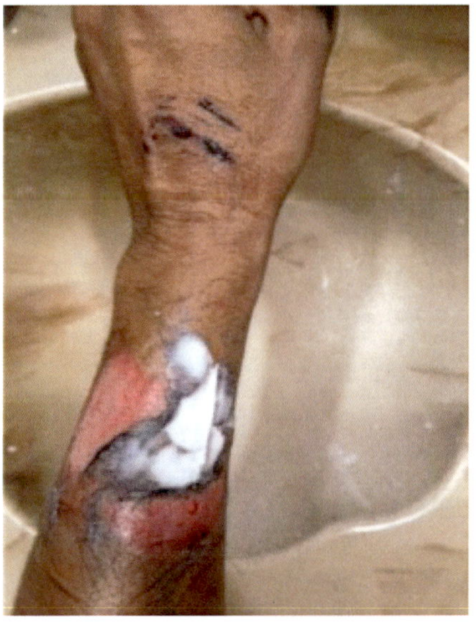

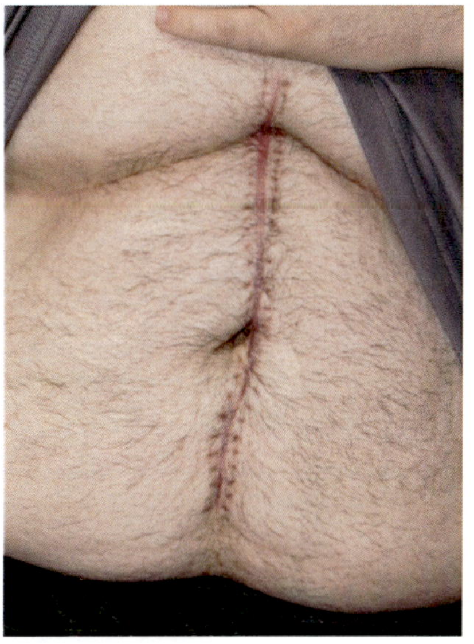

*Powerful post injury photos*

## Calling a Lawyer

I wrote an article titled, "If you wait until the dust settles, you've settled for nothing." There's a lot of cold, hard truth in that title. There is absolutely no reason NOT to contact a personal injury lawyer right after a wreck. None of us charge for consultations, and most of us would probably even visit the potential client in the hospital. Of course, there are good reasons why people are hesitant to contact a personal injury lawyer. The profession doesn't garner trust from the general population, most of the TV ads are offensive, and people associate injury lawyers with a certain stigma—to put it plainly, that we use loopholes, intimidation, or otherwise questionable business practices to get someone a check that they somehow don't deserve.

Most people want to stay as far away from that stigma as possible. The good news is that the truly talented lawyers among us feel the same. Your job, as one of those upper-echelon lawyers, is to ensure that your approach, your business model, your character, and your marketing all reinforce your honesty and integrity. This emphasis pays off in dividends, not just for your personal law practice, but for your clients. Getting a lawyer involved immediately provides many benefits to a case.

### 1. It Forces Preservation of the Defendant's Evidence

Let's assume a large company is facing a large financial loss because their video surveillance shows employees causing a terrible accident. That corporation will not go out of their way to keep that video preserved unless they must. It is a lawyer's job to force them to preserve that evidence. A lawyer will write "spoliation" letters to the Defendant or their insurance company, demanding that they preserve records, videos, photos, physical evidence, transcripts, recordings, all cell phone evidence, black box data, etc. The consequences for losing or destroying this evidence could be too damning and monumental for the Defendant to overcome at trial.

### 2. It preserves the Client's Evidence

I had a case where a client slipped and fell on a wet, slick surface in a supermarket and fractured his skull. He needed emergency care but was back on his feet a few weeks later. Two months later, after seeing the mountains of bills he owed, he called my office. I was most interested in what he slipped on, how long it was there, and how it got there. I was also concerned with what the Supermarket's defenses would be. I told him that I needed to take possession of the shoes he was wearing, and he told me he gave them to Goodwill a month earlier. At that moment, I knew that we could face a challenge in the courtroom: one possible defense would be that the client had old, worn, slick shoes, with no tread. In every injury or wrongful death case, preserving the client's evidence is critical. I tell my clients to write down everything they remember happening, take pictures of injuries, take pictures of the cars or property involved, and to find all witnesses and get their statements. If there is blood, I tell them to keep the clothes they were wearing. Every case is different and with each of my clients, I think of different pieces of evidence that will be helpful. The longer somebody waits, the harder it will be to preserve these valuable tools necessary to prove their case.

### 3. It Recognizes Time Sensitivity for Notice Requirements – Uninsured Motorist Coverage (UM), Homeowners, and Government Cases

Of more importance than the obvious two-year statute of limitations on injury cases is acting quickly enough to preserve every avenue of recovery possible.

What if the Defendant is underinsured or not insured at all? I had a case where my injured client was a "hit and run" victim and they hired me three months after the accident. Pursuant to the language of the insurance policy, the UM insurance carrier initially tried to deny the uninsured motorist claim. The UM insurer pointed out they never received actual written notice of the accident from my client within 30 days of the incident. They admittedly knew of the accident based on the numerous conversations with my client before the 30-day deadline, but never received actual written notice. They eventually paid the claim but attempted to use that issue as leverage in negotiations. A competent personal injury lawyer will send written notice to the UM carrier in all cases, with no exceptions.

Homeowner's policies have similar notice requirements. When the Defendant is the local government, "ante-litem notice" of the personal injury incident must be given typically within six or 12 months of the accident to recover. Not giving proper notice to the right parties could destroy a claim. These notice requirements will be discussed in more depth in Chapter 5.

### 4. It Halts Ruthless Creditors / Lienholders

Consider another case where my client, a young man, was seriously injured and incurred over $900,000 in medical bills. A month after the accident, he was moved to a rehab center. His mother was nearly drowning in collection calls and bills from creditors demanding a payment of $900,000. Good personal injury firms will immediately send cease-and-desist letters to these creditors telling them that their client is represented, and the case is pending resolution of a personal injury claim. This almost always will stop the calls and letters.

### 5. It Manages Insurance Companies Want to Close the Case Yesterday

Most well-run auto and casualty insurance companies call the victim or their family on the same day as the accident. They want statements, and they want to resolve the case as soon as possible—within days, if they can. They assure the victim that they will take care of everything and offer peanuts for the victim's pain and suffering. As soon as the victim starts acting questions, the claims adjuster's answers get shorter and nastier. They will continue calling until they close the case, or until they are represented by a lawyer. Insurance companies want to pay minimal claims and increase profit margins. An attorney's "letter of representation" provides peace of mind to the victim by forcing insurance companies to stop calling.

## Becoming the Delegate

Part of being an effective lawyer is providing as much value to our clients as possible. That includes taking the responsibility with keeping up with billings and collections, and even managing the treatment process. Certainly, interacting with and creating meaningful, trusting connections with family is a big part of this as well. In catastrophic injury cases I repeatedly see how families come together in dire circumstances. I have seen numerous distant family members fly from across the globe to help and assist after a beloved family member suffers an injury. Having the honor of becoming a part of that process is extraordinarily enriching.

## Memorializing Client Experiences

We have our clients write down as many details about their case as possible on an ongoing basis. This includes having the client keeping up with pain levels, what hurts, the treatment timelines, medications, witness names and numbers, etc.

Being injured is absolute chaos for the victim, their caregivers, and their family. In one second, the trajectory of someone's life changes—and for many, it changes forever. Making sure your client is making the right choices from the start is critical to the outcome of their case. At times, I must be very direct with clients when they are on the fence about hiring a lawyer. Whether they choose to hire us or not, we do everything we can within the rules of professional responsibility to protect a potential client from the pitfalls of not being represented, and ensure they are properly advised on how to handle the intricacies and nuances of personal injury. That's what this book is all about.

## CHAPTER 4

# What Makes a Good Case or a Bad Case (and what is it Worth?)

A big pitfall in handling injury claims is the real possibility of taking the wrong case. Just as one case can change a client's life for the better, a terrible case can destroy and bankrupt a great lawyer—and provide no benefit to the client. I strongly believe that good cases are functions of damages, liability, causation, and resources from where we can collect damages. If I were to add a fourth function to turn a good case into a great one, I would add the client variable. A likeable client that does everything they can do to help their case (and in turn, themselves) can have a tremendous impact.

I struggled with saying "no" in my early days of representing injury victims. In fact, I took any injury case I could get my teeth on. I wound up taking a lot of cases that had causation lacking or poor damages. As a result, I wound up disappointing the client, and underperforming for a case that was dead from the beginning. Unfortunately, we can't help everyone.

## Diagram of Damages/Liability & Causation Model

I created this model as a useful tool to objectively assess (and even share with colleagues) when I was on the fence about taking a case. Many lawyers have their own measures and guidelines, but this model allows me to review case-by-case over time and analyze objective value for our clients. For simplicity, I use the terms "liability" and "causation" almost interchangeably. Even so, I recognize their different functions in building a case: liability being the extent which I can prove a Defendant breached a duty, and causation identifying whether that breach of the duty was the proximate cause of my client's injuries.

*Note: The above graph is a general guideline and no lawyer should ever have any hardline rules on what case they would always or never take.*

## High Damages / Low Liability & Causation

This is a typical scenario where liability is hard to pin on the Defendant, but the damages are significantly high. We see these types of cases in head-on car accidents, where both parties say they had the green arrow or green light. Similarly, slip and fall/trip and fall cases will always have liability arguments, but can carry very high damages. Or, a daycare facility seems to be doing everything right, but children suffer serious injuries under their watch—to the extent it might warrant investigating negligence.

In cases where causation is unclear, but damages are high, further evaluation is always warranted. A good personal injury lawyer should start by looking into open records, available video, all reports, 911 recordings, prior conduct, etc. Many cases appear unpromising at first look, but a little bit of digging can provide substantial payoff for the client.

## Low Damages/High Liability & Causation

Some cases have high-enough causation, but too low of damages to consider them "good" cases. My sole requirement for representing anyone is that they must be hurt. If they aren't hurt, I can't help them. An example of a case with high causation and low damages could be a low-impact rear-end collision; although liability is clear, the Plaintiff has minimal symptoms of injury and doesn't need to see a doctor. Most of these cases won't be viable options for an injury lawyer. My non-lawyer friend recently was hit hard and went to a chiropractor for a few visits. He soon felt 100 percent better and discontinued his treatment. In total, he had $500 in medical treatment. The best advice I could give him was to ask for $5,000 from the liability carrier himself (even giving him a demand template citing applicable Georgia law). He submitted the demand himself and they gave him $3,000. He was able to successfully advocate for himself without paying for the benefit of a lawyer—and in truth, I'm not sure I would have done much better with his case.

### High Damages/High Liability & Causation

If the liability carrier in a high liability/high damages case is a commercial policy, consider this case a unicorn. Sign this case up immediately, as these types of cases can change the trajectory of a lawyer's career if handled properly. If a lawyer has limited experience with personal injury claims, they'd be wise to find an experienced injury lawyer that specializes in that area and work the case together. Splitting the attorney's fees is entirely worth it, particularly for lawyers with limited experience. One should never risk any mishandling of a case like this for the sake of their client. The best attorneys that specialize in high-stakes cases add incredible value to a case—so much so that it would never make sense *not* to associate with outside counsel. My team is always willing to reach out to the Trial Lawyers Association and mentors for guidance.

### Low Damages/Low Liability & Causation

Any injury lawyer would love to help a potential client that was unjustly treated or injured. In most scenarios where we have low damages and liability is questionable, we are unable to represent that client. There would be no use dragging them through the legal system if there is no benefit to be had. An exception would be in situations whereby taking the case, we would be furthering a worthy cause or constitutional issue (so long as the client is engaged with the objectives and likely results).

There are certainly exceptions to the rules, but here's an overview of general "cases to avoid" that I follow in my own law practice:

- Hit and Run/Uninsured Motorist (UM) with no visible third-party impact damage. If a single car wreck has no third-party visible damage and no corroboration, UM carriers will deny coverage alleging no evidence of third-party causation.

- Deer or dog in the road cases.
- Any case where someone seems obsessed with "getting a check" or begging for money up front.
- Slip and fall cases where the Plaintiff had traversed the area previously, or where anyone would expect to find a slippery surface.
- Any slip or trip and fall where the danger was open and obvious.
- Any car wreck where a potential client was cited for being at fault. (We have made exceptions where facts or witnesses suggest otherwise, and there are damages and policy limits to support taking the risk.)
- Any case where the client is an extraordinarily difficult person. Great clients make great cases, and difficult clients can destroy any value a case has. If it's a great case and I have serious client management issues, I'll consider referring the client to another lawyer that would be a better fit.

## The Property Damage/ Medical Causation Paradox

An insurance company's valuation of causation of the injuries as it relates to the wreck is based significantly on the amount of property damage sustained between the vehicles in question. The higher the property damage, the more likely they adequately value medical causation claims. The lower the amount of property damage, the more they will devalue a client's injuries. If a client sustained serious injuries, a long course of treatment, and a high amount of medical expenses, then we expect that case to be devalued and will likely need to be litigated.

Too often we will only have photographs of our client's slightly damaged vehicle and correspondence from the adjuster will all point to the unlikelihood of significant injuries when there is minimal property damage. We hear this same argument whether there's barely a scratch on the bumper or even if the bumper has fallen off without other body damage to the vehicle. If the property damage is less than $3,000, we expect a big medical causation dispute from the insurance company unless we have some heat in the case like a DUI. Thus, it is critical that we get photos of the other car as well in these cases. I have seen countless wrecks where the injured person's car is barely damaged and the rear vehicle has a crumpled front end with total loss type damage. Sometimes we can only get those photos after we file suit and request the production of documents from the Defendant.

Although it is rare that people are hurt in these low impact wrecks, the science certainly supports the plausibility of it. I have a three-page data synopsis (included in the appendix) that we include in our demands that cites countless studies that verify how serious car wrecks at even five miles per hour can be. I believe putting that language in the demand has no immediate effect on the pre-litigation offer, but it feels appropriate to let the adjuster know you are prepared to back this claim up with scientific evidence. I have personally heard clients detail what initially sounded like awful wrecks, but then see zero damage to either vehicle after going to see the wreckage. Automobiles made today are built to sustain impact and resist damage. The amount of apparent damage can be deceptive with how bad the impact was.

It is rare that my firm accepts these cases. Whether I accept them will depend on the credibility and likability of the Plaintiff, the seriousness of the injuries, and the course of treatment needed. If there is a case with a low impact that results in a spinal surgery then I will likely co-counsel with someone like Ben Broadhead who takes these cases on regularly and obtains numerous $1 million to $7 million results for people that adjusters initially scoffed at. A trial alleging a low impact caused the need for a spinal fusion could get expensive with biomedical defense experts and the need to call your own to prove your case.

*Injury case with no property damage*

## What is a Case Worth?

What a case is worth mostly depends on:

1 How bad the injury is,
2 The amount of reasonable medical special damages,
3 Other damages such as lost wages and pain and suffering,
4 Aggravating factors like punitive conduct,
5 The amount of property damage,
6 The extent we can prove liability and medical causation, AND
7 Whether there is enough coverage resources for the injuries and damages sustained.

The easiest way to know for sure what a case is worth is by measuring the data with case-specific variables. The best system and tool I have seen for this is Case Metrix. Kim White is one of the founders and she has done a tremendous job of securing data from judges, trial lawyers, the defense bar, and even insurance companies. I use Case Metrix for almost every case I have and even use it in my demands. Experience has taught the following:

### Non-surgical or "Soft-tissue" Cases

These are cases where the client heals without any invasive intervention, save for some pain-relief or similar injections. I've seen medical expenses cost anywhere from $500 all the way up to $150,000. The client starts with a chiropractor or orthopedist. They receive adjustments and/or physical therapy and might follow up with injections with a physiatrist. If that concludes the treatment with significant improvement to the client, most lawyers see one and a half to two times gross special damages. Damages can be in excess of three to ten times traditional resolutions when there are punitive facts involved.

In a soft tissue case where a client has $10,000 worth in chiropractor, PT, and ortho visits—and treatment is consistent and non-excessive—I would expect to see a settlement anywhere from $15,000–$20,000. Diligent lawyers will provide additional value at that point by negotiating the medical specials as low as possible to ensure the client's maximum net gain. In this scenario, maybe the lawyer can get everyone to agree on a one-third split; in the event of a $20,000 settlement, medical providers, attorney, and client might each net $6,333.66.

### Chronic Long-Term Soft-Tissue Cases

Some of these cases prevent using a simple multiplier for a client's damages—it just isn't fair. Injury lawyers will have cases where the MRIs show objective disc herniations or bulges and the client is in immense pain. Surgery is either not recommended, or the client doesn't want to take the risk. If a client's life has been devastated, they have high policy limits, and solid before and after witnesses, that case should certainly be litigated. The client likely doesn't have anything to lose.

My former partner Jason Ferguson, myself, and attorney Hampton Eadon had exactly this type of case in 2018. Our client, "Sam," had four-disc bulges that greatly impacted her life. She had been hit by a commercial truck and her car was a total loss. She had $40,000 in medical special damages and our highest offer pre-trial was $100,000. Our client had been out of work and could not find employment due to her constant schedule of doctor appointments, pain, therapy, etc. Surgery was recommended but she was delaying that as long as possible. We were able to obtain a $780,000 verdict for Sam against the commercial truck driver that hit her.

## Surgical Soft-Tissue Cases

Soft tissue cases can take on a life of their own. A client goes to the ER and follows up with a chiropractor. They show no signs of improvement after a month or two, so the chiropractor refers them to an orthopedist. The orthopedist orders MRIs and notices various impressions (such as disc herniations) that appear to be recent events, and the client is referred to physical therapy (PT). The client continues seeing the orthopedist and refers the client out for spinal injections to manage the pain.

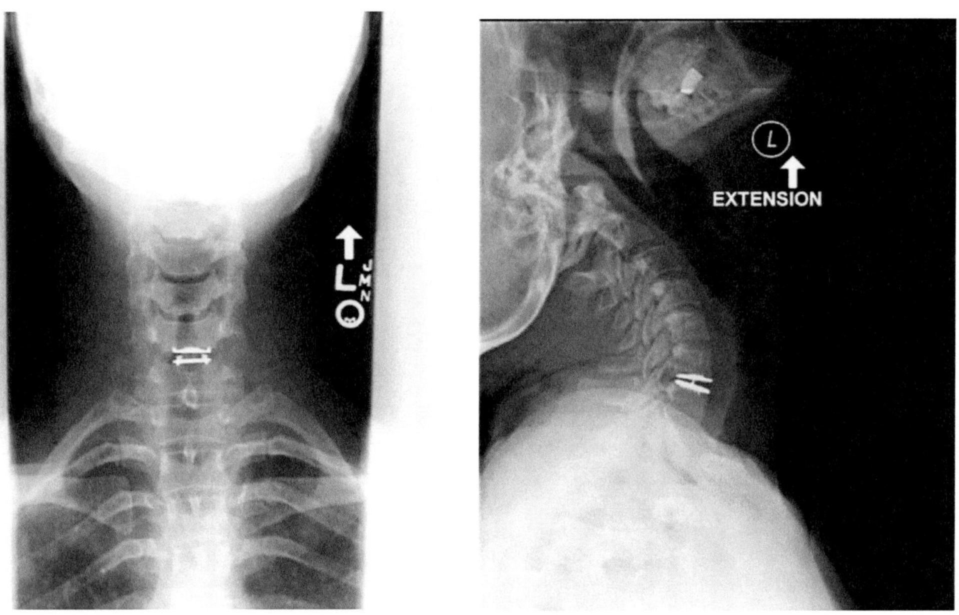


*Rear end case that was soft tissue in nature but evolved into a surgical disc replacement*

Assuming that doesn't work, the doctor orders more PT and follows up in a month or two. If the client is still in intense pain, the orthopedist will refer that patient to a spinal surgeon for a possible surgical recommendation. If the client has surgery, this case is now potentially worth seven figures (assuming adequate insurance limits or a possible bad faith action).

## Joint or Ligament/Tendon Surgical Cases

From my own experience, these cases vary greatly. If liability isn't in question, joint or ligament/tendon surgical cases can range anywhere from $75,000 all the way up to low seven figures. It likely depends heavily on the client's impairment and recovery.

## "Mild" Traumatic Brain Injury (MTBI)

These might be the hardest of them all (an important caveat: I don't believe that any brain injury can be classified as mild). There is no objective injury, and insurance companies will hardly ever put real money on the table. There are certain clues to where the lawyer should step in and direct treatment if they suspect MTBI. If I see any of the following, I owe it to my client to have them at least follow up with a neurologist or a neuropsychologist:

- Any loss of consciousness during accident
- Concussion diagnoses
- CT scans of the client's head at the hospital
- If family members say anything about the client seeming different or not themselves (i.e., temperament changes and mood swings)
- Skull fracture

If I suspect a client might have a MTBI, the case must be prepared and handled properly from start to finish, as it will most likely need to be litigated. I'll likely pursue a treatment or analysis from a neurologist or neuropsychologist that understands these injuries. These cases need treatment schedules that are consistent. Any evidence is helpful that shows life-altering damages, such as job loss because of poor performance. Having credible before and after witnesses that can attest to how different a victim has been since their accident can be powerful. There are outstanding lawyers that specialize in these claims—seek them out.

## Non-Surgical Fractures

The value of a non-surgical fracture case depends on impairment after the injury and to what extent the client makes a full recovery. When I hear a client suffered a broken bone with no surgery, I think at least $30,000–$50,000 in minimal value.

This can increase significantly depending on recovery, limitations, and impairment.

## Surgical Fracture Cases

I see these cases valued anywhere from $100,000 all the way up to high seven figures. Total value here depends on the case, the type of injury, the medical bills, future prognosis, lost wages, and impairment.

## Catastrophic Injury or TBI

By "catastrophic," I mean complete loss of use, paralysis, blindness, amputation, or TBI. If I have the right Defendant and policy limits to recover what my client deserves, I'll engage with vast resources to ensure that the case is handled properly. I won't hesitate to reach out to my fellow trial lawyers for their thoughts, guidance, or co-counsel. As of the writing of this book, if liability is not in question, any catastrophic injury should be worth at least seven to eight figures.

## Wrongful Death Cases

If liability can easily be proven, wrongful death cases (just like catastrophic injury cases) can bring immense value and closure to the family. Many times, where conduct is egregious enough, the family has no interest in settling a claim or financial gain and only want a jury to give them justice in court. Where liability is not an issue, I have seen juries award amounts as low as $250,000 all the way up to $100,000,000 for the loss of a life caused by a Defendant. Typical pre-trial settlement values can range from $500,000 up to $12,000,000. It goes without saying that the best lawyers will achieve the best results for their clients.

## Adding Heat

This is discussed in depth in Chapter 9, but I will briefly mention it here. Lawyers can enhance the value of their case if there are value-added punitive variables. They include:

- A Defendant arrested for DUI after causing the accident.
- Prior similar wrongdoings.
- Any conduct that might warrant punitive damages.
- Statements made by the Defendant.
- Social media posts making admissions.

## The Lawyer's Goal: Maximize Value and Minimize Costs

The obvious objective in every case is to maximize the value, but almost as important is minimizing the associated costs. A lawyer can employ a variety of strategies to maximize the amount the client is awarded. Again, these are discussed in much greater detail in Chapter 9, but an overview is warranted here. These strategies include:

- Evaluating collateral auto insurance coverages.
- Utilizing uninsured motorist coverage (UM coverage), including determining whether resident relatives allow for stacked coverages.
- ALWAYS negotiating medical bills as low as possible.
- Cutting the attorney's fee if needed.
- Analyzing whether the insurance company has engaged in bad faith.

Deciding what a case is worth is determined on a case-by-case basis. There are patterns and trends to value, and understanding all variables involved is critical. It is always helpful to call a fellow trial lawyer and review a case together, just to get an outside perspective. I have often asked multiple lawyers when I'm scratching my head. And while I've gotten better at evaluating the value of a case and saying no, I'm still learning how to gracefully decline a case. Remember that saying no to a case is hard, but necessary to ensure that the client's time, finances, and well-being are put first and foremost.

# CHAPTER 5

# Types of Injury Cases and What to Look For

When it comes to injury cases, it is not a one-size fits all type of practice. In fact, there are many types of personal injury cases, from the very common car and trucking cases, to slips and falls, medical malpractice, negligent security, work related accidents, childbirth injuries, nursing home abuse, defective products or devices, dog bite cases, or being injured while in the custody of police or while serving time at a jail. As you can see, there are dozens of different types of cases, and many lawyers may handle only a limited number of these cases, or even specialize in just one.

This chapter will offer you an overview of car wreck and trucking cases. The next chapter will offer you an overview of pretty much every other type of cases you might consider. This will help you to determine which, if any or if all, are the right fit for you and your practice. While the forthcoming chapters are not inclusive of every injury a Plaintiff might experience and pursue, it certainly gives you an overview so as to offer insight into how you might to decide to build your practice.

## Car Wrecks

Car wrecks constitute, by far, the most common personal injury cases. As a result, much of this book will focus heavily on these types of cases. In car wreck cases, liability is usually very clear, and the claim process is generally predictable. Most of these cases, if the right steps are taken, can be handled—and even litigated—at a relatively low cost when compared to more serious types of cases.

In the previous chapter, we discussed the primary types of injuries one might see in a car wreck case. These include the following: non-surgical soft tissue, surgical soft tissue, surgical joint/ligament tears, mild TBI cases, non-surgical fractures, surgical fractures, catastrophic injury, and wrongful death.

A car accident case is usually only worth what coverages are available under the policy limits available. The most common types of coverages are listed below.

## $25,000/$50,000

### *(max $25K per person/$50K max payable per incident)*

This is by far the most common policy coverage (minimum policy in the state of Georgia). In a serious injury case, I would almost never accept a client where these minimal limits were the only coverage available. There'd be nothing in it for the client and my office would be buried under massive amounts of medical liens, making this case impossible to work. Most non-surgical soft tissue cases should settle within these policy limits. If there are multiple people in a vehicle that are injured, the lawyer needs to move quick to represent the client's best interests and recover as much of that piece as possible.

## $30,000/$80,000

### *(max $30K per person/$80K max payable per incident)*

I have only seen this amount of coverage with Allstate. Marginally better than the $25,000/$50,000 policy above, it still gives many folks very little recovery to treat and be made whole for more significant injuries. As discussed above, most non-surgical soft tissue cases should settle within these policy limits. If there are multiple people in a vehicle that are injured, the lawyer needs to move quick to represent the client's best interests and recover as much of that piece as possible.

## $50,000/$100,000

### *(max $50K per person/$100K max payable per incident)*

These limits are still low, so if there are multiple Plaintiffs, it's important to get the first shot at available coverage. Keep in mind that even if 60 people are seriously injured, the maximum amount of liability available to pay out is $100,000.

## $100,000/$300,000

### *(max $100K per person/$300K max payable per incident)*

90 percent of car wrecks fall within these limits.

$250,000/$500,000

*(max $250K per person/$500K max payable per incident)*

When we see these limits on an auto policy, we can assume they have an excess liability umbrella policy for approximately $1 million (or higher in some cases). It's important to make sure all liability policies for the at-fault parties are requested, along with an affidavit affirming there are no other policies.

> Dear Paisley Law LLC,
>
> On 04/30/20 you asked for information regarding insurance coverag
> . This information is furnished pursuant to Official Code Georgi
>
> Policy Number: 0CJN -994
> Name of Insurer: Travelers Property Casualty Insurance Company
> Auto Liability Policy Limit: BI:250/500, PD:100
> Name of Insured:
>
> Sincerely,

*$250,000 in limits indicates a likely excess umbrella policy*

## Auto Claims Case Progression

With car wrecks, it is critical to understand claim management and making sure the client is doing everything they can to maximize the value of their injuries. Clients should be making all applicable appointments, following doctor's orders, filling prescriptions, and avoiding gaps in treatment. Having said that, managing a soft tissue injury case is different than managing a serious injury case.

The costs of treatment in an injury case often exceed the liability limits of a policy. At that point, a good lawyer will expose every avenue of recovery available. Questions to ask include (but are not limited to):

- Is there uninsured motorist (UM) coverage for the client, and do they have UM policies that can stack?
- Does the client have resident relatives with their own auto policy that could stack on their UM coverage?
- Are there liability policies that could stack?
- Was the Defendant driving for work purposes? Were they driving for Uber, Lyft, or another type of freelance work?

Every car accident case is composed of several phases. Each phase has its own distinct parts and processes that are individually critical. There are infinite ways to sabotage an injury claim by not being meticulous about the details of a case.

## Case Stages from Start to Finish

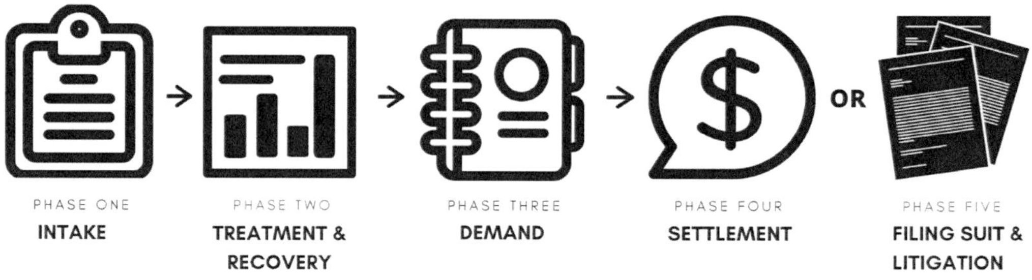


### Phase One – Intake

Intake can be broken down into three steps. Step One includes getting all relevant information about a case, establishing liability, and clarifying medical timelines. In Step Two, the lawyer will send out all letters of representation, spoliation letters, notice to UM or homeowner's carriers, anti-litem notices, and open record requests. Attorneys set up their initial investigation, experts, and inspections in the third step of this process.

The intake process can last several weeks, during which the attorney needs to ensure they are maximizing channels of recovery. They should investigate stacking liability and UM limits, exposing all UM coverages. Some cases might warrant punitive damages, and trucking cases could have multiple liable Defendants and sources of recovery. Making sure that Phase One is thoroughly completed will establish a strong foundation from which to build your client's case.

### Phase Two –Treatment

The client must see a doctor immediately if they are hurt. In some states, if an injured person waits more than a few days to see a doctor, they are barred from making a claim at all. Although I would rather the client decide their own treatment path, I certainly don't mind making the referral—in my opinion, any potential drawbacks of referring medical care are overstated. Managing treatment for clients in some degree is a necessity in every case. In the pages to come, we'll discuss in detail doctor referrals, letters of protections for the doctors, funding options for treatment or surgery, using health insurance, and when to utilize cash advances.

### Phase Three –Demand

Every lawyer has different philosophies on what should be included in demands. In Chapter 11, I will discuss my own philosophies, the auto accident demand statute, and first-and third- party bad faith.

### Phase Four – Settlement

The settlement phase is where the lawyer can provide the most value for their client. It is tedious and can mean engaging with lots of letters and phone calls. This book will briefly address ERISA self-insured plans vs. fully insured plans and whether payments provided by a health insurance carrier have to be paid back. We'll also take a closer look at negotiating with other providers like hospitals, private funding liens, medical doctors, and chiropractic offices.

### Phase Five – Filing Suit & Litigation

Litigation is covered anecdotally in Chapter 13, and not really the focus of this book. Filing suit can extend the length of a case by anywhere from a month all the way up to three to five years. Everything in this book is intended to optimize the length of a case so it doesn't get lost in the abyss of extended litigation.

## Ride Share Cases Involving Uber or Lyft

Whether a client was a passenger in an Uber or Lyft vehicle, or if they were hit by an Uber or Lyft driver, there are small distinctions that can determine the value of a case and what we can recover.

Here are the general steps to follow in ride-share cases include:

- Establish liability of the at-fault driver.
- Establish proof we are in a ride-share accident.
- Prove the app status of the driver and passenger (whether disengaged, "waiting for ride request," or "on their way").
- Pursue the full value of the client's case against Lyft/Uber policies.

If an injured person was hit by another driver who is working for Uber or Lyft, sometimes it's not even clear if the case even involves a ride-share driver. Clues we look for include but are not limited to looking at the passenger designations on the police report, viewing body cam and squad car footage, speaking with witnesses, etc.

After we have established our injured client's wreck was caused by a ride-share driver, the next variables we are concerned with are:

1. The seriousness of the client's injuries.
2. The ride-share app status of the driver, which determines how much insurance coverage is available.

If my client has very minor injuries and not a lot of medical expenses, then the ride-share status of the driver will probably be irrelevant. Any minimum auto insurance coverage should cover their injuries, pain and suffering, and other damages. Conversely, if injuries are serious, the status of the driver in the Uber or Lyft app has everything to do with how much we can collect on behalf of our client. In Georgia, Uber and Lyft ride-share insurance is governed by O.C.G.A. § 33-1-24.

We want to know whether a driver's personal insurance coverage (usually low or state minimum policy limits) or their commercial Uber or Lyft insurance policies will cover the wreck.

## App Status: Disengaged or Driver Mode Off

If the Uber or Lyft driver causes a wreck while his app is not activated or his driver mode is off, then his personal insurance will cover the wreck and the injuries endured by the people he hurts. Just because they drive around with that well-lit sign in their window, doesn't mean they are on duty and covered by Uber or Lyft. On a personal insurance policy, this coverage is likely to be $25,000 per person, and $50,000 per accident.

### Uninsured/Underinsured Motorist Situations (UM)

If a ride sharing driver is disengaged from his network or not logged on to the app, then he's just another driver for personal reasons and his own UM insurance policy limits will cover him.

## App Status: Driver Mode On/ Waiting for a Ride Request

If the driver causes a wreck when the driver's app is on, but no match has been made to a rider, then the Uber or Lyft liability policy will cover up to $50,000 per person and $100,000 per accident.

### Uninsured/Underinsured Motorist Situations (UM)

What if it's not the ride-share driver's fault? If someone hits the Uber or Lyft driver, and that at-fault person is underinsured or uninsured, then O.C.G.A. § 33-1-24 states that Lyft or Uber shall be responsible for $50,000 per person of bodily injury claims and $100,000 per accident if the driver has a non-ridesharing passenger in the car.

## App Status: On Way to Pick Up Driver/Match Notification Made/Dropped Off Passenger

Pursuant to O.C.G.A. § 33-1-24, if an Uber or Lyft driver causes a wreck during the period of time a driver accepts a ride request on the ride-share company's digital network, until the driver completes the transaction or the ride is complete—whichever is later—the Uber or Lyft policies will kick in and pay up to $1,000,000 for the bodily injuries they cause (to pedestrians, occupants of other vehicles, or ride-share passengers).

*Rideshare wreckage – full airbag deployment w/ multiple impacts*

### Uninsured / Underinsured Motorist Situations (UM)

If another car other than the Uber or Lyft driver causes a wreck and injures the ride-share driver or his passengers, from the moment a match notification is made and until that passenger's ride is completed, Lyft or Uber policies will cover up to $1,000,000 of bodily injury damages per accident to the driver or his passengers.

## Can I Sue Uber or Lyft?

How would you be able to pursue an action against Uber or Lyft directly? An example might include situations where the driver is so poorly skilled or intoxicated and has a terrible driving record with significant safety violations and causes serious injuries or death; or where there are multiple offenses and public complaints on the app about the driver's terrible skills; or even where the driver assaults or commits some other intentional tort against his passenger. In any of these situations, is it possible to sue the Uber or Lyft Corporation?

Not likely, but yet to be seen, as ride-sharing is still relatively new in the U.S. and Georgia. Most of the case law in Georgia asserted by ride-share defense lawyers claim the same law that should apply to them is what applies to taxicab companies. It is well settled that the drivers for taxicab companies are independent contractors. So far, no higher court in Georgia has made a distinction between ride shares and taxicab companies.

Uber and Lyft disclaim any semblance of being a transportation company and refer to themselves as mere communication companies that pair drivers with passengers. We know this is a flawed argument because there is a safety and background check when a driver applies to Uber, passengers and drivers have rating systems that people depend on, and both companies both have certain claims to quality depending on the type of vehicle you order. At some point there will be a case that goes on appeal with relevant facts, and I would hope that if Uber or Lyft shows that they undertook screening yet failed to take action with a knowingly dangerous driver, that they will be held at least somewhat responsible.

## DUI Injury Cases

DUI and punitive conduct from a Defendant is mentioned several times in this book. If an injured client is injured by a drunk driver, that case no matter how minimal the medical treatment is, it's worth $25,000 or much more. In minimal liability insurance cases where the injuries are soft tissue and minor in nature, I will keep track of the medical bills and make sure they don't get over $3,000 - $5,000, and immediately send a Holt Demand for the $25,000 policy. This maximizes the payout to the client with minimal reimbursements to medical providers.

In cases with more serious injuries, if we are still dealing with a minimally insured Defendant, then the case will likely involve the client's (Underinsured Motorist) UIM carrier. The problem with settling the claim against the liability carrier is that the DUI would then not be admissible in the UIM case if it had to be litigated (punitive facts aren't generally admissible in cases against the UM/UIM carrier). If a lawyer doesn't let the liability Defendant out of the case and accept their tender of limits, the evidentiary argument could be made that the inflammatory DUI evidence would be admissible in trial versus the Defendant's carrier and the client's UIM carrier. Even though it might be tempting to accept that quick liability payout, it might be more benficial to keep the Defendant in the case as leverage on the UIM carrier.

If a DUI is accused in a commercial trucking case, then this is an ultimate gamechanger. I would expect damges to exceed five to ten times special damages.

## Trucking Cases

Trucking accidents have similarities to car wrecks, but the more years I practice, the more I realize the differences are oceans apart. If a lawyer is new to personal injury and has a trucking case that comes in the door with serious injuries or death, the absolute best practice is to co-counsel that case with a law firm with deep experience in trucking cases. These lawyers will add tremendous value to the case. The referring lawyer can learn as much as they want, and it ensures the best possible outcome to the client and their family. A good injury lawyer is a humble team builder, never selfish, and puts the client's interests first—always.

### Recognizing a Trucking Case

You must take immediate action when a commercial truck is involved in an accident. Even in cases where a client might have been allegedly at fault or cited for the accident, if the injuries were bad enough, it might warrant further investigation and expense.

A trucking case can generally be described by any accident case involving a potential Defendant that should be governed under the Federal Motor Carrier Safety Rules (FMCSR). 49 C.F.R. § 390.5 defines a commercial motor vehicle as "any vehicle used on the highway in interstate commerce transporting people or property with a gross vehicle weight rating or gross combination weight rating or gross combination weight of 10,001 lbs. or more." Practically speaking and per the book on *Understanding Federal Motor Carrier Claims,* the FMCSR applies to any "owner and/or operator of any business vehicle and/or trailer with any load which in combination weighs more than 10,001 lbs. .... Straight trucks, work vans, large pick-up trucks with trailers, landscaping vehicles, HVAC work vehicles, plumbing trucks and utility may fall within this definition of a commercial vehicle."[1] If a lawyer isn't familiar with trucking cases, they should get on the phone with a trucking lawyer.

## Minor v. Major Trucking Cases and How to Handle Them

Minor impact cases involving an 18-wheeler are rare. Even if someone who has been hit thinks they are okay, they must see a doctor immediately and, at the very least, undergo an MRI of their spine (if their doctor advises). If the case is in fact a minor impact with minor injuries and client retains a lawyer, these cases can be handled much like a car wreck with a few exceptions, such as sending out

---

[1]Fried, Rogers, Goldberg, *Understanding Motor Carrier Claims, 5th Edition.*

spoliation letters. I have had two such clients recently, with only minor bruising. The biggest indicator that they were not seriously injured was that they had little inclination to attend their doctor appointments and wanted their cases closed immediately. In these minor trucking cases, maybe I could gamble and handle them like regular car wrecks, but it's smart to still send out spoliation notices and understand all parties involved. If injuries are minor, the settlement values on commercial policies can be much greater than typical auto liability carriers. In my experience, typical minor soft tissue trucking case settlement values range from two to ten times medical special damages, depending on aggravating factors.

*Clients rear-ended by 18-wheeler. Claimed minimal injury*

I once had a client that was rear-ended hard by a commercial driver. He suffered a herniated disc and had to get an epidural spinal injection to relieve the inflammation in his back. He made a great recovery after some lengthy physical therapy. In a case where he incurred $50,000 of special damages, we were able to recover over $500,000 on his behalf pre-litigation due to the aggravating factors in the case. Turns out after impact the commercial driver ditched his tractor trailer on foot and fled into a nearby clothing store where he hid in a dressing room and tried to change his appearance. Bystanders ran after him and called police and they were able to detain him in the fitting rooms. That punitive conduct greatly enhanced the value of this otherwise modest case.

Major impact cases with serious injuries or death are another battleground entirely. If an inexperienced lawyer is smart and cares about their client, they will associate with outside expert counsel. Consider the basics of handling a trucking case:

## Initial Response

In a serious case, the trucking companies know they have everything to lose and they have response teams to intervene and investigate the accident. Their insurance carriers have investigators, lawyers, and a risk management team on call 24/7 and they are usually on scene no later than two hours post-accident to investigate the wreck.

Right away, the attorney needs to send out spoliation letters to the trucking company. This prevents them from losing or destroying vital information about the wreck. We always demand preservation of six-month driver log reports, maintenance records one year before and six months after the accident, vehicle inspection reports, and whatever else is relevant. If a case is serious enough, the lawyer must facilitate a response team of its own. Accident reconstructionists, mechanics, safety compliance experts, photographic investigator, load securement specialist, human factors expert, and an expert to download the ECM data from the truck should all be considered. None of this can wait and must be done immediately, or the data is lost and gone forever. Skid marks disappear quickly, as does electronic evidence like ECM data, the black box, and evidence of mechanical failures. It's never safe to rely solely on the police.

## The Parties

To further explain the complexity of these cases, it's worth noting who the parties to a suit might be. The driver, the common carrier, the owner of the trailer, shipper, consignee, broker, insurer, and the logistics company can all be viable Defendants in a commercial trucking case. During litigation, the attorney might need to depose the driver, safety director, risk manager, maintenance director, training director, dispatcher, route specialist, and the information specialist.

## Establishing Liability

It's always helpful to understand how to establish liability and/or increase the value of a case. First, find out whether the truck driver was drinking or on drugs. Having a list of all rules of the road that were violated (as well as all potential violations of the Federal Motor Carrier Safety Regulations) is critical in proving liability. This is where bringing in a trucking case expert can be incredibly helpful: they can ascertain whether more specific FMCSR violations were contributory in the wreck. The expert can opine on the driver's background, the logbooks, required inspections, loading requirements, braking, conspicuity, other safety equipment, and all other documents required.

The FMCSR rules are most important because they establish the standard of care a truck driver must use. The standard is higher than a regular driver because of all the training and testing, inspections and logging of procedures. In fact, truck drivers must use extreme care in the fog, rain, sleet, or snow.

Expert trucking lawyer, Joe Fried of Fried/Goldberg believes the most simple and valuable tool in establishing liability in a trucking case is using the specific state's CDL manual. It specifically combs through every rule the driver must follow. The rules have basic language that is easy to understand, and they are hard to refute. Joe Fried suggests getting a copy of the CDL manual where the accident happened, the manual of where the Defendant resides, and a copy of a manual in the state where the Defendant company resides. Most CDL manuals are the same from state to state but there will be some variations. That manual will address the following:

- When to inspect, how often to inspect, and what to look for during inspections
- The 7-step methods of starting up the truck
- Basic control procedures while driving that include:
    - Seeing
    - Controlling speed
    - Distance perception,
    - Managing space between vehicles
    - Night driving strategy
    - Distracted driving
    - Being alert and safe
    - Understanding the load and cargo and its effects on the way one drives

The manual also addresses the safety of transporting passengers, air brakes, combination vehicles, double and triple trailers, tank vehicles, hazmat, and school buses. The CDL driver must have completed a rigorous licensing process, their daily procedures before they can drive are lengthy, and they have to know the mechanics of their trucking systems (unlike drivers of regular vehicles). Based on all this, they must be held to a higher standard. Use the CDL manual to show that CDL driving is a higher standard that what other drivers are held to.

## Resources in Trucking Cases

CDL trucking cases are highly specialized, and expensive to litigate. In 2018, my firm spent over $30,000 in expert fees, depositions, and litigation expenses in a case that was non-surgical and soft tissue in nature. More serious cases could easily cost a law firm between $50,000 and $250,000 just to get the case to trial. Unless a lawyer specializes in these types of cases, I would almost consider it malpractice to not associate with specialty outside counsel.

Perhaps the best resource for trucking cases here in Georgia is the law firm of Fried/Goldberg. This firm gives away everything they know at no cost and expecting nothing in return. Consider signing up for the monthly breakfast notifications or webinars at their website. Their firm also has a lawyer portal that is dense with anything one might need for litigation resources. It includes copies of all things written discovery, video depositions of Defendants, safety directors, and expert witnesses. The resources are limitless, and I highly recommend them. Their website is friedgoldberg.com.

Do not go about these cases alone. There is a lot at stake, and they are significantly different then the common car accident case. The addition of Federal Regulations, significant and substantial injuries, and the likelihood of a tremendous investment in prosecuting the case can make it an easy decision to call in the expert and share in the case. In fact, you owe it to your client to ensure that you maintain the correct level of expertise when accepting any new matter.

## Pedestrian and Bicycle Cases

There can be horrific injuries and death when a car strikes a pedestrian or a cyclist. Beyond establishing liability and obvious medical causation, uncovering insurance monies can be difficult. The at fault driver who wrongfully hits a pedestrian or cyclist due to negligence will ideally have liability insurance that covers the claim. If the driver runs from the scene and is never found or does not have enough liability coverage to compensate the client, then we must look elsewhere. Whether a client is a pedestrian or a cyclist, if a motor vehicle hits them, then their own uninsured/underinsured motorist coverage will cover their claim. This includes other coverages like medical payments coverage. After the client's policies are examined, we will then look to see if they have any resident relatives that can apply excess coverage.

## Pedestrian Laws and Common Cases

When pedestrians are lawfully in the roadway, they will almost always have the right of way. Therefore the driver of the vehicle that hits them is usually at fault and liable for their injuries.[2] If a pedestrian is hit in a crosswalk, they will almost always be able to recover for their injuries as they will have the right of way. When pedestrians are hit outside of the crosswalk the question becomes whether they entered the roadway already under safe conditions. [3]

In these situations, I think of cases where someone would be walking in their

---

[2] O.C.G.A. § 40-6-91and O.C.G.A. § 40-6-22.

[3] O.C.G.A. § 40-6-92.

neighborhood and there is no sidewalk, or situations where a car is parked on the side of the road, and they are hit while standing next to their vehicle. Applying the crosswalk law to these situations doesn't make sense. Another common pedestrian accident is when someone is backing out of their driveway or exiting an alleyway. In these situations, drivers have a responsibility and duty to yield to pedestrians on the sidewalk.[4]

I had a case in Tift County where my client and her friend had broken down on a rural, flat, well-lit, and straight farm road but it was late at night and dark out. They abandoned their car and walked along the fog line on the right edge of the road to go get help. Several minutes later a farm truck was speeding through the area, didn't see them and hit them causing serious injuries and hospitalization. There was no crosswalk or sidewalk for the pedestrians to traverse. They had entered the roadway lawfully under safe conditions. In establishing liability, we also found it helpful to establish that any reasonable person under the conditions would have seen the two women in the roadway and passed them safely.

## Bicycle Law and Common Cases

Bicycles are considered vehicles and thus subject to many of the same rights and restrictions by which motor-vehicles are governed.[5] The injuries are usually serious, so establishing liability and finding coverage can be tricky. The irony in cycling cases is that jurors can be sympathetic to the Defendant driver in these cases. Most people in Georgia have cars they rely on for transportation; they don't know what the bike laws are; bikes are much slower so they can be publicly perceived as a nuisance on the roads. Having a good case with clear liability makes a huge difference. It's my opinion that most cycling wrecks occur because cyclists are hard to see, and a driver isn't typically looking for cyclists to avoid when entering a roadway or while turning at an intersection – they are looking for motor vehicles.

When taking on a bicycle injury case it helps to rule out any wrongdoing by the client. I usually will focus on typical points of defense from insurers where they might try to deny liability, assert contributory negligence, or point towards alternative causation theories. Although helmets are not required for riders 16 and older,[6] a jury would likely hold that against our client if there was a resulting head injury.

We handled a cycling death case where an insurer initially evaded liability based

---

[4] O.C.G.A. § 40-6-144

[5] O.C.G.A. § 40-1-1(14)(75).

[6] O.C.G.A. § 40-6-296(d)

on my client not wearing a helmet. Once the State Patrol extracted the ECM data and ascertained the Defendant's vehicle was traveling 60 miles per hour when he hit our client on the right edge of the road, they relented and paid the amount we demanded. It was clear a helmet would have been useless in a collision at 60 miles per hour with a full-sized pick-up truck. The State Patrol didn't help us when they mentioned in the report that "although there were lights on the front and back of the bike, they were not working upon my arrival, and I cannot verify if they were working before [the cyclist] was struck." It was dark out and my client was required to have a white light on the front of his bike (a red steady or flashing light on the rear is not required under Georgia law). Based on numerous bike cases I have had, I believe police also have a bias against cyclists.

Other cycling laws in Georgia have a lot of gray area. For example, a rider should always stay to the right edge of the right lane on the road but there are many exceptions for when the cyclist is turning left, avoiding hazards, traveling on small narrow roads, traveling the same speed as traffic, exercising due care when passing a slowed or stopped vehicle, or if there is a right turn lane and the cyclist is not making a right-hand turn.[7] These are broad exceptions that would likely apply to most cases.

In the cycling death case mentioned above, the Defendant should have noticed my client and per O.C.G.A. **§ 40-6-56,** safely passed on the left with at least three feet of distance between his truck and the bike. If a driver hits a cyclist traveling on the right edge of the road, that is a good indication that the three-foot rule was not followed.

## Roadway Bike Collision Cases

Consider if one cyclist ran into another on a street, and one of them was clearly at fault and didn't yield when they should have. It is safe to assume that the at fault rider's auto liability policy would not cover damages caused to the other person since the bicycle will not be insured on an auto policy. The only plausible coverage from the Defendant would be his homeowner's liability coverage, or a general liability policy (like an umbrella policy). If there is no coverage or limited coverage, then the next place to look is the injured person's UM coverage. Since bicycles are considered vehicles by statute, the argument could be made that since the injury was caused by a vehicle in the roadway then the damages should be covered. This issue would be highly contested and litigated so the case would have to be a high damages and high UM coverage situation to warrant moving forward with the case.

---

[7] O.C.G.A. § 40-6-294

## Non-Roadway Bike Collision Cases

Although bicycles are considered vehicles, a collision with another cyclist or pedestrian would not be covered by auto liability or uninsured motorist auto policies where the accident occurs on a non-roadway like a sidewalk or the Atlanta Beltline. Insurance companies will cover accidents involving a motor vehicle on a roadway. The Beltline or any other non-roadway would be excluded from the policy. Insurance companies will also argue the bicycle is not a motor vehicle and therefore would not be covered under a UM policy.

*The Atlanta Beltline*

I found this out the hard way. Along with the firm of Litner & Daganian, I took on an interesting issue in Fulton County, Georgia. A cyclist was riding on the Beltline in the opposite direction of our client. The Defendant was distracted by something and went into the left side of the beltline and his helmet hit our client's face causing some serious injuries. The Defendant had no homeowner's or liability coverage, so the only place left to look was the client's UM policy. Although Arman Daganian superbly handled the case, opposing counsel successfully argued on summary judgment that by its very definition, the Beltline was not a roadway and should be excluded from coverage. The UM carrier's alternative argument was that the bike was not a motor vehicle and shouldn't be covered. The Court in its ruling did not have to address the latter issue. Sometimes, you learn the legal lessons the hard way. But that doesn't change the value in advocating for your client. In this case the seriousness of the injuries justified taking the risk to overcome the legal concerns. Fortunately for the client, he recovered and suffered no long lasting debilitation.

## Statute of Limitations in Auto Claims

The statute of limitations in injury cases (excluding ante-litem issues in government cases) is two years from the day before the wreck. If an accident occurred on January 1, 2020, then the statute will run on December 31, 2021. Tolling of the statute can occur with injured minors until they reach the age of majority, or cases where the Defendant was accused of committing a crime.

In Georgia, almost any traffic violation is a criminal offense. Therefore, the two-year statute will begin on the date the criminal traffic violation was closed and signed off on by the judge. In cases around the metro-Atlanta area, many traffic citations aren't resolved for up to two to three years, prolonging the statute for a lengthy period. Consider the circumstance where a Defendant collided with my client's vehicle on January 1st, 2020, was issued a citation for following to closely, and resolved that case with a no contest plea on July 1, 2020. The statute in this case would run on June 30, 2022.

## Injured by Someone Else While Driving for Work

I mention companion worker's compensation (WC) and third-party claims as they relate to liens in Chapter 14. In cases where someone is driving for work and is injured by a third party, they have two different claims: one against the third-party liability insurance carrier that hit them as well as the worker's compensation claim with their employer. Usually, the worker's comp claim will get them money faster so it's hard to pass this up. Before the client starts the WC claim I will let them know a couple things. First, if they proceed with the WC claim and it settles, then they will likely be forced to resign from their job as a condition of their settlement. Second, I will tell them they will have very little control over who their doctor is in the WC case. The WC defense team has to agree who the injured worker treats with. They also play a role in approving any necessary treatments, imaging, or surgeries. In cases where it makes sense with third party liability limits, if we see that the WC treatment has stalled out or not getting approved, we will consider having the client treat with a different provider on a lien that WC will not pay for but we'll likely get it paid for with the third-party settlement or verdict.

If the WC claim is being handled by a different lawyer, it helps to tell that lawyer if they settle, they must have the employer waive their rights to subrogation. Although their subrogation rights are weak in Georgia, they still can assess a lien and create headaches at settlement time. My understanding is that the employer will waive subrogation rights 95 percent of the time.

*HVAC technician driving company van was injured by a third party*

Now that we have unpacked car wrecks and trucking accidents, we can turn to the remaining types of injury cases you may handle. That is the topic of the next chapter.

## CHAPTER 6

# Non-Vehicle Injury Cases

In the previous chapter we spent time focusing our energy on car wrecks and truck accidents. While they often encompass the majority of an injury attorney's caseload, there are many other cases personal injury lawyers often accept and litigate. This chapter will help to provide an overview of those cases and brief insight into how we handle them. Remember, many of these cases require specialized knowledge and training, so either spend the time becoming an expert in the specifics of these cases or ensure you bring trusted counsel in that does have this experience.

## Homeowner Claims and Slip/ Trip and Falls in Businesses

Homeowners claims can have broad coverage for a wide range of negligence, even if the negligence occurred outside of the Defendant's home. These claims often become a catch-all for negligence committed by someone outside the scope of an auto or boating accident. For example, someone's child might accidentally seriously injure one of his friends, and even though the injury did not occur inside the insured's home, the policy still will likely cover the negligent act and the damages that followed. I have even seen homeowners claims cover bicycle accidents that occur away from the home.

I would suggest anytime a lawyer sees negligence committed by an individual that injures another outside the scope of an auto claim, consider pursuing a homeowners or umbrella claim against the negligent party. The worst the insurance company can do is deny coverage while citing specific policy language on why it will not be covered.

## Homeowner Claims Governed by O.C.G.A. § 51-3-1 and § 53-1-2

Georgia homeowners (or those charged with managing the property) have a duty to keep the home reasonably safe. However, their liability will depend on whether the injured person was invited to the property, had a license to be there, or was simply trespassing.

### Invitees - O.C.G.A. § 51-3-1

O.C.G.A. § 51-3-1 specifically reads. "Where an owner or occupier of land, by express or implied invitation, induces or leads others to come upon his premises for any lawful purpose, he is liable in damages to such persons for injuries caused by his failure to exercise ordinary care in keeping the premises and approaches safe."

Invitees are those who have been invited to a property and generally include family, friends, co-workers, and neighbors. That invitation can be express or implied. The owner of the property has a duty to keep it reasonably safe. Customers in stores and businesses are usually invitees too.

### Licensees – O.C.G.A. § 53-1-2

O.C.G.A. § 51-3-2 reads as follows:

*Duty of owner of premises to licensee:*

> *(a) A licensee is a person who:*
> *(1) Is neither a customer, a servant, nor a trespasser;*
> *(2) Does not stand in any contractual relation with the owner of the premises; AND*
> *(3) Is permitted, expressly or impliedly, to go on the premises merely for his own interests, convenience, or gratification.*
>
> *(b) The owner of the premises is liable to a licensee only for willful or wanton injury.*

Licensees therefore are those who have a license to be on the property. They generally include those who are there for their own financial benefit, such as gardeners, housekeepers, and yard and pool maintenance workers. In this situation, the owner must only warn of non-apparent dangerous conditions that may create an unreasonable risk of harm.

### Trespassers

Trespassers have no right to be on the property. Therefore, the owner typically does not have to keep the property safe or warn others about dangers. (Though obviously, the landowner is not allowed to maintain traps to intentionally harm trespassers.)

In Georgia, property owners and occupiers have a duty to keep their premises safe. While legal standards vary depending on the relationship between the injury victim and the landowner, generally, a Plaintiff can recover for injuries caused by a known hazard on the landowner's property.

In a typical slip/trip and fall case, the Plaintiff carries the burden of proving two elements.

1. The Plaintiff must prove that the Defendant had actual or constructive knowledge of the hazard superior to the Plaintiff, and
2. Despite exercising ordinary care, he or she lacked knowledge of the hazard.

Some of the most common types of Georgia premises liability lawsuits arise from:

- Carpeting or rugs which have worn or frayed and creates a tripping hazard.
- Any blatant structural problems in the home that result in injury.
- Deck collapses.
- Loose railings and banisters.
- Burns suffered because of a fire caused by the homeowner's negligence.
- Stairways or uneven floors which are not clearly marked and cause a slip and fall accident.
- Walkways, driveways, or pathways which have not been maintained due to weather conditions, ordinary use, or simply due to age.
- Dog bites from animals which were not leashed, fenced in, or otherwise controlled.
- Swimming pool accidents, including drowning, which were due to the negligence of the owner or the person who was in control of the property at the time.

## Slip/Trip and Falls in Businesses also Governed by O.C.G.A. § 51-3-1 and § 53-1-2

Georgia businesses or landowners (or those charged with managing the property) have a duty to keep their business reasonably safe. However, their liability will depend on whether the injured person was invited to the property, had a license to be there, or was simply trespassing. This is the same statutory analysis covered in the homeowner claims above. Invitees can include shoppers in a store, patrons in restaurant or bar, someone hired to do work by the owner, etc.

## Areas Owners are Responsible For

Property owners are required to keep the area within their premises free from unsafe static defects or foreign substances. This also applies to surrounding areas and approaches that are adjacent and under the control of the owner. Approaches are considered areas directly contiguous, adjacent to, and touching entryways to the property of the owner. To be considered a covered approach under the definition, the owner must be able to foresee a reasonable invitee finding it necessary or convenient to traverse while entering or exiting the premises for which the invitation was extended.

Within these areas of owner responsibility, slip/trip and fall cases can be divided into foreign substance cases and static defect cases.

## Foreign Substance Cases

A foreign substance is something on the ground not ordinarily present. This might be considered smaller particles, small puddles of water, waxes, cleaning products, food pieces, or other objects that can create a slippery or dangerous surface. Business owners have a duty to regularly inspect (but not necessarily discover) hazards that might be dangerous. If an owner can prove that the area that caused the accident was regularly inspected, they will likely win their case. Similarly, the owner would also likely win if a foreign substance would have been too hard to detect by ordinary inspection, as it would not have been discovered regardless of inspection.

In these types of cases, the Plaintiff must show that:

1 The Defendant knew or should have known of the foreign substance, and
2 The Plaintiff either had no knowledge of the danger, or the Defendant prevented the Plaintiff from discovering the danger.

Since no business owner will ever admit to having actual knowledge of a foreign substance danger, the burden often relies on the Plaintiff to show the owner had constructive knowledge. To show constructive knowledge of the dangerous substance or item, a claimant would show that employees were close by and could have easily seen and corrected the hazard. Absent proof of proximity of employees or staff, a Plaintiff could prove the substance had been on the ground for an extended period, that a reasonable inspection would have revealed the dangerous substance, and upon that revelation, it would have been promptly cleaned up. The longer the substance was on the floor, the more likely the Plaintiff would win at a summary judgment hearing. Cases showing an inspection period every 30 minutes are deemed to be adequate inspection intervals to reasonably discover a foreign substance. If someone falls because of a substance was there for merely a few seconds, courts will generally side with a Defendant on summary judgment.

In cases where a Plaintiff alleges that a defectively waxed or polished floor caused their fall, the Plaintiff has the burden of showing that the Defendant was negligently using certain materials or applying them in a way that was negligent. In rainwater cases, the burden becomes almost impossible to overcome because a reasonable person already knows areas in a store will be slippery because of other patrons tracking in water. This brings up defenses of equal knowledge that would bar the Plaintiff from recovery.

The most common types of foreign substance cases include:

- Wet floors with employees nearby in areas that would not ordinarily be wet.
- Walkways, driveways, or pathways which have not been maintained due to weather conditions, ordinary use, or simply due to age.
- Small produce left in the aisle in a grocery store for a long period of time.
- Small boxes or tripping hazards left in the aisles at stores.

## Static Defects

Static defects are fixed and unmoving. They have been in place for weeks, months, or years, and are subject to the same analysis that the Defendant knew or should have known of the danger, and the Plaintiff had no knowledge of it. In all cases, a business owner will claim lack of knowledge of the danger and a Plaintiff may have to show other people were injured there, or that people had complained about it in the past. In cases where dangers are obvious, such as potholes, or any structures or walkways that do not comply with building codes (such as uneven walkways or non-compliant ramps), knowledge is presumed. In serious injury cases involving static defects, getting an expert early on to evaluate code compliance could be critical to recovery for a client.

Some of the most common types of static defect cases arise from:

- Carpeting, flooring, or rugs which have become damaged, worn, or frayed and creates a tripping hazard.
- Uneven walkways where the height differential of one section to the next exceeds building code regulations – usually ¼ of an inch.
- Any blatant structural problems in the business that result in injury.
- Loose railings and balusters.
- Stairways, ramps, or uneven floors which are not clearly marked and cause a slip and fall accident.

## Defenses and Facts that will Kill a Homeowner's/Business Slip/Trip and Fall Case

Facts are incredibly specialized in any premises negligence case. If a case has any of these issues, an attorney should ensure that the injuries justify the risks of going forward. In addition, make sure case law is on the client's side to get past summary judgment. Some affirmative defenses to watch out for:

### Equal or Superior Knowledge

Intuitively, one might not find it just or equitable to hold a business owner liable for a danger the Plaintiff knew about and chose not to take precautionary measures while traversing the dangerous areas. For this reason, courts will regularly grant Defendant's summary judgment if the facts support that the Plaintiff knew of the dangerous conditions. Therefore, if the Plaintiff knows of the dangerous condition, there is no duty to warn imputed to the Defendant.

### Assumption of Risk

If a Plaintiff had traversed an area several times or had been there numerous times before and still chooses to traverse the area, the law will deem that they have assumed the dangers of their actions and would be barred from recovery. This is a component of having equal knowledge and being required to prove the Defendant must have had superior knowledge of the danger or defect.

### Prior Traversal

If the client had traversed the dangerous area before they hurt themselves, proving negligence becomes more complicated. By prior traversal they will have garnered equal knowledge of the potential dangers or the defect or surface and would be barred from recovery.

## Open and Obvious Defect

If the obstruction or danger of a static defect was open and obvious, recovery becomes much more difficult. When there is nothing that obstructs or interferes with a Plaintiff's ability to see a static defect, the owner is justified in assuming that the Plaintiff will see it, realize the potential risks involved, and change their course of action accordingly. An open and obvious static defect provides a complete defense to an owner's liability.

## Contributory Negligence and Causation

In every personal injury case, a defense attorney will look for any opportunity to assert that the Plaintiff was partially or more than 50 percent at fault, thus limiting or barring them from recovery. If a Plaintiff gets past summary judgment, they will surely try to argue to a jury that the Plaintiff knew or should have known of anything dangerous. Similarly, the defense will always look for ways to allege that any injuries the Plaintiff is seeking recovery for were not—and could not have been—caused by the slip and fall. Whether they had preexisting pain or injury, or there were previous or supervening events, a good defense lawyer will look for any defense available in these cases.

As one can see, foreign substance and static defect fall cases are hard, and the law is not favorable for an easy recovery at all. Many stars must align for one of these cases to be viable. There almost always will be a strong affirmative defense and oftentimes the insurance defense team will not offer a penny until a Plaintiff is lucky enough to get past summary judgment. Only then will a Plaintiff see any real money offered.

## Should I Hire an Expert?

Just as in any other case, the more serious the damages are, the more likely a competent attorney should consider hiring an expert for whatever the issue is. If the injuries are minor or soft tissue, treating the case like a low-damage car wreck case is more than reasonable. If the case is serious with catastrophic injuries and there are the policy limits to support it, a lawyer should certainly consider hiring an expert pre-litigation.

For code or structural issues, hire a well-respected structural engineer familiar with modern commercial or residential building codes to assess the case. We had a client catch fire because a 45,000 BTU commercial grade propane heater was placed too close to him while he slept, and we had to rule out any contributory causes to the fire. We hired Frank Hagan, P.E. to assess the burn patterns and all pictures we had, and he concluded the heater was placed within 18 inches of our client. Maybe we could've sent the demand without that expert report, but if there are substantial damages—and you want to ensure recovery of a big policy limit on demand, rather than burden a client with years of litigation—the expert could be a small price to pay. That case settled on demand for the maximum of $1,000,000.

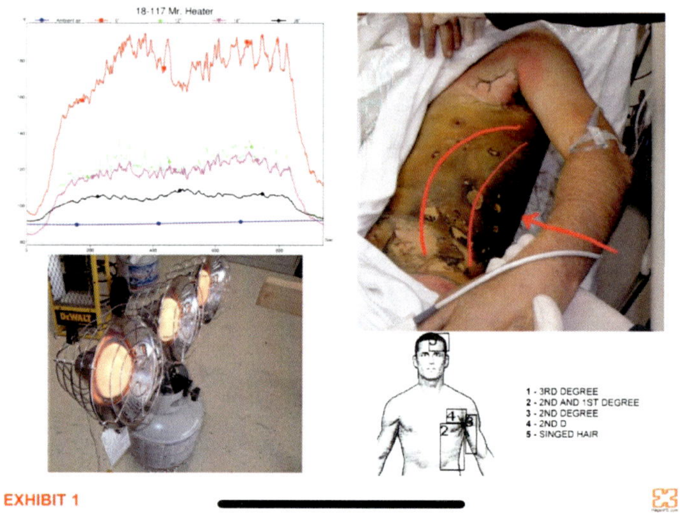


*Expert report - exhibit on burn patterns*

## Dog Bite Cases

Dog bites can be complex and highly specialized. Not only does a lawyer have to work their way through various statutory elements, but they also must find insurance coverage that will adequately pay the damages. Dog bite injuries can be tragic, and sometimes there is no insurance coverage for the most horrific of injuries. The legal hurdles on a bite case can generally be overcome with some diligence. Dog bite laws are a tangent on basic premises liability laws and duties for homeowners and landlords. Landlords and homeowners already have a duty to invitees to keep the premises and approaches safe.[8] The dog bite laws further clarify specific elements we must show and extend to, even when an incident doesn't take place on the homeowner's property.

To prove liability in a Georgia dog bite homeowners case, the Plaintiff must show either:

1. Prior aggression or viciousness,[9] OR
2. That a leash law type of ordinance was violated that led to the bite

[8] O.C.G.A. §51-3-1
[9] O.C.G.A. §51-2-7

## Showing Prior Aggression or Viciousness

O.C.G.A. 51-2-7 says *"a person who owns or keeps a vicious or dangerous animal of any kind and who, by careless management or by allowing the animal to go at liberty, causes injury to another person who does not provoke the injury by his own act may be liable in damages to the person so injured."*

Because of this wording, Georgia is classified as a "one bite free" state. It might be hard to prove liability if a dog is inside his home, a friend comes over and gets bitten while sitting on the couch. If there was no prior aggressive behavior, recovery could be problematic.

So how creative can we get showing prior incidents of aggression? Georgia courts have ruled that a dog barking, growling, or showing its teeth is not enough to show prior aggression.[10] The Plaintiff must show a prior lunge, a chase, a prior bite, or even the killing of someone's household pet. There is no breed-specific, strict liability standard to stereotypical aggressive breeds.

## Ordinance Violation

The statute goes on to say: "In proving vicious propensity, it shall be sufficient to show that the animal was required to be at heel or on a leash by an ordinance of a city, county, or consolidated government, and the said animal was at the time of the occurrence not at heel or on a leash..."[11] Any county or municipality will have leash law ordinances that prohibit a dog from being off a leash or outside of an owners' control.

Abusers or those who provoke a dog are barred from recovery. Trespassers are also excluded, but there are exceptions for small children that might be too young to understand whether they are trespassing. If someone is bitten by a police dog, they typically would not be able to recover.[12]

Affirmative defenses in premises cases often apply to dog bite cases. If a dog bite victim knew a dog was dangerous and then voluntarily put himself close to the dog, he could be barred from recovery. I had a close friend recently go over to a neighbor's house where their neighbor had a dog that had recently bit the owners own child. This was generally known by most of the neighbors. While my friend and his child were at the house, the dog got scared and just slightly bit my friend's child. The child was okay and the injuries were not worth a doctor

---

[10] Huff v. Dyer, 297 Ga.App. 761 (2009)

[11] O.C.G.A. §51-2-7

[12] O.C.G.A. §4-8-21

appointment. Had it been more serious, the prior knowledge my friend had of the dog's prior aggression would have been a legitimate defense.

### Finding Insurance Coverage

A viable dog bite case (or any injury case) is only as good as the insurance coverage that might exist; this coverage is often elusive, as homeowners are non-responsive when asked for home insurance information. Most homeowners will have general liability coverage. In my experience, getting in touch with the homeowner is impossible when they know I'm a lawyer about to sue them. We will send letters telling them they are required by law to send us insurance information, but they never seem to respond. If knocking on their door and calling them fails, we will file suit, hoping for a response. If I get a chance to speak with them, I am very clear that I want nothing to do with their personal assets and all we are looking for is insurance coverage. When we file suit, we are usually able to ascertain quickly whether there is insurance.

## Dog Bites Cases against Landlords and Multifamily Properties

Let's say John is walking his dog through the courtyard of his apartment complex, and out of nowhere, the dog lunges at Bill (another tenant), biting him. John is a renter and even keeps rental insurance as required per his lease, but his policy excludes dog bite incidents. If John has an umbrella policy, then maybe Bill could recover from John if the dog bite statutory elements are met. Otherwise, Bill might be stuck seeking liability against the property owner/landlord if the landlord knew of the dog's prior aggressive incidents.

O.C.G.A. § 44-7-1 addresses civil liability for landlords who have fully parted with rights of possession to a property and says they are not liable for the negligent actions of their tenants to third parties. Conversely, property owners have a duty under O.C.G.A. § 51-3-1 to keep their premises and their approaches safe for invitees. A multifamily landlord can logically part with rights of possession to all the interior units in a multifamily apartment complex, but still has a duty to keep the common areas safe. Single family residence home rental cases are much harder to prove against landlords because they have usually parted with their rights of possession and have no public common areas for invitees so O.C.G.A. 44-7-1 would apply.

In addition to showing the bite happened in a common area, the property owner/landlord must also have knowledge of the dog's viciousness or prior attacks. Without proof of the landlord's knowledge of the dog's aggressive tendencies, motion for summary judgment would likely be granted and a Plaintiff would be barred from recovery.

To recover from a property owner or landlord for a dog bite case, the victim would have to show:

1. The bite or attack occurred in a common area where the landlord had a duty to keep the area safe under O.C.G.A. § 51-3-1, AND
2. The landlord had knowledge of the dog's aggressive tendencies.

### Finding Evidence of Prior Aggression or Bites

I have a recent case where we were easily able to show prior aggression by doing a search on the county court clerk database with the homeowner's name. We also submitted an open records request for all police reports filed at that property and determined the dog had bitten at least two people prior to the incident with my client. Other ways one could investigate prior events is talking to neighbors or to the animal control officer and see if they had contact with the landlord.

After filing suit, much can be discovered during litigation. Requests for production of documents could reveal prior complaints, as well as current and former employees and other tenants that made complaints.

## Injured While Working but Caused by a Third-Party

It's common knowledge that if a potential client is hurt at work, then their exclusive remedy to recover under O.C.G.A. 34-9-11 is through their employer's worker's compensation benefits. Tort claims in this circumstance against the employer wouldn't be viable.

There are tangential circumstances where an injured person at work still has a tort claim. When hearing that a potential client was hurt at work, it makes sense to ask lots of questions to understand if there were other parties involved that could be liable to provide the client with additional recovery options.

If a worker at a property is injured by a third party that is not their employer, then they likely have a tort claim against that party. An example might be if a FedEx delivery driver is delivering packages to a home and the homeowner's dog gets out and bites the delivery driver. The FedEx employee has a worker's compensation claim with her employer as well as a third-party dog bite negligence claim against the homeowner and their insurance company.

Lawyers must be careful though that the third-party property owner isn't so closely connected to their immediate employer that the property owner might be considered a principal contractor or statutory employer and thus not liable for a tort claim.

I had a client who was a Registered Nurse (RN), and she worked out of a local hospital. She was a "statutory employee" of the hospital even though the hospital was not her immediate employer. Her nursing services company she worked for was contracted out by the hospital to provide RN services for the hospital's patients. She was walking down a hall that was freshly mopped. There were no yellow "wet floor" signs posted. Thus, she slipped and fell with her entire nurse workstation falling on top of her. She was badly injured and could not work for several months.

When I took this case on, I had never heard of the statutory employer law in Georgia under O.C.G.A 34-9-8. I figured I had a case against the hospital for premises liability negligence regarding their floor maintenance. After all they were not my client's employer and in effect, they were a negligent third-party. Opposing counsel for the hospital sent me some good law saying that my nurse client was a statutory employee of the hospital. The hospital's contractual relationship with the nursing services company in the facility was of the nature that rendered the nurse essentially an employee for the purposes of injury claims.

The hospital, although they were owners of the facility, maintained they were the principal contractor of the nursing services company, and while hiring them to perform nursing duties for patients, this was also their contractual obligation to other subcontractors in the hospital (e.g., physician's groups that needed nurses to perform their duties). Therefore, the hospital was a principal contractor to the subcontracting nursing services company, and even though the hospital was not the immediate employer of my client, they were the statutory employer of my client.13 Pursuant to O.C.G.A. 34-9-11, worker's compensation benefits provided by my client's immediate employer as well as the hospital were the exclusive remedy for which my client could recover. My third-party claim against the hospital was dead.

Thankfully we didn't give up there. Turns out the hospital also sub-contracted their housekeeping and cleaning duties to another third-party cleaning company. I called up the hospital's lawyers and told them I would immediately dismiss the case against them if they would tell me the name of the company hired for cleaning services at the hospital. They happily obliged and we then initiated a

---

[13] Carr v. FedEx, 317 Ga. App. 733 (2012)

third-party tort claim against the housekeeping company. We sent a demand for payment to them, and the case was resolved for a meaningful recovery for my client.

If you hear someone was injured at work, don't just stop there, and refer them to your favorite worker's comp lawyer. Try to ascertain all the parties involved to see if there are multiple claims available to the potential client.

## Medical Malpractice

It is hard to mention or even think about medical malpractice (commonly referred to as "med mal") without mentioning tort reform. In the early 2000s war was waged on the 7th Amendment. This was probably felt the most by the medical malpractice bar. Across the U.S., caps on damages, heightened burdens of proof, additional hurdles to file a case, and widespread propaganda has had the effect of severely crippling access to the courts by victims of medical malpractice. Since 2005, most Plaintiffs' lawyers avoid medical malpractice cases because they are so specialized and are cost prohibitive.

Ironically, the war on medical malpractice cases was pointless. According to the Congressional Budget Office, medical malpractice premiums, litigation, and verdicts accounted for only 2 percent of overall healthcare spending.[14] Furthermore, tort reform has had no effect on access to healthcare.[15] The propaganda was well received in the U.S. because healthcare costs were rising fast and the healthcare lobby (malpractice insurers, doctors, hospitals, well paid executives, etc.) jumped at the chance to scapegoat trial lawyers.

Their argument was an easy one to make: healthcare costs are driven by greedy trial lawyers filing frivolous suits and getting excessive verdicts. They argued these massive and frivolous verdicts were driving up the costs for everyone else and limiting the middle class' access to affordable healthcare. The results of tort reform have done nothing more than limit victim's access to the courts, increase incidents of medical negligence, and have failed to lower healthcare costs at all. Even doctor's malpractice insurance premiums haven't decreased.[16]

No novice injury attorney should ever handle a medical malpractice claim alone. If a potential client consults with a non-medical malpractice lawyer, and the case is even remotely viable, that lawyer should immediately call an expert medical

[14] Congressional Budget Office, *Limiting Tort Liability for Medical Malpractice* (January 8, 2004).

[15] Government Accountability Office, *Medical Malpractice: Implications of Rising Premiums on Access to Health Care* (September 29, 2004).

[16] Forbes Magazine: *On Tort Reform, It's Time to Declare Victory and Withdraw* (March 2, 2015).

malpractice lawyer. In my experience, I must decline representation on 99 percent of the medical malpractice claims for those that call my office. To proceed on these cases, one must bear in mind that it takes $100,000–$500,000 to litigate these cases. A viable case must have substantial damages and liability must be clear—at least at first, because it almost never is actually "clear cut."

## Evaluating the Case

What does medical malpractice look like? Here are just a few examples of how a doctor, hospital, or nurse's negligence can seriously injure or kill someone:

- Failing to diagnose deadly medical conditions such as heart attacks, strokes, and infections.
- Failing to timely diagnose or treat surgical complications.
- Failing to diagnose and treat testicular torsion or ovarian torsion.
- Hypoxic ischemic encephalopathy (HIE) birth injuries caused by failing to promptly perform a C-section, leading to cerebral palsy or death.
- Birth injuries such as brachial plexus damage.
- Maternal deaths during deliveries.
- Medications errors caused by physicians, nurses, and pharmacists who ordered, approved, or gave the wrong medication, the wrong dose, or administered the medication to the wrong patient.
- Anesthesia deaths and brain injuries caused by prematurely removing a patient's breathing tube, failing to be prepared for a difficult airway, and intubating patients in the esophagus instead of the trachea.
- Serious injuries or death caused by airway fires during medical procedures.
- Patients being awake or waking up during surgery due to the mismanagement of anesthesia.
- Failing to provide timely treatment of infections, leading to extensive tissue loss or amputations of one or more limbs.
- Performing unnecessary medical procedures that cause serious and catastrophic injuries.
- Failing to monitor IVs, causing IV infiltration and serious injuries to a patient's arm.
- Leaving surgical instruments and sponges in patients that should have been removed.

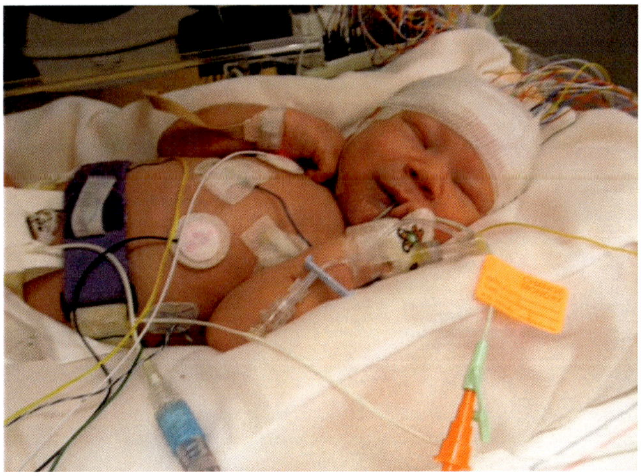

*Newborn recovering from induced hypothermia following HIE birth injury*

## Medical Malpractice Statute of Limitations

In the state of Georgia, O.C.G.A. § 9-3-70 through § 9-3-74 governs the statute of limitations involving medical malpractice in Georgia. A claimant generally has two years from the date of injury, but no longer than five years with the statute of repose. The statute can be tolled for various issues like whether the Plaintiff was a minor at the time, for incapacitation, or even fraud. Statutes of limitation are critical in every case, so always read the statute and know what dates a case is bound by.

## Should I Even Bother with a Demand Letter?

In my experience, demand letters to doctors or hospitals are pointless, as they are often just completely ignored. Invariably, suit must be filed to get any substantial recovery on a medical malpractice claim. Of course, if a case is litigated and it has substantial value, one should always consider an Offer of Judgement fulfilling the requirements enumerated in O.C.G.A. § 9-11-68.

## What Needs to Be Proven?

To prove a claim for medical malpractice, a claimant has to prove the doctor deviated from his/her standard of care. The standard of care for a physician is based on the degree of care and skill ordinarily exercised by physicians in the U.S. (not just locally or in the same state) under the same or similar circumstances.[17,18] (See Further accentuating this uphill battle in malpractice cases is that there is rebuttable presumption medical services were performed in an ordinary and skillful manner.[19]

---

[17] Murphy v. Little, 112 Ga. App. 517, 521 (1963)

[18] Summerour v. Saint Joseph's Infirmary, 160 Ga. App. 187, 188 (1981)

[19] Beach v. Lipham. 276 Ga. 302 (2003)

When alleging medical malpractice, the law requires the attorney to submit with the complaint a standard of care affidavit, written and signed by a licensed physician. As one can imagine, the costs of having a skilled physician review thousands of pages of medical records is high.

The potential parties in a medical malpractice case include: the treating doctor, other supervising doctors, the hospital, nurses, anesthesiologist, or whoever else interacted with the patient/client.

Given that these cases are so costly, damages must be extraordinary in a malpractice case to rationalize bringing a case.

## Daycare Negligence

Child Care Learning Centers (daycare and pre-schools) are governed by Georgia's Department of Early Care and Learning or DECAL. Their website is decal.ga.gov, and is a great resource for parents interested in laws, rules, open records, licensing, and disciplinary history of a particular facility. O.C.G.A. § 20-1A-1 – Creation of DECAL, reads as follows:

> The Department of Early Care and Learning is created as a department of the executive branch of state government and shall have the duties, responsibilities, functions, powers, and authority set forth in this chapter and otherwise provided by law. The Department of Early Care and Learning is the successor to the Office of School Readiness and shall have the duties, responsibilities, functions, powers, authority, employees, office equipment, furniture, and other assets formerly held by the Office of School Readiness. The Department of Early Care and Learning shall be a separate budget unit.

Based on this statute, DECAL created the regulatory governing body, Bright from the Start, and all rules and regulations are codified under Ga. Comp. R. & Regs. R. 591-1-1. This set of rules formally known as the "Rules and Regulations for Child Care Learning Centers."

Chapter 591 creates strict rules for many areas of childcare, including animals, bathroom conditions, health, records, health records, diaper changing areas, toy approval, hygiene, field trips, sanitation, kitchen operations, medications, and many more. We encourage every parent to be armed with knowledge about these rules so they may properly vet an establishment. The 92-page Bright from the Start PDF document covering all these rules is public and may be read at this link: http://decal.ga.gov/documents/attachments/cclcrulesandregulations.pdf.

The more the public knows, the more children will be protected. The most common violation of these rules is when a daycare knows and is informed of an injury or incident in their facility, and they fail to self-report the incident to DECAL. We find the best facilities often over-report even the most minor of violations or incidents.

## Negligence Law for Daycare Facilities

A daycare facility is held to an ordinary negligence standard as set out in O.C.G.A. § 51-3-1, described as duty of owner or occupier of land to invitee:

> "Where an owner or occupier of land, by express or implied invitation, induces or leads others to come upon his premises for any lawful purpose, he is liable in damages to such persons for injuries caused by his failure to exercise ordinary care in keeping the premises and approaches safe."

"Failure to exercise ordinary care" might include any of the following:

- Providing an unsafe environment, such as leaving sharp or dangerous objects or broken equipment on the playground.
- Having knowledge of a hazardous condition and failing to remedy the hazard.
- Repeated safety violations.
- Negligent supervision, such as staff leaving children unattended who may fight each other, touch hazardous objects, or run away.
- Inadequate hiring, such as failing to conduct background checks to weed out applicants with a criminal record of child abuse.
- Intentional physical or emotional abuse.
- Understaffing the facility, which can lead to a lack of supervision or neglecting children's needs.
- Poor organization, which can lead to giving a child the wrong medication, serving expired food products, or causing an allergic reaction.
- Car or bus wrecks during field trips.
- Unsanitary conditions.
- Poor and careless cleaning practices where exposing dangerous chemicals to the children injures or burns them.

I have handled many cases involving many of the above incidents and they all are heartbreaking and highly emotionally charged situations.

## Do the Research During Intake

Ask the tough questions when laying the groundwork for a daycare case. We always try to ascertain the following:

- Whether the facility was insured per the statute for injuries to children. If they are not, was notice of no insurance posted conspicuously at the entry way of the facility? (Typically, more insurance means a more rule-following culture.)
- Do they strictly adhere to Chapter 591 and the rules governing daycare centers?
- Do they consistently report any incidents on their premises?
- What is their hiring protocol for running background checks of prospective employees?
- Did they run a background check in the case with the employees involved?
- Have they had any major violations in the past, or ever had their license / accreditation ever suspended or revoked?

One great aspect of the Bright from the Start system is parents and the public can look up violation and license information on any licensed childcare facility in Georgia on this link: http://families.decal.ga.gov/ChildCare/Search. One can obtain a wealth of public information on a facility including, but not limited to: address, ownership data, locations, pre-K availability, but also license status, violation notices, and prior enforcement actions.

Any information NOT included by DECAL might be obtained by completing an Open Records Request to Bright from the Start, which can be found here: http://decal.ga.gov/BftS/OpenRecordsRequest.aspx.

## Report a Safety Violation/ Incident to Bright from the Start

If a client's parent is aware of a dangerous incident at a facility and they want to make sure the daycare is held accountable by DECAL, they can make an anonymous complaint to the childcare services department of Bright from the Start. DECAL will investigate any report concerning a licensing violation at a childcare center, group day care, or a family childcare home. To file a complaint, they can call 404.657.5562 or 404.656.5957.

## Parties to a Daycare Negligence Case

In a daycare negligence case, the business (rather, their insurance company) is the primary party the attorney is up against. Secondary to that, one could name the owner personally or even staff members that were involved and drop them from the case later as more information regarding liability is learned. In a serious injury or death case, one should always be cognizant on whether the cause of the injury was a dangerous product. If so, consult with a products liability expert to ensure money isn't left on the table.

### Demand

In a childcare facility case, I send a Holt demand to the insurance company the same way I would in an auto case with similar requirements. If the value of the case exceeds $15,000, the settlement will have to be filed and signed off on by a Probate Judge in Georgia. Sometimes that can take anywhere from two to 12 months depending on the venue and case. If the case is complex with serious injuries, then any novice lawyer should associate with more experienced counsel in order to provide top value to the client, as well as making sure the claim and suit are handled properly.

## Products Liability

As this book is introductory in nature, we won't go in depth on products liability, but here are some basic points one must understand.

First, PL cases might be the most highly specialized and expensive cases to get to trial. (Recent estimates I've heard are $250,000–$500,000 at least.) Furthermore, Defendants are usually some of the biggest international corporations that have infinite resources to litigate and prolong a case into eternity: car makers, gun makers, chemical companies, etc. Just like other specialty areas of injury law, the damages and injuries must be massive to justify taking a case like this on. The analysis on damages and necessity of litigation on these cases is like the medical malpractice cases mentioned earlier.

The Statutes of Limitation in Georgia are covered in O.C.G.A. § 9-3-33. Generally, in products injury cases (excluding minors and legally incompetent), the statute is two years from the date the cause of action accrues. Under O.C.G.A. § 51-1-11, the statute of repose for Georgia product liability tort actions against a product manufacturer is 10 years from the date of the first sale for use, or consumption of the personal property causing or otherwise bringing about the injury. A Plaintiff must also be able to show that the alleged defective product was not merchantable and not reasonably suited for its intended purpose, and the product's condition when it sold was sold was the proximate cause of the Plaintiff's injury. Exceptions to this 10-year statutory repose period include negligence actions alleging that a manufactured product caused disease or birth defects, or negligent conduct manifesting willful, reckless, or wanton disregard for life or property. Georgia courts hold that the 10-year statute of repose for products liability tort actions also does not apply to a Plaintiff's "failure to warn" negligence claims.

## Negligent Security Cases

Think of derelict property owners and managers that know the property is dangerous because of criminal activity, but do not protect their residents, or invitees. These cases include apartment complex shootings, or shootings in any public area, strip malls or locations controlled by a business where they know there is dangerous criminal activity but chose to do little or nothing to protect bystanders.

When a hardened criminal walks into an apartment building to commit burglary and then kills an innocent person when confronted, why should the apartment building owners and property managers be liable for that man's actions? Apportionment of liability is a huge hurdle in these cases.

Negligent security cases can be tremendously complex, expensive, and litigious. They are the subject of ongoing tort reform efforts. Any serious injury or death case should be handled by competent counsel.

### Negligent Security Claims in Georgia

People expect to be kept safe from harm when visiting another person's property. In order to do so, many office and public buildings have security systems, cameras, or security personnel in place to help prevent crime on that property. However, when these systems are not in place, or if they fail and a person is injured, the property owner may be held civilly liable for the resulting injuries.

Lawsuits against landowners and property owners whose inadequate security leads to harm are most often pursued using the legal theory of premises liability. This tort alleges that a property owner's negligence led to the injury of a visitor.

### Duty of Property Owners

Georgia law is clear in stating that property owners have a responsibility, or duty, to protect visitors to their land. However, the extent of this duty depends upon the reasons for the visitor being on the property. The law recognizes three classifications of visitors: invitees, licensees, and trespassers Each of these classifications affects the duties of landowners to keep people safe.

The most protected people are those who enter a land as invitees. According to

O.C.G.A. § 51-3-1, landowners here must exercise reasonable care in keeping the premises safe.

### Other Classes of Visitors

For licensees and trespassers, the landowner must only refrain from intentionally or recklessly causing harm. Since it is very rare that a landowner intentionally causes an injury through poor security, most inadequate or negligent security cases apply to those people considered invitees.

Landowners have an obligation to take reasonable care to protect invitees. This includes ensuring that their property is safe, and measures are taken to prevent the criminal activities of others. Installing security cameras, hiring security guards, and limiting access to residents are all examples of steps that can be taken to maintain safe premises.

### Breach of Duty in Negligent Security Claims

For a negligent security claim to prevail, a Plaintiff often must show that the breakdown, or lack of any security system, was the proximate cause of their injury. In order to do so, a Plaintiff can illustrate there was a breach of a landowner's duty by proving that:

- The victim entered the land with the permission of the property owner. This can include shoppers in a store, patrons in restaurant or bar, and even tenants and guests in an apartment building.
- The owner or property knew or should have known of the dangers presented and the owner had superior knowledge of the danger, AND
- But for the inaction or poor and negligent security measures taken by landowner, the victim would not likely have been injured. This can involve introducing evidence that a lock was broken on a common area door, that the landowner did not employ proper security measures, there were numerous previous burglaries, frequent gang activity, or even that the area had inadequate lighting.

## Suing the Government

Some time ago, I had the pleasure of having attorney Seth Eisenberg, a specialist in seeing the government, as a guest on my *Jim Paisley Podcast*. He took a deep dive into the caveats of taking action against the state and federal government. Much of what I write here is based on the material we covered, but he goes into much greater depth on the podcast. This is all from Seth's materials:

## Suing the State

The Georgia Constitution grants the state and all its departments and agencies sovereign immunity. In Georgia, sovereign immunity is defined as a legal protection that prohibits an agency of the government from being sued without their consent. A 1991 Constitutional Amendment empowered the Georgia General Assembly to waive said immunity by enacting a State Tort Claims Act. The Georgia General Assembly enacted O.C.G.A. § 50-21-23, commonly referred to as the Georgia Tort Claims Act (GTCA), waiving state immunity for acts of state employees and officers acting within the scope of their employment.

The GTCA makes it clear that the exclusive remedy for injuries caused by negligent employees is an action against the State agency, not the employee personally. Waivers of sovereign immunity, and the extent of such waiver, are strictly construed by Georgia courts. Only an act of the Georgia General Assembly can waive state, county, and municipal immunity.

The GTCA represents a limited waiver of sovereign immunity and caps certain monetary damages depending on the type of occurrence. There are special exceptions and limitations regarding the types of actions, ante-litem notice of claim, venue and service that must be followed or else claims against the state will be barred before a jury gets a chance to decide a case. In claims against the state, ante-litem notice deadline is 12 months from the date of the incident and is governed by O.C.G.A § 50-21-26. The laws governing state claims are much stricter than the laws for cities and counties. A plaintiff must provide ante litem notice within twelve months of their injury. The notice must also be written, and hand delivered or mailed (via either certified or overnight delivery), to both the Risk Management Division of the Department of Administrative Services, and the government office that is the basis for the claim. While the state attorney general does not have to receive the ante litem notice, he does have to be served with a copy of the lawsuit once you bring the actual claim. Suit cannot be filed until the State responds or 90 days has passed with no response. And per the statute there are numerous agencies that must receive the notice. The notice must articulate the name of the government entity accused and the acts that are the basis of the claim along with the date, time, location, nature of the loss suffered, the amount of loss claimed and what exactly caused the loss. The statute is long and convoluted and requires a thorough analysis while drafting and sending the notice to the appropriate parties.

## Suing a County

The Georgia Constitution grants counties sovereign immunity, and therefore you can only sue a Georgia county with proof of a waiver of sovereign immunity. The waivers provided in the GTCA do not apply to counties. Georgia counties enjoy broad immunity with few exceptions. An important exception is the statutory waiver codified in O.C.G.A. § 33-24-51 for car accidents caused by the neglect of county employees. Additionally, while the county is insulated from suit for the wrongful acts of its employees, in certain circumstances county employees can be sued in their personal capacity.

Like the State, there is a specific 12-month window of opportunity for ante-litem notice after an accident for injured victims to act. Although the ante litem notice requirements for suing a county are less strict, it is much harder to sue a county than a city or the state in Georgia, as there are less claims that are actionable. Ante litem notice for suing a county is governed by O.C.G.A. § 36-11-1. The statute covering county claims requires them to be presented within twelve months after your injury. A plaintiff must notify the county in writing of the intent to file a lawsuit within twelve months, and lay out basic information of the reason for the claim. The statute only requires that the county receive sufficient information about a potential claim, in order to give the county an opportunity to investigate the claim and gather evidence prior to suit.

## Suing a Municipality

O.C.G.A. § 36-33-1(a), in conjunction with the Georgia Constitution, establishes that it is the public policy of the State of Georgia that there is no waiver of the sovereign immunity of municipal corporations except as expressly waived by the Georgia General Assembly, and implied waivers of a municipality's sovereign immunity are not favored. The important distinction for understanding when a municipality is liable is whether the action causing the injury was the neglectful performance of a governmental function. An example of a governmental function is garbage collection done for the public benefit. In contrast, there is no immunity for an accident related to the operation of a municipality's water works (a proprietary function).

Unlike counties, there are several express waivers of a municipality's sovereign immunity. There is a statutory waiver for car accidents caused by the neglect of municipal employees. The Streets and Sidewalks doctrine, codified at O.C.G.A. § 32-4-93, sets forth a municipality's liability for defects existing in a municipal street system. Municipalities are not immune from nuisance causes of action. It is a Plaintiff's burden to prove that a city is liable for negligence.

O.C.G.A. § 36-33-5 governs municipal ante litem notices. Claims against a city have stricter guidelines than a county claim but less requirements than suing the State. Per the municipal statute, you must provide a written ante litem notice to the city within six months of the injury. The notice must be in writing to the governing authority of the municipal corporation for adjustment, stating the time, place, and extent of the injury, as nearly as practicable, and the negligence which caused the injury. No action shall be entertained by the courts against the municipal corporation until the cause of action therein has first been presented to the governing authority for adjustment. The governing municipality shall consider and act upon the claim within 30 days. After 30 days a claimant can file suit if the action hasn't settled upon ante litem notice. The statute of limitations is suspended during the time that the demand for payment is pending before such authorities without action on their part. The anti-litem statute for municipalities is long and convoluted, requiring careful analysis before sending notice to all of the required recipients.

## Suing a Cop for Excessive Force or Federal 1983 Actions

Police brutality or civilly holding law enforcement accountable for over-aggression is an entirely different animal. This gets into Federal 1983 actions where police are personally liable for intentional torts, like battery or an ensuing wrongful death. Recent examples of this include George Floyd, Rayshard Brooks, and older cases like Rodney King.

The Civil Rights Act of 1871 is a federal statute, numbered 42 U.S.C. § 1983, that allows people to sue law enforcement or any other government agency for civil rights violations. It applies when someone acting for the government has deprived a person of rights created by the U.S. Constitution or federal statutes.

Lawyers I know refer to these cases as "1983 actions." These claims are most often invoked when someone claims to be the victim of excessive police force, or police brutality.

Pursuant to 42 U.S.C.A. § 1983 (2020), for it to come into play, the Defendant must have acted "under color of any statute, ordinance, regulation, custom, or usage, of any State…" Courts have determined that the "under color of" clause requires that the tortfeasor qualify as a representative of the state when depriving the victim of civil rights. Essentially, the clause refers to people who misuse some kind of authority that they get from state law. Police officers who use excessive force generally fit this bill. When a 1983 action has to do with an arrest, a court will normally consider the officer to have acted under color of state law, and therefore meeting that requirement.

Judges can consider several factors to decide whether an officer was acting under the color of state law when violating someone's federal rights. Among them are whether the officer was on duty, was wearing a police uniform, used police equipment (like a taser, his squad car, or handcuffs), flashed a badge or otherwise claimed to be an officer, or simply carried out an arrest.

## Bivens Actions Under Federal Authority

The U.S. Supreme Court established a similar kind of legal claim to the Section 1983 lawsuit in **Bivens.**[20] A "Bivens action" is comparable to a Section 1983 case, the key difference being that the person accused of wrongdoing is an official of the federal—rather than a state or local—government. In a 1983 case, for example, the Defendant might be a city police officer, whereas the Defendant in a *Bivens* case could be a U.S. FBI agent.

As one can see, cases against the government are highly specialized areas of law that I would not hesitate to associate with an attorney like Seth Eisenberg or a civil rights specialist to make sure nothing was missed or overlooked.

There are many different shapes and sizes for injury cases. As you build your practice, it is imperative to first choose the areas you intend to focus and specialize. That will give you a leg up on the competition, as you can begin to build your brand and represent yourself as an expert in your practice areas. If you choose to be a jack of all trades, ensure you have competency in each of those areas of practice. If not, you are opening yourself up to tremendous risk and likely ethical and bar complaints.

---

[20] Bivens v. Six Unknown Named Agents of Federal Bureau of Narcotics, 403 U.S. 388 (1971).

# CHAPTER 7

# Client Intake

The first two weeks of a case are often the most crucial. This two-week window is often the point where witnesses have the greatest clarity of mind, when videos haven't been looped over, when evidence can be preserved, and—of course—where lawyers can document injuries via photographs. A laundry list of intake protocols ensures that we, as zealous advocates, are doing everything we can to preserve the value and efficiency of a case. What follows is an example of a typical intake protocol that we employ at our firm, and that you should consider employing at yours.

## Get to Know the Client like Family

I always request to meet new clients in person. This gives me an idea of how their injury has affected them, any resulting limitations, and the amount of pain they are enduring. It also helps me get a good understanding of their character—a crucial step in any new case If someone is seriously injured or if they've lost a family member, I will always travel to them to make the process as smooth and as accommodating as possible.

Having said that, most clients with minor injuries aren't terribly interested in sitting down for an in-person visit within the first two weeks. Seeing them at work or home is usually too personal, and they may not want to go through the headache of scheduling an in-office appointment. Though the strong preference is always to sit down face-to-face, there are certainly exceptions that can be made; in these cases, getting to know the client via phone can suffice.

## Collect Client Information and Background

Good people make good clients. Our forms go deep into everything relevant about the case and the client's history. This includes name, date of birth, location of accident, medical history, health insurance information, auto insurance information, previous accidents and claims, relatives that live with them, and a medical timeline of treatment providers. This is also your best opportunity to gather any relevant pictures from the accident.

## Obtain Accident Info and Report

Accident reports are a great starting point for a case. The accident report contains names of drivers, owners, insurance information, contact information for all involved, diagrams, locations, how the wreck happened, officer's names, witness contact information, whether citations were written, the weather, etc. Accident reports can also tell us whether there was a video of the investigation. In every case, one should always do an open records request for video, audio, 911 calls, and all reports from investigators. The best place to get reports in Georgia is buycrash.com.

## Establish Liability

The police report is often helpful here. If there's any gray area, we go to the scene and take pictures, call witnesses listed on the report, and ask them to email us their version of what happened. If liability is questionable, we look at video (if available) and listen to what witnesses say on 911 tapes. We explore all aspects of the case until clear liability begins to fall into place. Should the evidence suggest that our client was likely at fault, we will shut the case down sooner, rather than later. There's little use in stringing the case along and wasting the client's time.

## Send a Firm Introduction (i.e., CYA) Letter

This letter is usually attached to the engagement contract. It explains to clients that they should use common sense on social media and limit what they post about the accident. The CYA letter should also cover all the obvious bases: establish an open door of communication about doctor's visits and diagnostics and remind them to keep up with their doctor's appointments. Additional advisement in the CYA letter should state whether they've ever declared bankruptcy, a request for any related bills and records, HIPAA releases, shared details on any prior injuries, and—of course—an invitation to contact us with any new information or questions.

## Engagement Contract

Any contract needs to establish the contingency fee. (I usually keep mine at 1/3 pre-litigation and 40 percent after filing suit unless it's closed soon after filing.) Our contracts state that the attorney's fee will never exceed the net proceeds the client receives at the end of a case, even if I must cut my fee to ensure this result. The agreement also establishes that we don't get paid our fee or expenses unless we win.

We also include two standard clauses in our engagement contracts. The first is a termination clause that allows us to assess a lien for attorney's fees if we are fired unjustly. The second clause allows us to co-counsel with another attorney and lets the client know that it will not affect the contingency from their end.

Other things to add include a power of attorney giving us the authority to settle on their behalf, and a statement establishing that we don't practice tax law and cannot advise on whether the settlement will result in any tax implications.

## Health Insurance Information

Health insurance is an incredible value driver for an injury case. I make copies of each client's health insurance cards and, in most cases, try to have most treatment run through their health insurance. This will have a net effect of driving costs down and providing bigger margins for our clients.

### How Health Insurance Works in Injury Cases

To understand how health insurance can benefit personal injury victims, it is first necessary to briefly discuss how health insurance works. Most health insurance plans are designed to cover a certain amount of medical bills once a deductible has been met, with the insured responsible for covering the remaining portion. The reason health insurance can help drastically reduce out-of-pocket expenses at the end of a personal injury case is because the insurer will have a contract in place with a medical provider to pay a predetermined amount for a treatment rendered. Once the insurance pays their contractual portion to the provider, members then are usually required to pay a copay amount. The provider usually adjusts the remainder of the bill to satisfy the total amount charged for the services rendered.

A hypothetical scenario illustrating how health insurance works would be to consider a client we will refer to as "John." John was rear-ended in a car accident and incurred a $10,000 hospital bill as a result. John's health insurer, who was in-network with the hospital he was treated at, has a contract in place which outlines that John will pay a co-pay of $500 while the insurer will pay 30 percent of the bill ($3,000, which might have to be paid back later), and $6,500 will be adjusted (i.e., written off) by the hospital. The benefit that health insurance provides in this instance is that it saves John at least $6,500 off a $10,000 bill. John satisfied the debt in full and only had to pay $500 because he had health insurance and went to an in-network hospital.

### How Can Health Insurance Yield a Greater Recovery?

Continuing with John's example above, let's assume he files a claim against the person who rear-ended him for his hospital bill ($10,000) plus pain and suffering. His case settles for $25,000. When it comes time to distribute settlement funds, John will walk away with a significantly larger recovery amount than he would have if he did not have insurance. Here's an example of what his settlement statement would look like:

- **Settlement amount** – $25,000.00
- **Payment to hospital** – $0.00
  *(John paid his copay and his health insurance covered the rest)*
- **Attorney's fee** (33.3 percent) – $8,333.33
- **Subrogation amount** – $3,000.00
  *(If the Health Insurer is ERISA-protected, we might have to pay back this amount. It can be negotiated or tossed if there's no right to recovery. More on ERISA in Chapter 14).*
- **Net recovery check to John** – $13,666.67.

Without health insurance, we would have had to negotiate directly with the hospital to pay off the entire $10,000.00 balance. Hospitals have all the leverage and typically refuse to reduce more than 15–33.33 percent. Health insurance is a big advantage for the client and their ability to collect on a case.

## Auto Declarations Pages

We ask our clients to print out or show us their auto declarations policy. We inquire whether they have any resident relatives with their own uninsured motorist policy that might stack on top of the client's. We'll send a letter to the uninsured motorist (UM) carriers as well as the liability carriers, demanding they tell us the liability and UM policy limits of the parties involved in the wreck. If they have a traditional/reduced by UM policy, we make sure to request a copy of the form they signed waiving add-on UM coverage. We are also looking for indications of medical payments benefits.

**Coverage Information**

Your total annual policy premium for all covered vehicles is shown below. A premium is shown for each type of coverage you have purchased for each vehicle. **Where no premium is shown, you have not purchased the indicated coverage for that vehicle.**

| COVERAGE | LIMITS | | PREMIUM PER VEHICLE |
|---|---|---|---|
| | | | **VEH 1 2016 KIA FORTE** |
| **A. Liability** | | | |
| Bodily Injury | $ | 25,000 Each Person | $337 |
| | $ | 50,000 Each Accident | |
| Property Damage | $ | 25,000 Each Accident | $285 |
| **B. Medical Payments** | | | |
| | $ | 1,000 Each Person | $55 |
| **C. Uninsured Motorists** | | | |
| Uninsured Motorists | $ | 25,000 Each Person | $108 |
| Bodily Injury | $ | 50,000 Each Accident | |
| Property Damage | $ | 25,000 Each Accident | |
| Property Damage Deductible | | | |
| Veh1: $250 | | | |

*Clients declarations page – looking for UM coverage and Medical Payments*

## HIPAA's and Medical Record Collection

While tedious, these forms are very important. Our HIPAA forms address not only authorization of our collection for the client, but also the power of attorney to sign it on their behalf, as well as consent to transpose their signature on other medical collection documents. This means we can use the form to collect the records ourselves, hire another record collection company to collect them for us (more on that below), or use their signature on a medical provider's own paperwork if they insist. The timing of medical record collection can also be important, an issue discussed in more depth in Chapter 10.

### Outsourced Medical Record Retrieval

We outsource most of our record collection. There are several effective and reasonably priced companies that automate this process, such as American Retrieval and Legal Monkeys. Without a doubt, this is one of the biggest cost- and timesavers for our law firm. If we can cut our paralegal's time spent on collecting records, they can instead focus on client satisfaction and working their cases up. These collection companies can get records much faster than a paralegal can. Their processes have been automated and refined with AI technology that can't be replicated by a legal staff.

The average cost of collection is $30 per record (plus whatever the medical provider charges), and $30 per bill collected if it's not included in the records. If it is a small provider, like a private orthopedic clinic or chiropractor, we don't bother with outsourcing record collection. In these cases, we should be able to contact someone directly.

## Establish a Medical Timeline

Once we have collected the names of all known medical providers for the client, it is important to establish a medical timeline of treatment. A good timeline will include information such as date of service, name of provider, type of provider, and type of treatment rendered. The timeline can be as detailed as needed, but keep in mind that a brief timeline will make it easier to quickly obtain a high-level view. Most importantly, this timeline will be a great reference source when it comes time to draft a demand and final settlement statement.

## Prior Medical Treatment and Claims History

In every personal injury case, it is almost certain that insurers will run our client's insurance claims history. As a personal injury lawyer, it always better to be a step ahead and ask clients about prior claims filed. When asking about their claims history, we want to find out if they have filed any type of personal injury claims in the past, including (but not limited to): claims such as workers compensation, premises liability claims, medical malpractice claims, auto accident claims, etc. Find out how long ago the prior claim was filed, what type of injuries were involved, and if the claim has been resolved. In general, the more extensive the claims history for a person is, the more insurers will try to use this to their advantage in painting the client as a litigious person.

In many cases it makes sense for lawyers to run their own claim history through a C.L.U.E. Report through LexisNexis. We usually run it on their portal, or you can email them at **consumer.document@lexisnexis.com**.

Likewise, we also want to discuss and note a client's prior injuries. Prior injuries are not uncommon and don't always have to be detrimental to a case. For example, some people are asymptomatic and only become symptomatic after enduring trauma, such as an auto accident. In other cases, some people endure soft tissue injuries in a prior accident and those injuries are later exacerbated by a subsequent auto accident. Some people are in an eggshell state when they are hit. They might be recovering from a surgery, are pregnant or elderly, and an auto accident aggravates prior issues.

Upon discovering evidence of prior injuries, insurers will do everything in their power to undermine our client's case. We never volunteer evidence of prior injuries unless we are trying to show an insurance company that our client's injuries are now worse than they were before. The types of injuries we make a special note of are the injuries that our client specifically sought medical treatment for. Particularly, we want to find out the type of injury sustained, and the extent of treatment performed. Did the client's injury get resolved through soft-tissue physical therapy/chiropractic means, or did the client undergo injections or surgery? Has the client gotten an MRI of a specific body part in the past which may be in question now? How long ago was the prior injury or treatment? The longer period of time since they were treated for a similar injury, the better.

Just as we want to uncover our client's prior claims history, we also want to know their injury history so that we are prepared for anything the insurance company may bring up later. There is nothing more frustrating than having an insurer reveal something about a client that you should have known beforehand.

## Pitfalls (e.g., Bankruptcy)

We had a client once that filed for bankruptcy unbeknownst to us. We spent months on this client's case establishing coverage, overseeing treatment, and even litigating the case. It was not until we were knee-deep in litigation that defense counsel asked for this case to be dismissed based on a pending bankruptcy, for which she did not list her pending personal injury action. Whenever a person is in bankruptcy and they have a personal injury action pending, they must list that matter in their proceedings.

This is one instance where the CYA letter mentioned earlier comes into play. In said letter, the client is advised to notify us of any bankruptcy proceedings that they become involved in. Unfortunately, the consequences of failing to do so can quickly derail a case, regardless of how compelling it may be.

## Establish a Case Management System

Now that we have collected all pertinent information from our client, we need to input this information for safekeeping. Every firm needs to have a case management system to keep accurate records, quickly access files, and track progression. Programs such as Filevine, Casepeer, and Clio exist to help law firms manage their case load. Case management software programs provide everything from intake forms to electronic databases, fax services, calendaring, accounting, CRM data, and telephone services. Creating a "master list" of cases is also helpful because we can constantly stay abreast on case statuses, lead types, and case values.

While these programs can cost $200+ per month, the ability to have streamlined case organization and management is well worth it.

In our office, once we implemented a good case management system, we began calendaring bi-weekly follow-ups with every single case. The number one complaint against lawyers is "I haven't heard from him/her" or "He/she doesn't answer my calls." Keeping a regular channel of communication with a client eliminates 99 percent of client issues and allows us both to stay informed of any new developments. It also gives the client an opportunity to ask us questions about the case that they might not ask otherwise. Keeping a consistent pattern of communication helps avoid unexpected surprises with cases and has the added benefit of keeping clients happy.

The importance of having a streamlined, detailed, and organized intake process cannot be overstated. Not only does this provide your best opportunity to create a personal connection with a client, but this two-week window is crucial to ensuring that the foundation for a case is built without cracks or impediments. Establish a solid intake process, follow up on any missing pieces, and you'll find that bringing new clients on board becomes much more efficient.

## Social Media Scan for the Client and the Defendant

In my intial client advisement letter, I advise clients to stay off social media altogether. At the very least I'll advise never to post anything involving the wreck, injuries, and to refrain from posting any photos or videos of the client engaging in anything active that might prejudice their claims of injury later on. In addition I will ask for social media handles and I will perform my own search on their profiles to make sure nothing is posted that could harm the merits of their case. I have represented sex workers, Instagram models, Youtube personalities, and other social media "celebrities," and each scenario requires a case by case analysis on what could prejudice them later in the event of litigation.

Conversely, the intake team at my law firm will always do a Google and social media check on the Defendant. The fruits of a Defendant's social media scan can be worth a lot of money. I have had several cases where a Defendant was at a party with photos and videos of them drinking with time stamps on the posts, and even though they may not have been arrested for DUI, we use their pictures and their captions as admissions in the case against them as circumstantial proof of impairment. I handled an apartment shooting case where my client was murdered on the grounds of his apartment building. Later that very day the property management company made numerous statements on social media announcing that they were absolutely not responsible for anyone's safety on the premises. Those self prejudicial statements were useful later on.

## Assisting a Client with Their Property Damage Claim

Unless a client is catastrophically injured or killed in an auto wreck, one of their top priorities is getting their car fixed or replaced. They may care about their means of transportation more than their injuries, and this is understandable. It might be the family's only car and they cannot maintain any measure of their livelihood without it being replaced. Assisting them with their property damage claim is necessary, even if it is just to make sure they have the ability to get to and from their doctor appointments. I tell my clients that I do not represent them for their property damage claims, however I will guide them and give advice where necessary based on my experience with these companies. The reason for this is that it doesn't make sense for me to represent them and charge them on a contingency fee that would eat up a significant portion of their car money.

When we must represent clients on both the property damage and bodily injury claims if the liable insurance carrier denies coverage altogether, or just refuses to pay anything. I will advise the client to keep any receipts relating to rental car payments, rideshare drives to work or the doctor, or monies paid for out-of-pocket fixes to their vehicle. In addition, I inform them that the insurance company is only liable to pay them the cash value of their vehicle. If their car is not totaled, I will advise them they are entitled to make a separate diminished value claim for their car. This might warrant having the diminished value assessed by a third-party appraisal company.

Lastly a client will invariably ask me if they should make their property damage claim through their insurance company or the liability carrier's policy. This advice is entirely subjective based on my opinion and is more practical than anything legally based. My answer depends solely on whether their car is legally drivable. If the car can be safely driven and meets equipment standards, then they should be patient and wait until the liability carrier is advised of the claim, investigates, accepts liability, and helps arrange and pay for the repairs. This process usually takes two to three weeks depending on the insurer.

If the client is in more of a hurry or if their car has been severely damaged and undriveable, they should make the claim through their own insurer. The response time will be much faster, and they will be put in a rental until the vehicle is totaled out. At that point they will be given a check for the cash value of their vehicle minus their deductible. When liability is finally accepted, opposing insurance companies will often reimburse drivers in two to four months when their own insurance company resolves their subrogation claim against the liability carrier for the deductible amount. The client must know that they cannot make the claim against their own insurance company unless a police report has been made within 24 hours of the wreck.

# CHAPTER 8

# Key Letters to Send

Now that you've gathered your client's background information and entered the case management system, it's time to send out initial letters of representation (LORs). Aside from providing notice of representation, LORs typically include a brief synopsis of the type of claim, date, time, and person(s) involved. They also act as a formal request for a copy of the insured's policy limits. There are different types of LORs based on the type of case and information received from a client, but the most common letters are listed here:

## Letters of Representation to Liability Insurance Carrier

If an insurance claim has not yet been filed, one should call the insurance company and file a claim on the client's behalf. It's important to establish a claim number, adjuster name, contact phone number, fax, and mailing address for the LOR. We can often obtain the insurance company name and policy number of the driver/insured from the accident report.

Along with this letter, an Affidavit Requesting Policy Limits should be submitted to the liability carrier to follow the statute and force them to reveal the policy limits. Having the Defendant's policy number isn't always necessary. If we are aware of the liability carrier, the name of the Defendant, and perhaps the date of birth or driver license of the driver, it is likely they can find the policy.

## Notice to the Client's Uninsured/Underinsured (UM)/Medical Payments Carrier

This is where novice attorneys get themselves in malpractice trouble. I once took over a case where the bulk of the claim was UM coverage and the previous derelict attorney never sent notice to the UM carrier. The case was over a year old, and many UM carriers would have denied coverage. They have provisions in their contracts (which are routinely upheld) that bar coverage if notice is not sent within 30-60 days or "as soon as practicable." It is imperative that a notice of UM/MedPay claim is sent with all other initial letters of representation. If a claim has not been established yet, we follow the same protocol outlined for the at-fault insurance carrier in establishing a claim.

Depending on the case, there might be stackable policies (liability or UM), so a lawyer must send appropriate LORs to every insurer. Resident relative policies will likely stack.

## Notice to Resident Relatives UM Carriers

I cover this numerous times throughout these chapters, but it bears repeating. If a client has a relative that lives with them and the relative has their own car with their own auto insurance policy, then whatever UM insurance that relative has will be excess, meaning it will be considered as stackable (i.e., add-on coverage) for a client's injuries. This UM carrier must be put on immediate notice to make sure benefits are protected if needed.

My cursory reading of Georgia law is that even distant relatives can become stackable. I've seen in-laws covered, and stepparents/stepchildren as well.

Resident relative UM coverage is by its nature an excess policy. That means it is irrelevant whether the policy is a traditional or add-on. Traditional UM policies are only reduced by liability coverages, not other UM coverages.

## Homeowner's Notice

In a homeowner's personal injury case, make sure to file a claim if one hasn't been filed yet. Send an LOR to both the homeowner and their insurer, putting them on notice of the incident and asking for policy limit information.

## Spoliation Letters in Trucking, Premises, and Products Cases

We send spoliation notices in products liability cases, premises liability cases against a business, and auto accident cases involving company or commercial vehicles. We demand preservation of evidence to both the company involved and their respective insurer. Furthermore, we include general LOR information, which demands insurance coverage documents.

## Ante Litem Notice on Government Cases

If suing a government entity, we send an ante litem notice to them as soon as possible. There are different time limits to send a notice depending on which type of government entity we are filing against. The Ante Litem notice, LOR, and spoliation notice can be included all in the same letter. Specifically, when filing a claim against a city or municipal corporation, we pay specific attention to the statutory language requirements outlined in O.C.G.A. § 36-33-5. For example, per the statute, we must send the letter to the mayor, the entity within the city/county, and/or the city commissioner's board. Lastly, as a catch-all, we consider including a clause in the letter that states: "In the event that you find something in this letter that does not meet the statutory requirement, please contact us immediately."

Government entities and agencies (such as police departments) have specific protections afforded to them in the law. We want to thoroughly research who we are making a claim against, and what protections exist in the law for that entity. We need to know if there are any relevant statutes concerning time limits for filing complaints and/or language to include in the initial LOR to them. ***The deadline for ante litem notice for State and County is 12 months from the date of the incident; if dealing with a city, the deadline is six months.***

The ante litem must also demand a specific amount of money, as its purpose is to allow the government agency a chance to settle pre-litigation. The ante litem is a quasi-demand and in many ways, it even reads like one. The statute says we must list the amount we are demanding—and although this seems simple in nature, many lawyers mess this up. On my podcast (*The Jim Paisley Podcast*) episode with government Plaintiff's lawyer Seth Eisenberg, he is baffled by how many lawyers screw this up. They will write "an amount potentially exceeding $5 million…" Courts in Georgia have said this doesn't comply with the statute. It must say, "I am demanding $5 million for full compensation for my client's injuries…" In many pre-litigation government cases, the information we have is limited, or the scope of a client's injuries is unknown when the ante litem deadline is approaching. Therefore, to satisfy this requirement, the lawyer must shoot high to make sure the requirement is met; if they do choose to pay it, it will be a fair amount for the client no matter what.

Read O.C.G.A. § 36-33-5 and talk to GTLA members to make sure this notice satisfies the statute.

## Open Record Requests to Law Enforcement and Court Dispositions

Sometimes it's not possible to get a copy of the police report on buycrash.nexislexisrisk.com. We'll be forced to send a formal open records request via U.S. mail to the appropriate law enforcement agency. The request should give notice of representation concerning the client; details about the date, time, and place that the incident occurred; and should request records such as police reports, body cams, dashcam, supplemental reports, witness statements, and/or 911 calls. Police departments, fire departments, and 911 departments may require separate requests for records. For court dispositions, I will call the clerk of court's office in the court that has jurisdiction over the traffic ticket that the at-fault party was issued in order to coordinate obtaining a copy of the disposition of the case.

## Google Maps and Google Earth

While not an official form, utilizing Google Maps and Google Earth can be extremely helpful to a case. I like to get a printout of the place that the accident took place for my own records. Simply put, it helps to have a visual representation of the accident scene when trying to acclimate ourselves with a client's case.

## Access to Forms and Letter Templates

By far, the most comprehensive personal injury form database is Michael Goldberg's ***Library of Georgia Personal Injury Forms, 5th Edition. It covers over 300 possible forms needed in a personal injury case and just about any form needed that applies to topics in this book. I highly recommend this form database! Forms in his database not covered above include:***

- Law Enforcement Misconduct Spoliation Letter
- Escalator/Elevator Spoliation Letter
- Nursing Home Spoliation Letter
- Spoliation Letter to Preserve Surveillance Tapes
- Letter to Insurer Requesting Client's Recorded Statement
- Open Records Act Request to Police for Entire Investigative File
- Open Records Act Request for 911 Tapes/CAD Report
- Letter Requesting Certified Copy of Guilty Plea
- Letter to GBI Requesting Autopsy Report
- Letter to GBI Requesting Toxicology Reports
- Freedom of Information Act Request to Federal Governmental Entity

- Freedom of Information Act Request to Federal Motor Carrier Safety Administration
- Open Records Act Request to MARTA for Elevator/Escalator Incident
- Open Records Act Request to Department of Human Resources
- Open Records Act Request to Animal Control
- Open Records Act Request to Police for Criminal History of Property
- Open Records Act Request to Internal Affairs/Police Department for Excessive Force
- Open Records Act Request to Department of Labor

NOTE: All of the forms listed in this chapter, except for the Open Records Request letter, should be sent via U.S. Certified Mail, Return-Receipt Requested per applicable Georgia law. If available, a copy of the accident report should be attached as well.

Sending written correspondence is an effective way to preserve evidence, request important and key documents, and providing you with overall insight and investigation into your case. It is important to send correspondence out almost immediately, as you never know what is out there at the forefront of the case that may otherwise disappear when it is time to litigate. Document your files, ensure you protect your clients interests, and use the key letters outlined in this chapter to create leverage and the potential for a successful resolution.

***My Top 30 most often used forms are on my website, PaisleyLaw.com, and can be accessed for free. Of course, anyone using these should be competent in the law they are practicing and make changes to the forms depending on the law and facts in their case.***

***There are many more form letters one might need than the ones mentioned above, but these mentioned are by far the most common.***

## CHAPTER 9

# Building the Foundation of a Claim and Maximizing Recovery

Personal injury lawyers may find themselves spending a significant amount of time exchanging documents with clients, insurance agencies, and opposing counsel. Rest assured that those letters of representation are not in vain! In the weeks to follow, you will receive letters from various entities be many incoming letters concerning the case. You can expect to receive letters from medical providers, responses to open records requests, and correspondence from insurance companies. The most common letters we receive during the first month of handling a case are outlined below.

## Declarations Pages, Reservation of Rights, and Denial Letters

These letters will either outline available coverages for a client's loss or deny coverage based on the policy. Common reasons for insurance coverage denials are unpaid insurance premiums, unlicensed drivers, and/or excluded drivers from the policy. On occasion, the insurance company will deny a claim based on causation and liability dispute issues. If a denial of coverage is not asserted, you will need to find out exactly how much applicable policy coverage is available to your client. In Georgia, the minimum amount of liability bodily injury insurance available as of this writing is $25,000 per accident and $50,000 per person.

I always recommend asking the insurance company to provide an affidavit verifying coverage from the at-fault party/policyholder. Likewise, if our client's damages end up being more than the liability limits cover, we typically look to our client's uninsured motorist policy for additional coverage. Later in the chapter, we'll go into more depth about what to look for on the declarations pages to maximize recovery potential.

## Medicare Reporting Notices

All auto insurance companies are required to report a claimant's Social Security number in their system to Medicare by law. Medicare is strict about protecting their interests in a personal injury case when they pay for someone's medical care. They expect to be reimbursed accordingly from any settlement and must immediately be placed on notice by the insurance company. As a result, the insurance company may send the attorney a letter asking for a client's personal information so that they can comply with their respective reporting requirements. We coordinate with the insurer to allow them to get this information to Medicare as soon as possible. Having Medicare or Medicaid footing the bill for a client's medical bills is beneficial for both the client and for our firm. Their involvement drastically reduces inflated medical bills that would otherwise be payable to the hospital.

## Police reports, Videos, and Open Record Requests

These publicly available records help us prove liability and frame the narrative for our client's case in the demand stage. If a Defendant receives a citation for their negligence after the crash, we can find out whether he entered a guilty plea to close the case. If the Defendant pleads guilty to rules of the road or a moving violation, establishing negligence per-se is complete. We will then get a certified disposition from the local court.

| **Traffic Control:** 7 | | **Device Inoperative:** ¨ **Yes** ý **No** | | **T** |
|---|---|---|---|---|
| **Citation Information:** | | | | **C** |
| **Citation #** | E03927001 | **O.C.G.A. §** | 40-6-391(a)(1-5) | **C** |
| **Citation #** | E03927003 | **O.C.G.A. §** | 40-6-123(a) | **C** |
| **Citation #** | | **O.C.G.A. §** | | **C** |
| **COMMERCIAL MOTOR VEHICLES ONLY** | | | | |

*DUI citation listed againt the Defendant. A cue to do an open records request for video and arrest report.*

Likewise, if the Defendant's case is pending, we want to know the status of the case and if there are any upcoming court dates, etc. If it's a serious case with high limits, we will contact the prosecutor and make sure they are aware of a pending civil claim. Prosecutors can be a very helpful ally in getting more information on a case, as well as in leveraging the criminal case to achieve better results on the civil matter.

## Supplemental Information from Clients

Supplemental information includes photos, medical bills, and property damage correspondence. As the case unfolds, the client should also be receiving various correspondences. The client should be informing counsel of any releases or other correspondence from the insurance company, as well as sending a copy to ensure all parties are staying up to date. This responsibility is outlined in our client advisement letter and discussed in detail prior to signing. From time to time, we also may need to help a client coordinate property damage and diminished value claims.

Keeping a consistent line of communication with a client helps avoid pitfalls in the early stages of a case. The biggest drawback to a lawyer not having enough information from the client is that the lawyer is unprepared. They might not have all the facts (both good and bad) to bring the most compelling case forward and won't be ready to defend the weakest parts of their case. I preach early on to my clients that if there is any information that could hurt our case, I must know about it immediately.

I had a wrongful death case recently where the decedent was riding his bike on a rural road and was killed instantly when he was hit by a truck driving 60 miles per hour. The family was ashamed and reluctant to tell me of their son's recent mental health struggles. Knowing these issues forced me to strengthen my analysis of the cause of death being attributable to the Defendant and not something more sinister, like a suicide. Had I not known about his mental health, I could have been blindsided later in a deposition or in court.

## Lien Notices from Hospitals

Many hospitals outsource their lien recovery services involving auto accident cases to consumer collection law firms. Since the hospital is likely unaware of our representation, our client may receive correspondence from this law firm or subrogation company. We typically advise our clients to avoid speaking with these entities while the case develops. If the client has private health insurance, we encourage them to limit their inquiries to the health insurance copay amount and to verify that the hospital has billed health insurance to date.

Many times, these law firms are seeking MedPay coverage information; it's the hospital's gimmicky way of maximizing their recovery of their inflated bills. I always avoid giving the hospital MedPay information, as they have overinflated bills and are incredibly reluctant about reducing them during settlement. If the client does not have health insurance, we still make a note of the law firm in their records. Eventually, we will need to negotiate the bill with the contracted law firm prior to settlement (Chapter 14 discusses resolving healthcare liens in greater detail).

The foundation of a claim is built not in bricks and stone, but in paper. This makes it crucial to create a solid, dependable, and fool-proof system to ensure that the proper paperwork is both sent and received. Use documentation to your advantage, and you'll find yourself building stronger and stronger cases. And once you do that, you can begin to maximize your recovery. Remember the foundation of a case is defined by the receipt and sending of documentation – but a truly great personal injury attorney knows how to properly analyze that paperwork. Leaving no stone unturned will maximize recovery for a client's case. As a personal injury lawyer, you have a range of creative recovery options to explore in liability and coverage to ensure that your client is adequately compensated.

## Liability

You should have a police report, the client's testimony, a disposition copy, case status knowledge for the at-fault party's ticket, and any 911 calls/dashcam footage. The next step is to look for any signs of aggravated liability which could lead to punitive damages. You may find extenuating circumstances that change the course of the case as a result.

Consider a former case where a client was struck in his driver's side door by a vehicle at 2:00 AM. The at-fault party was not cited for DUI, but upon further investigation of the 911 tapes and our client's testimony, we discovered that onlookers had called 911 minutes prior to the accident. These callers complained about an erratic driver that appeared drunk. Further bodycam evidence showed that the driver exhibited signs of nervousness and slurred speech but was not breathalyzed or investigated for DUI by the police.

Numerous CT scans had created an expensive ER bill for our client, and his recovery included months of visits to orthopedist. The insurance company initially tried to downplay this case, but after asserting evidence of drunk driving, the insurance company tendered full policy limits of $25,000. As a rule, we will assert punitive conduct whenever it's remotely plausible. Like the aforementioned case, an insurance company would be afraid of an excess verdict (leading to a bad faith claim) if a jury had to decide the outcome.

## Insurance Coverage

If we have the declarations pages of the at-fault party and our client's UM coverage, we will need to accurately determine the amount of available coverage for the client's loss. Below are different scenarios in which coverage exposure can potentially be increased:

### Liability Stacking

If a client is hit by a person driving someone else's vehicle, the amount of liability coverage could be increased if the at-fault driver has an auto liability policy of their own.

Similarly, let's assume our client is the first in line in a three-car accident. They are hit once by the car immediately behind them, and again when the third vehicle forces another collision into our client's car. Our client may be able to assert a claim against *both* vehicles, not just the car immediately behind them.

A third example would be an adult child that lives with his or her parents. If the child causes an accident and does not have insurance of their own, they could potentially be covered under the parent's auto liability policy if they reside in the same household.

## UM or Underinsured Motorist Coverage and Resident Relatives

When I receive a copy of my client's declarations page in the mail, I'll make specific notes about the available UM coverage. There are two types of coverage I am looking for:

### Add-on Coverage

Add-on coverage is the best UM/UIM coverage anyone can have. In a situation where the at-fault party is underinsured, the add-on UM policy will help cover the rest of the value of the case. As the name suggests, this coverage will be added on to whatever liability coverage is available. If the liability carrier has a $100,000 policy and our client has $50,000 of UIM add-on coverage, the total coverage would then be $150,000.

### Traditional Coverage

The second and most common type of UM coverage that clients have is "traditional" or "reduced by" coverage. This limits the amount that our client can recover because it is contractually offset by the amount of available liability coverage. Insurance companies are required to have their insured sign a written waiver stating they knowingly are waiving add-on coverage. We always demand a copy: if they cannot produce this signed waiver, the coverage is converted to add-on by default.

The worst-case scenario is when the client has no UM coverage available. In Georgia, drivers are allowed to choose which type of UM coverage they desire. As noted above, the insured must waive UM coverage in writing. If the signed waiver can't be produced by the insurance company, the insured is entitled to the state minimum coverages.

To illustrate the crucial difference between UM coverages, let's analyze a recent case. Our client, "Angela," was rear ended in an auto accident and had to undergo major neck surgery as a result. Her medical bills totaled over $100,000. The at-fault party only had $50,000 in liability coverage, but the client had an "add-on" UM policy of $100,000. We were able to get the maximum settlement of $150,000 on this case because the client had the "best" type of UM coverage.

If Angela only had "traditional" UM coverage, her maximum recovery would have been limited to $100,000, because the UM coverage would be offset by the $50,000 in liability coverage available. If Angela declined UM coverage altogether, the maximum recoverable amount would only have been $50,000.

In each instance, the differences are steep. The best advice we can give any client or is to always get as much UM (add-on) insurance as they can afford. As tempting as it may be to save on insurance costs by minimizing coverage, we never know when an uninsured or underinsured person can cause damage or injury.

## Can a Client's UM Carrier Cancel, Non-Renew, or Increase Rates if Client Was Not at Fault and They Make a UM Claim?

Invariably, clients are worried if they give notice to their insurance providers, or make a claim on their own UM/UIM policy, then they will then have to pay increased rates, or their policy will be cancelled. Clients that have USAA insurance are especially weary of this. I will show clients two different statutes that address this issue and alleviates this concern.

O.C.G.A. § 33-9-40 articulates that insurance companies may not surcharge premiums or cancel the policy of their insured based on involvement in a wreck that was not their insured's fault. This clearly stands for the proposition that being a victim of a wreck alone is no basis to increase rates or cancel a policy. Based on this statute I advise clients that at the very least they must put their UM/UIM carrier on notice and protect their right to recover from it if necessary. This statute does not address the scenario where an insured might make several or excessive claims from wrecks that are not their fault. Putting them on notice of an accident is fine, but what are the consequences when a client needs to make a UM/UIM claim?

O.C.G.A. § 33-24-45(c) addresses what an insurer may do when there are numerous claims within a three-year period that stem from a wreck that is no fault of my client. The statute is long and confusing but eventually addresses this issue. In a wreck that is not my client's fault, an insurance company may not increase rates, cancel a policy, or choose to not renew the policy if there are less than three (two or fewer) of the following claims within a 36-month period:

1 For accidents involving two or more vehicles where the insured driver was not at fault.
2 Uninsured/underinsured motorist claims
3 Comprehensive coverage claims
4 Making a towing or roadside service claim.

Let's unpack this. None of this says an insurer must cancel or non-renew someone for multiple claims, it just allows them to. This is a classic "three strikes and you're out" statute. Two of the above claims in three years are acceptable, but when a client hits the third, they could be vulnerable. The first exception appears to suggest just by being in a wreck that isn't your fault and noticing the UM carrier could count against an insured. Exceptions two through four address reporting claims. If an insured is in a wreck that is not their fault (strike one), and then makes two more of the listed claims, then they could be vulnerable to an insurance company canceling the policy or raising their premiums. In theory, a UM carrier could meet the exception to the statute in the scenario where my client is rear-ended and injured by an uninsured driver, and my client must make a comprehensive coverage claim to cover the cost of replacing her vehicle.

In most cases, clients will not have to worry about a rate increase or cancellation but advising them on the law is helpful. If they are genuinely hurt, then I will express that getting the healthcare and compensation they need is much more advantageous than a potential rate hike on their policy. Most likely a recovery for their injuries would dwarf any potential rate increase.

## State Farm UM Coverage

When State Farm is involved, I always question how many vehicles a client has insured with the company. State Farm is the only insurer that I know of that insures each car under a different policy, so each car insured with that one family or person stacks on top of the other coverage. My first injury client ever (Ryan – mentioned earlier in the book) had parents that owned five vehicles. Each vehicle was insured for $25,000 per person/$50,000 per accident. Any other carrier would've had maximum UM policy limits of the 25/50, but since those are all different policies under the State Farm plan, they were stackable and we recovered the $125,000 of UM coverage available in that case. State Farm also calls their traditional coverage "difference in limits" coverage which means it is offset by liability coverage.

## Other Types of Coverages

Liability and UM coverages are most common in personal injury cases, but there are other coverages that could help maximize the value of a client's claim: MedPay, umbrella, and commercial policies.

### Medical Payments (MedPay) Coverage

MedPay is an elective and inexpensive no-fault auto insurance coverage. In a personal injury case, MedPay can provide significant benefit: this coverage typically covers medical bills with little to no questions asked. Even passengers in other vehicles who are injured can potentially benefit from MedPay. MedPay coverages range anywhere from $1,000 to $50,000, or even more. Hospitals love MedPay because they see it as guaranteed money, allowing them to balance bill even after collecting MedPay proceeds.

For example: if a client has a $10,000 hospital bill and $1,000 in MedPay coverage, the hospital will bypass their patient's health insurance, collect the $1,000, and try to bill the client for the remaining $9,000 balance when the personal injury case settles. MedPay coverage is only limited to paying for medical bills and is exhausted once the coverage limit has been met. If used prudently, MedPay can be used to a client's advantage in covering medical bills for which health insurance may not cover. Some of these bills might include EMS bills or even health insurance co-pays. The beauty of MedPay for the personal injury attorney is in mitigating the client's out-of-pocket medical costs at settlement time.

In referring to the prior scenario, if the client had a $50,000 MedPay policy, their $10,000 bill would be covered completely by MedPay. The client would yield a greater recovery amount because they have one less provider's bill to worry about reimbursing. Some MedPay providers may assert a subrogation lien, but in practice, few of these liens ever are enforceable. Georgia's "made whole" doctrine must be met in order for subrogation rights to apply. We'll discuss this doctrine further in Chapter 14.

A lawyer should be aware that if UM or UIM is covering the claim and pays the UM/UIM policy limits, the carrier is entitled to an offset of whatever they paid in MedPay coverage. For example, if a client exhausted $10,000 of their MedPay coverage and their UIM carrier had policy limits of $25,000 and tenders it, the most the UIM carrier would have to pay out for the bodily injury claim is $15,000.

## Managing MedPay Funds

MedPay is easier to collect than any other source of medical compensation or funding. It's a no-fault policy that has little oversight from insurance adjusters on whether the billed amounts are excessive or unnecessary. Because of this ease of collection, providers want the exclusive access to the funds. Plaintiff's attorneys can almost always be the decision maker on which provider receives the MedPay funding.

In my practice I will guide funds to the provider that is going to provide the most care to the patient and be the most willing to be reasonable with their billing practices and reductions on the back end of the case. This is usually the rehab provider – the chiropractor, physical therapy clinic, or the orthopedic clinic.

I have approached MedPay funding management in two different ways. First, one could send a provider the claim number and have them bill the MedPay provider directly. The advantage to this is it's less to keep track of for the law office or attorney as the MedPay provider will mail the attorney a notice when the MedPay limits have been exhausted. If that amount paid by MedPay is equal to or anywhere close to the total balance originally owed by that provider, then we will make sure to request that provider accept the MedPay payments as full compensation for their services. It's one less provider to worry about with resolving liens and hopefully less work for the attorney's admin staff.

The second approach is for the attorney to send all unpaid bills to the MedPay carrier and demand payment. They would most likely tender the MedPay limits, and the attorney would demand the check be written to his trust account. This balance would remain in the trust account until the case was ready to settle (or upon payment of verdict). The attorney would then use this amount to pay off outstanding medical liens as needed. I've known a few attorneys that believe this method is best practice for gaining leverage to reduce bills and liens as much as possible.

I will never provide a hospital with MedPay claim information. They will exhaust the limits immediately, avoid billing health insurance, and will send our firm a bill for the balance ("balance billing"). Furthermore, the hospital will offer only a minimal reduction to their highly excessive bill. In cases where clients have health insurance, some hospitals will require the attorney provide proof of no MedPay or proof that the funds were exhausted before they will bill health insurance. If this happens, my office will make sure one of the rehab providers submits a MedPay claim as soon as possible to make sure a hospital's health insurance claim is still viable per the health insurance company's submission deadlines.

## Umbrella Policies

We once settled a million-dollar case that didn't appear to be a million-dollar case upon initial review. Our client was a passenger when the driver decided to drive recklessly and totaled the vehicle. The car hit a tree trunk at a high rate of speed and our client's leg was crushed as a result. Thankfully, the client was able to walk again after multiple surgeries and a long rehabilitation. The driver only had a $250,000 liability policy. After further investigation, it was uncovered that the father of the driver had an excess umbrella liability policy of $1,000,000—on top of the initial $250,000. Would there not have been an umbrella policy, our client would not have even been able to pay for his medical bills.

Make sure to pay special note to how much insurance coverage a person has. Coverage of $250,000 typically reaches the upper limits in auto liability coverage, and is a good indicator that there may be an umbrella policy present. Therefore, it is crucial to have the insurance company provide an affidavit to us verifying "no additional coverage" in every case. Similarly, if a person is a celebrity or if we have reason to believe they are very wealthy and woefully underinsured, it could also be a red flag to explore excess recovery avenues for our client.

## Commercial Policies

Commercial coverage is another type of supplemental or excess coverage to look out for. In these cases, we specifically want to know if the at-fault party was engaged in the course of business at the time of the crash. If so, then the employer's insurance coverage could potentially become involved. In the case of rideshare services (Lyft, Uber, etc.) drivers are usually required to carry a distinct commercial policy that covers them in the course of business. We always send letters of representation to the employer and the employer's insurance company to at least put them on notice of the incident. Most commercial insurance policies are written for $1 million or more, so exploring this avenue is another way to maximize recovery for a client.

## Turn Up the Heat: Punitive Damages

As stated earlier, sometimes a higher case value is warranted simply because the at-fault party's conduct was above and beyond egregious. Specifically, Georgia law allows for punitive damages when a tortfeasor's conduct is "reckless, willful and wanton or shows a conscious disregard for the consequences of his actions."[21] Similarly, when a driver causes an accident while intoxicated, the issue of punitive damages for his or her conduct is always for the jury to decide.[22] Punitive damages in Georgia are capped at $250,000. If the Plaintiff can show that the Defendant's actions, or failure to act was done with the specific intent to cause harm or while under the influence of drugs or alcohol then the punitive damages are uncapped.[23] There also is no cap on punitive damages for products liability cases.[24]

Common examples of auto accident cases that invoke punitive elements are cases that involve conduct such as DUI, reckless driving, and hit and run. An arrest does not necessarily need to occur to assert a claim for punitive damages. Many insurers will try to claim a defense against paying for punitive damages; however, under Georgia law, punitive damages are covered by "any insurance policy issued to a person within this state."[25] Since insurers are obligated to pay for punitive damages, make sure to maximize the value of a client's case if punitive elements are present. The purpose of punitive damages is to punish the wrongdoer and deter the behavior from occurring, and is distinct from the general damages our client sustains.

## Trucking Cases

Trucking cases can include numerous Defendants, including (but not limited to) the driver, the common carrier, the owner of the trailer, shipper, consignee, broker, insurer, and the logistics company.

All Defendants in a trucking case will have varying degrees of liability and insurance coverage that will cover their claims where they are responsible. All must be explored for possible culpability.

[21] O.C.G.A. §51-12-5.1

[22] Craig v. Holsey, 264 Ga. App. 344, 590 S.E.2d 742 (2003)

[23] O.C.G.A. §51-12-5.1(f)

[24] O.C.G.A. §51-12-5.1(e)

[25] **Lunceford v. Peachtree Cas. Ins. Co.**, 230 Ga. App 4, 495 S.E.2d 88 (1997)

## Mitigating Out of Pocket Damages

The final stone to uncover involves mitigating out-of-pocket damages. It is a fact that clients will incur medical bills if they are injured. The item of most concern for a client is, "How are these bills going to get paid?" The ideal scenario is if a client has both MedPay and health insurance coverage. Think of these as two prime coupons on the "retail price" of medical treatment. To illustrate, let's look at an example of a summary of special damages on a prior case:

### Josh S. Medical Expenses

| | |
|---|---|
| Ambulance | $2,110.50 |
| Hospital | $58,891.20 |
| Orthopedist | $1,330.00 |
| Chiropractor | $3,620.00 |
| ER Physician | $1,400.00 |
| Radiology | $331.00 |
| TOTAL: | **$67,682.70*** |

The client in the scenario above had a health insurance policy which covered the hospital visit. Because of the type of health insurance, the hospital was contractually obligated to discount his bill by $56,891.20 and he was required to pay a copay or balance of $822.42. His insurance paid their contractual portion of $567.58. When the client's case finally settled, he only had to pay back $10,000 to the remainder of providers. Health insurance is a huge cost saver for our clients and can be the difference is settling a case and spending years in litigation.

Success stories like this in maximizing recovery are only possible if the handling of paying medical bills is done correctly and strategically. It is imperative that we find out what kinds of coverages are available to our client and then seek how to use those coverages to our client's advantage. Had the client in our example had MedPay limits of $10,000, we could have paid the rest of his bills with MedPay, leading to an even higher recovery.

Pursuant to Georgia's Collateral Source Rule, insurance companies in Georgia are not entitled to mitigate the value of a claimant's bill because the claimant had health insurance pay for the bill.[26] Otherwise, people would be penalized for having health insurance. Had this case gone before a jury, the jury would not be allowed to know how much the client actually paid for the $58,000 hospital bill. If

---

[26] **McDonald v. Simmons**, 207 Ga. App. 692, 428 S.E.2d 690 (1993)

anything, the jury should operate under the pretense that the client is fully liable for the total amount of the bill. This collateral source rule will be discussed further in Chapter 11.

In all, leaving no stone unturned involves becoming well-acquainted with three factors: liability theory, the amount of insurance coverage available, and the amount of special damages due out of pocket. If we can optimize each one of these areas, we will be prepared to seek the highest compensation possible for our client.

## CHAPTER 10

# The Treatment Process: Schedules and Payments

Over the last 15 years, I've learned that most people hate going to the doctor. Even those who are hurt will still find ways to avoid treatment by "riding through it" or "just giving it a few days." Doctor's appointments are inconvenient, time consuming, and logistically complicated with work and other family obligations. But failing to seek medical help is incredibly detrimental to an injury case. Every day that passes without treatment gives the insurance company fuel to dispute a client's injuries, whether it be causation or a superseding cause.

Simply put: if a client is truly hurt, they must see a doctor immediately. Timely medical care establishes a record of treatment, verifying that the incident they hired us for was the actual cause of their injury. Always encourage clients to get to the doctor as soon as they can, as this is the crucial first step in the treatment process.

## Avoid Gaps in Treatment

Pain is a great motivator for keeping appointments. In addition to getting treated immediately after the wreck, a client needs to maintain the recommended treatment schedule. This is true whether it's a brain injury or a soft tissue whiplash case. Regular treatment validates injuries, tracks trends in pain levels and progress, shows a commitment of the patient for improving their health, and more importantly, it helps them recover.

Even those who are truly hurt and suffering can struggle with maintaining a regular schedule of treatment. Sometimes, keeping up with a treatment schedule complicates their desire for a normal life. Other times, they feel the rehab care isn't helping (or progress is moving too slowly), making doctor appointments feel like a waste of valuable time. A best practice to adopt is to call the client bi-weekly, at minimum, to check on treatment status. This provides an opportunity to not only help keep them accountable, but to address any problems early on and ask if you can help get them back on track.

## Consequences of Gaps in Treatment

Insurance companies are fickle. Even if a client follows the doctor's orders and completes all rehab care appointments on schedule, the insurance adjuster will argue the treatment was excessive. Conversely, if the client misses appointments, the insurance adjuster will immediately assert a gap in treatment and attempt to discard any medical bills after the gap.

I generally see this gap argument asserted after a two-week lapse in treatment. We always avoid that gap, encourage the clients to make the appointments, and look for ways we can help them. If they have no transportation, we encourage them to use a ride-sharing app and save their receipts. If they don't have the means for ride-sharing, their health provider may arrange for transportation through Uber or Lyft. Ideally, assuming the doctor orders it, a client/patient will attend at least one or two rehab care (physical therapy, chiropractic, or both) sessions a week. They will also have periodic follow-ups with the primary medical doctor responsible for directing treatment. In the client's best-case scenario, this treatment schedule lasts for 60–90 days, after which they feel significant improvement.

If gaps do occur (which they invariably will), then we look for credible ways those can be explained or diffused. At the time of writing, there is a global pandemic, and I cannot imagine a better reason for missing appointments. The client could be high risk, concerned about contracting the virus, or perhaps the doctor's availability and office hours are limited. Whatever the reason, the client must relay this to the doctor and ensure it is noted in the medical records. If the client is undergoing therapy and doctor-directed exercises at home, that should be recorded to show the client was at least keeping up with treatment. Pregnancy, sickness, and surgery are also valid reasons for missing necessary medical treatment.

My professional experience with juries is that gaps can be explained and mitigated most of time if the issue is addressed in the forefront during voir dire. We don't hide it; we are transparent and address it head-on. Jurors understand that life happens and sympathize with the difficulties involved in maintaining a regular schedule of doctor appointments.

## Doctor Referrals

Should a lawyer make recommendations for treatment providers? If a lawyer is recommending treatment providers, it could be argued that a doctor and lawyer have an arrangement to pad the bills and drive the cost of a claim into the stratosphere. This is problematic for a few reasons, the first of which is that as lawyers, we are called upon to do good for others. Throughout my years of practice, I have met hundreds of spinal surgeons, orthopedic surgeons, neuropsychologists, neurologists, physiatrists, psychiatrists, general practitioners, chiropractors, physical therapists, etc. My network of doctors is expansive, and I know very well who treats people the best and who doesn't. I want my clients seeing someone who cares about them and is highly competent. Therefore, I would never hesitate to refer a client to doctor that I felt was the best for their circumstances. If there is ever an inkling of doubt over whether this could become an issue at trial, practicing transparency in voir dire or before the defense attorney is certainly a best practice. However, if the client has their own doctors they trust, I always encourage them to be autonomous in their healthcare. Their choice will always supersede mine.

I think it's great when clients insist they want to treat with their doctor and entirely guide their own treatment plan, but my job at that point is just to make sure their doctor is being highly attentive and focusing on all of my client's complaints. I had a client in a car wreck that clearly suffered some neurological problems after the wreck. She was suffering from tremors, dizziness, irritability, headaches, and feeling lightheaded. She wanted to go to the neurologist her primary care doctor recommended. The problem was that although she told her neurologist about all these problems, all he wrote down were the tremors he noticed. When I looked over the records, I noticed the lack of notes from the doctor. I asked the client about him, and it turned out that he was incredibly disorganized in his office, disheveled, and unprepared for their visits. We were lucky that every time she went to the physical therapist, they would note all the symptoms presented above.

What about case value and not driving treatment costs up? My philosophy is that I want clients to heal and improve as soon as possible while doing a great job on their case; I want to become a trusted resource for them for years to come. Former clients are the best referral sources. If they are overtreated by bad doctors and used as a pawn to get the lawyer a bigger fee, that client will regret ever meeting that lawyer. The concept is incredibly basic but it's what makes sense: we advise our client in a way that is best for their short- and long-term health while making sure they have the financial means to cope with the physical and emotional ramifications of their accident for years to come.

One last thought on gaps in treatment and directing medical providers: a recent client, "Vivian," was hit on the interstate and suffered air bag burns, facial lacerations, PTSD, and numerous painful, lasting whiplash injuries. She went to the ER and was released that day. I had a network of providers. I wanted to refer her to an orthopedist, a chiropractor, a neuropsychologist, and a plastic surgeon. She would have none of it! She only trusted her concierge primary doctor to direct treatment. I was apprehensive when he was prescribing her PTSD medication, telling her how often to go to PT, and reading her MRIs. I was worried he wasn't "staying in his lane." Furthermore, he was only seeing her once a month and there were numerous two- to four-week gaps in treatment—all at his direction.

Luckily, based on his lengthy treatment notes, it was obvious this doctor took his time and did what he thought was best. We were able to support a solid claim on her case and closed for the maximum policy limits. When in doubt, I try to let go and let the doctors do their job while keeping in touch with the client and ensuring the doctor is being attentive to the concerns of the client.

## Which Doctor Should I Refer My Client to?

I would guess that 90% of injury cases are spinal and whiplash related. In that case, there are numerous options for who I would suggest a client see for help. But I have noticed patterns after doing this several years. As the lawyer I am most concerned with getting the client the help they need and being able to prove their injuries were a result of the Defendant's negligence. In auto wreck cases if a client requests a referral, I generally have two options: chiropractic care or an orthopedist, who will likely refer my client to physical therapy.

Many injury attorneys I know choose not to associate with chiropractors because the insurance industry's unfavorable analysis of their treatment. I find that chiropractors can be very effective at treating neck and back injuries after a wreck. I know several medical doctors that believe a combination of physical therapy and chiropractic tends to yield the best results for patients. If a client complains of stiffness, pain, lack of mobility, or soreness, I will not hesitate to refer them to a chiropractor if that clinic regularly treats injury patients, keeps comprehensive patient records and bills, and is willing to refer out to a medical doctor when appropriate for treatment, validation, and advanced imaging.

If a client is telling me they are having some of the more significant symptoms after their wreck then I will refer them to an orthopedist for treatment and imaging. When a client tells me they are experiencing numbness in their extremities, shooting pains down their arms or legs, numbness when sitting or standing, or extraordinary sharp debilitating pains, crippling headaches, alarms will go off in my head. Those cases invariably will indicate disc herniations or bulges that are compressing on the nerves coming out of the spinal cord. Often times an MRI will indicate whether the herniation or bulge appears to be of a recent acute-type event. If they still really want to see a chiropractor, I will support that 100% but I will encourage them to also see the M.D. to validate that the chiropractic care is needed.

If a client has suffered visible lacerations or airbag burns that leave scars, then I will refer them to a plastic surgeon for an estimate on scar revisions. These estimates will almost always exceed $25,000, and I find that insurance companies take these seriously.

## M.D. Validation – Chiropractic Care and Physical Therapy

Although I personally appreciate the health benefits of chiropractic, professionally, the insurance industry does not value their diagnostics and treatment as they should. Even the chiropractors I know that take the most detailed treatment notes get slandered, devalued, and belittled by insurance companies. It is difficult to get a large chiropractic bill covered, especially if there is no medical doctor validating the treatment. Right or wrong, this is how insurance algorithms evaluate the claim. And it doesn't stop with chiropractic care: insurance companies will attempt to devalue the most exhaustive medical treatments even by renowned medical doctors in their specialty.

Any chiropractic bill over $5,000 or $6,000 will pose a challenge in pre-litigation. I have seen chiropractic bills ranging from $10,000 up to $30,000 for treatments as long as 12–18 months while never having a referral to an orthopedist, let alone an MRI. To maximize the legitimacy of a chiropractor bill, it is helpful to first have the client treated by a chiropractor for four to six weeks. If they have not significantly improved, they'll need to get a chiropractic referral to the orthopedist validating what the chiropractor has done, as well as recommending continued chiropractic treatment. The orthopedist will then recommend a revisit in four to six weeks and order an MRI if symptoms indicate the need.

In more serious cases where there are objective injuries like fractures, ligament and tendon tears, and surgeries, the M.D. validation is relatively pointless, as insurance companies tend to value these cases more appropriately. The objectivity is less questionable and more obvious. In post-surgical cases, there can be excessive physical therapy bills, but if they are documented appropriately, they are not typically hard to recover.

Any non-medical doctor should not provide treatment for more than two to three months without revisiting the M.D. to validate that treatment. Not only does it make the pre-litigation argument easier, but the treatment also holds up better if the case is litigated.

## Attorney Communication with Healthcare Providers

The golden rule of communicating with the office of a provider is that we ALWAYS assume everything we write in an email, letter, text, or voicemail will be seen by the opposing side at some point. I will not write, "I'm sending client XYZ over to you – she needs an MRI." Instead, I will write that I am referring them "because I love the way you treat my clients," say how bad the wreck was, what he/she is telling me hurts, and to "see if the doctor thinks these symptoms warrant more advanced imaging." If a jury sees the former, all kinds of collusion arguments would be made by the defense. The latter implies a working relationship of a team that deeply cares about the well-being of their client/patient.

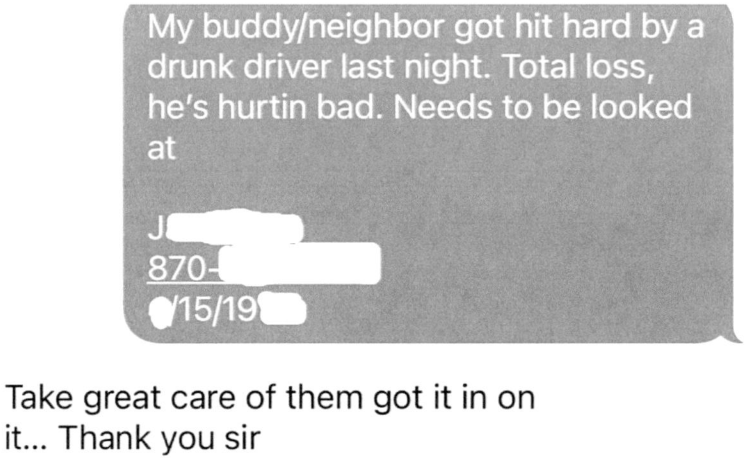


*Quick text to orthopedic scheduling contact for a client needing a doctor*

If I refer a client to a healthcare provider, I prefer working with healthcare providers and doctors that are approachable, and that keep an open line of communication with my office. Having a doctor you can call and ask for elaboration on injuries and treatment can be monumental in understanding what a client is going through.

Any healthcare or rehab provider treating the patient on a lien will ask the attorney to either send in a letter of protection or a lien agreement, which states that they will not distribute any funds to the client without first settling the balance with the provider. This is standard in every case where any client treats on a lien.

## Funding Treatment and Surgery

I emphatically dislike using funding companies, but in some cases, they are an absolute necessity to get my clients the healthcare they deserve. Physical therapists, chiropractors, and most orthopedic medical clinics will treat injury victims without demanding money up front and will assess a lien on the client's case. When it comes to surgeons or specialists like neurologists or neuropsychologists, they will almost always refuse to treat on a lien. If a client has no health insurance, private medical funding becomes the only viable option.

I am no expert on medical funding, but it typically works like this:

Sam is hurt in a car wreck and has no money or health insurance. His back pain is so serious, he's on an office chair getting around his kitchen, because lightning pain goes through his legs if he tries to stand up. Sam sees an orthopedist and after an MRI is ordered, he has a follow-up with a spinal surgeon who finds several lumbar disc herniations. The surgeon recommends immediate surgery before the damage is catastrophic. Sam is broke, so a funding company is his only option.

His lawyer must arrange for the surgery to be paid through the funding company. The funding company will pay for the surgeon, the facility, the nurse team, and the anesthesiologist. The amount to be paid is predetermined between the funding company and the healthcare provider. What the funding company pays is much lower than what is billed. Sam's surgery may be billed at $100,000 and the funding company could arrange to pay $40,000 up front. Sam has his surgery and then settles his injury case, where the total policy limits are $150,000. Sam's lawyer will beg the funding company to reduce their $100,000 lien. Hopefully, the funding company would reduce as much as 30–50 percent to maximize Sam's net payout when the case closes.

It's not ideal, but as of now, the disclosure on total amount paid by a funding company is not legally required and industry standard is for non-transparency. Although the total payment amount is not disclosed to lawyers or clients, we know the difference is substantial. I would love to see more regulation in this industry. In the example above, the funding company provided an invaluable resource to save the client from ongoing pain and a surgery that would've never happened if the funding was not available.

Again, I will only use a funding company if health insurance and other avenues are not available. This is not to say that all funding companies are bad. They are in a competitive industry, so there are several that provide value-added services. Funding companies will manage treatment schedules, arrange transportation, and regularly check in on clients to ensure they are doing everything to maximize their claim.

### Bankruptcy and Funding Companies

If a client is currently in bankruptcy proceedings and is faced with using a funding company, their lawyer should reach out to someone who specializes in bankruptcy, as there are rules against borrowing money for medical treatment. Alternatively, there could be cases where the value of an injury case is so high, it might be prudent to drop the bankruptcy proceedings so that treatment can continue. Any outstanding debt can be resolved with net injury proceeds from their case.

## Cash Advances

In 2018, The Georgia Supreme Court affirmed the Court of Appeals decision in *Cherokee Funding v. Ruth*, 342 Ga. App.404 (2017). The facts alone give a cautionary tale on why a client should only use cash advance funding as a last resort. Ruth was a Plaintiff and had borrowed various cash advance installments of approximately $5,500 (plus various fees) as a non-loan sales contract with interest rates compounding at 4.99 percent per month. Three or so years later, when Ruth's case settled, Cherokee sought to collect over $84,000. The Court ruled this was not a loan and therefore not subject to usury regulatory laws because of all the contingencies associated with the contract.

One can see how $5,000 becoming $84,000 could destroy any good relationship with a client. This drastically reduces their net payout. Most good funding companies (including Cherokee) will now cap their repayment obligation at 150 percent of the borrowed amount. Without legislative regulation, we can only hope competition self-regulates these practices.

There is one more pitfall of cash advances to consider: they can force a case into an early settlement that is far below its value. If Martha is advanced $2,000 to make a down payment on a vehicle so she can go to work, but the attorney is only offered $7,000 on her $25,000 case after her pre-suit demand, then it becomes obvious that the $2,000 could grow exponentially if the case is litigated. If $2,000 becomes $6,000, this might force the client into seriously considering a low offer if their pre-suit net payout wouldn't be drastically different compared to litigating the case for a long period. We only associate with funding companies that cap their payoff amount at a reasonable amount.

Cash advances are an absolute last resort, but they are necessary in some cases. They can be useful for people with no savings to pay their necessary living expenses. They can also be used to fund an expensive deductible while still using health insurance. Choosing the right company makes all the difference. It's important to ask for a spreadsheet that articulates what the balance will be in six months, one year, and even two to three years out. Look for companies that cap their balances once it reaches a certain amount. Lastly, keep in mind that everything is negotiable. None of these amounts are final and if case margins are small, the good companies will reduce the owed amount accordingly.

## Job in Jeopardy

One of the saddest parts of an injury case—and an ultimate reminder that life isn't fair—is when someone can't work and provide for their family because they were seriously injured. I am not aware of any law prohibiting an employer from terminating an employee who is unable to work due to an injury in a non-work-related incident. Most people tend to use their vacation time, then turn to short-term disability, and then FMLA. Self-employed and independent contractor clients have the hardest times in scenarios like this.

I always tell my clients to work if they can. Making a lost wages claim under Georgia law is complicated, not to mention navigating the views a jury might have toward missing work. If a client had back pain and rants on the stand about how working was impossible, fate will have it that there will be a paraplegic juror that works every week 50-60 hours. Just because a client can make a lost wages claim doesn't mean they should—especially at trial.

Driving costs lower on a case should be almost as important as achieving a high number for a client. Perhaps the biggest takeaway from the treatment process is your role in ensuring that each client receives expert guidance through the best treatment schedule and means of payment. Though there are certainly alternative options, wherever possible, use health insurance. If a large deductible needs to be paid before surgery, get the deductible funded through a funding company that caps the payback amount.

My philosophy is that I want clients to heal and improve as soon as possible while doing a great job on their case; I want to become a trusted resource for them for years to come. The concept is incredibly basic but it's what makes sense: we advise our client in a way that is best for their short- and long-term health while making sure they have the financial means to cope with the physical and emotional ramifications of their accident for years to come.

## When to Collect Medical Records

Your client is done treating and either healed up, rehabilitated or their prognosis and permanent impairment is mostly known. Now it is almost time to put all this together, write a demand, and settle the case. There might be seven medical providers stemming from the EMS transport all the way to the physical therapy provider. Or maybe many more depending on the seriousness of the injuries. Timing the collection of health records and bills can cause significant delays in resolving a case. The timing is subjective, depends on the provider, whether the client is done treating with that provider, and how long it will take for your team to get the records.

The easiest rule of thumb is if the client is done treating with a provider, we immediately request those certified bills and records. The bigger the medical provider, the longer records and bills will take to retrieve. If a client went to the hospital and was released with no admission or surgery, chances are the client is done treating there and will not return. With hospitals, we almost always request records and bills as soon as we can. As there is ongoing treatment with any provider, we will only request bills and records after they are done treating with them. With any trip to the hospital, a client will have several providers with different bills and records. EMS will likely have a $1,500 + bill for their services. The hospital will bill for their facility fee, imaging, treatment. There will be another bill for the ER physician as they are separate entities. The radiology department will bill for their readings of the images as well.

In surgical cases or those involving catastrophic injury, figuring out the providers can often require a detailed search through individual records and bills that leads to the names of additional providers. In serious injury/surgical cases, I would speculate there might be approximately 25 different medical providers that we need to track down. In addition to looking through operative or hospital records, I would suggest looking at health insurance estimation of benefits ledgers as well as bills and paperwork sent to the client. Now that you've got all the bills, records, open records, police reports, photos, videos, witnesses, etc., it is time to demand the insurance company pay your client what they deserve.

## CHAPTER 11

# The Demand

The client finally completes treatment, or at least there is an accurate prognosis on how the client's injuries will affect them the rest of their life. We've collected all medical records and bills known to us. We've tracked down all necessary 911 tapes, body cam footage, powertrain module information, police reports, witness statements, Defendant citation dispositions, photos of the property damage, and photos of the client's injuries. Now we get to put this together in a tangible narrative that illustrates what the client's injuries, pain, suffering, loss wages, and just about anything else the accident caused.

## The Time Limited Demand

The purpose of a Time Limited Demand is to force an insurance company to act or negotiate in good faith. Before getting into stylistic preferences of a demand, this necessitates a brief discussion of bad faith laws. There are broad consumer protection laws that punish insurance companies if they act in bad faith.

There are two types of insurance bad faith: third-party (common law) bad faith, and first-party (statutory) bad faith.

## Third-Party or Common Law Bad Faith

Let's look at a typical third-party bad faith scenario using an "A" driver and a "B" driver. A hits B in the rear, causes B serious injuries, and B needs surgery on his neck. B goes after A's auto liability insurance policy and asks the liability insurance carrier to settle for the full $100,000 limits. After reviewing all medical records and bills, A's insurance company refuses to settle for the full $100,000 limits.

B appears to have a great bad faith case against A's insurance company for third-party bad faith, and they could be liable for the full value of B's injury.

The Plaintiff must first get a judgment against the tortfeasor and then go after the actual Defendant for the excess (assuming it exceeds the policy limits that were not paid previously). The Defendant will then initiate a contractual bad faith action against his own insurance company for the excess amount plus any punitive damages if they apply.

Practically speaking, the Defendant could assign his claim to the Plaintiff and the same Plaintiff's lawyer could handle everything. There is a significant downside here: if the bad faith claim is assigned to the Plaintiff, they cannot recover punitive damages. Juries will not hesitate to slap insurance companies with punitive damages in bad faith actions.

In a perfect world, one lawyer would get the judgment; if the excess isn't paid and accepted immediately, the claim should be handed over to another bad faith specialist lawyer. That lawyer would approach the Defendant and file the bad faith action in their name against the insurance company, usually in federal court.

## First-Party or Statutory Bad Faith

Let's use the sample case above and adjust for a first-party bad faith scenario. In this version, B's insurance company pays the $100,000 in limits. A then goes after their own first-party underinsured motorist coverage with limits of $25,000. If B's UM coverage denies the full $25,000 payout, B might have a first-party bad faith action. Unfortunately, this type of case can be difficult to win. The truth is that Georgia does not have strong first-party bad faith laws, meaning that insurance companies often leverage this against a Plaintiff.

Under Georgia UM/UIM law, if a carrier refuses to pay a claim within 60 days, and that refusal was made in bad faith, the insurer is liable for a 25 percent additional penalty in excess of the limits or $25,000 (whichever is greater), and all reasonable attorney's fees.[27] Furthermore, the bad faith action against the insurance company would have to be made in a separate action filed by the insured only after a judgement has already been rendered against the uninsured motorist in the initial tort action.[28]

As one might notice, there is quite a bit of legwork to collect a secondary action of attorney's fees. I know many Plaintiff and defense lawyers that unequivocally say

[27] O.C.G.A. 33-7-11(j) (revised in 2021 to include the $25,000 penalty language)
[28] O.C.G.A. 33-7-11(j)

that UM bad faith does not exist. If limits are $25,000 and we get an excess verdict of $2 million, the most the insurance company could be on the hook for is an additional $25,000 (plus attorney's fees).

In my own practice, I find that where damages are obvious and irrefutable (e.g., surgical cases or catastrophic injuries), insurance companies tend to pay immediately on UM claims. On soft tissue cases, they tend to put up more of a fight.

## Last Thought on Bad Faith

We never advocate "setting up" an insurance company for bad faith, as this approach could certainly backfire later. An example of this could be if I submitted a bare bones demand that undermined the seriousness of a wreck and the resulting injuries to lure an insurance company into rejecting a demand. Then, assuming I was fortunate later to get a large verdict and judgment against the Defendant and pursued a bad faith action against the insurance company, a higher court could review the initial demand along with the language and tone used with it. If it was clear that the demand was written to bait an insurance company into rejecting said demand, the entire award could be thrown out. Even worse, getting a poor appellate decision on something like this would be fuel for the tort reformist groups trying to limit the people's access to a trial by jury for their injuries. In the grand scheme of things, it's better to let the facts be the facts and neither downplay or exaggerate them. I'm highly in favor of first-party bad faith legislation that protects UM claims, but beyond that, the Plaintiff's bar should be careful.

## 2013 Auto Accident Demand Statute

Prior to 2013, third-party bad faith actions based in common law led to different interpretations on timeliness of a demand, including the conditions set forth for payment and release, called "Holt Demands."[29]

To clarify and set forth basic acceptable conditions, the General Assembly passed O.C.G.A. § 9-11-67.1 that applies to actions for personal injury and death resulting from motor vehicle wrecks. The statute makes it clear that the demand must:

- Be made in writing
- Specify the period of review and consideration is at least 30 days from the date of receiving the demand,
- The demand must specify the amount of the monetary payment sought,

[29] **Southern Gen. Ins. Co. v. Holt**, 262 Ga. 267 (1992)

- Specify what type of release (general or limited), and which parties they will release in the event of acceptance, AND
- Which exact claims will be released

Furthermore, the statute is a guideline on the acceptable means of accepting the claimant's offer. The insurance company may seek clarifications of terms, definitions, liens, subrogation claims, medical bills/records, or other relevant facts. Merely seeking clarification is not considered a counteroffer. The statute articulates that a demand shall be sent by certified mail or statutory overnight delivery, return receipt requested, and shall specifically reference the demand statute.[30]

The person or entity providing payment to satisfy the demand may elect to provide payment by cash, money order, wire transfer, cashier's check, bank check, or electronic funds transfer.[31] Any party accepting the offer to pay must be provided at least 10 days to pay from the moment of written acceptance to get the funds to the claimant.[32]

The more I read this statute, the more I am considering how it applies to each case and adjusting my demands accordingly. I recommend any lawyer read it at least 20 times before sending out a demand that might be wrongly rejected. I find it helpful to reach out to the many mentors in GTLA for guidance on these provisions.

## Non-Auto Wreck Demands

The Georgia legislature gave us solid guidance on auto claims, but what about all the other cases involving insurance companies like homeowner's claims, premises liability, daycare negligence, or dog bite claims? From talking with many other of my fellow trial lawyers, I would guess the consensus is that we follow the same rules spelled out in the auto liability demand statute. It appears that all the conditions required are the gold standard of what the higher courts would uphold on assessing a potential bad faith claim.

## Outline of a Demand

There are six key components of any demand: Facts of Loss, Determination of Liability, Bodily Injuries and Pain and Suffering, Summary of Expenses and Medical Bills, Additional "Heat," and finally, a Demand for Payment with Conditions. We'll go through each in turn below.

---

[30] O.C.G.A. § 9-11-67.1
[31] O.C.G.A. § 9-11-67.1
[32] O.C.G.A. § 9-11-67.1

## Facts of Loss – put in photo of accident diagram and car crash

We outline the facts here with as much detail as one prefers with an advocacy for the client. I like to include excerpts from the police report; photographs of property damage; pictures of the scene; quotes from witnesses or the Defendant; road diagrams from the police report; citations issues to the Defendant, etc. Of this list, photographs can often tell the most powerful story. Insurance algorithms govern most of what they can pay, but I believe favorable pictures trend a case to the top of those numbers.

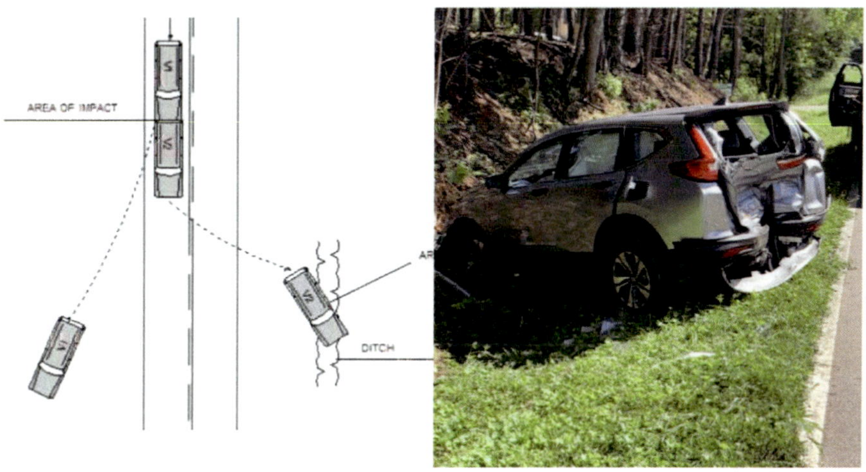


*Diagram and accident scene photo in the demand*

## Determination of Liability and Causation

This section is straightforward law school torts. Here, the lawyer briefly explains why the Defendant's negligence is the proximate cause of the client's injuries.

## Bodily Injuries and Pain and Suffering-

This section requires a good deal of detail and focused attention. As I build this section in my own demands, I first detail exactly what injuries were noticeable on scene and then establish a treatment timeline, including all providers with dates and ranges of treatment. I also include all ICD-10 diagnostic codes from the doctors, treatment plans, anything notable the client tells their doctor that bolsters their case, and highlight anything serious. When anything noteworthy by a doctor is listed, such as impairment ratings, I like to circle it in red or underline it. I detail the entire sequence of treatment to date, and I conclude with what the client is experiencing today. They may be experiencing chronic pain or the inability to complete everyday activities like shower, put clothes on, pick up their grandkids, brush their hair, go for walks, or even the inability to sleep. Pictures of injuries here are, again, very powerful. I will include any pictures of pre- or post-surgical wounds that visualize what my client experienced.

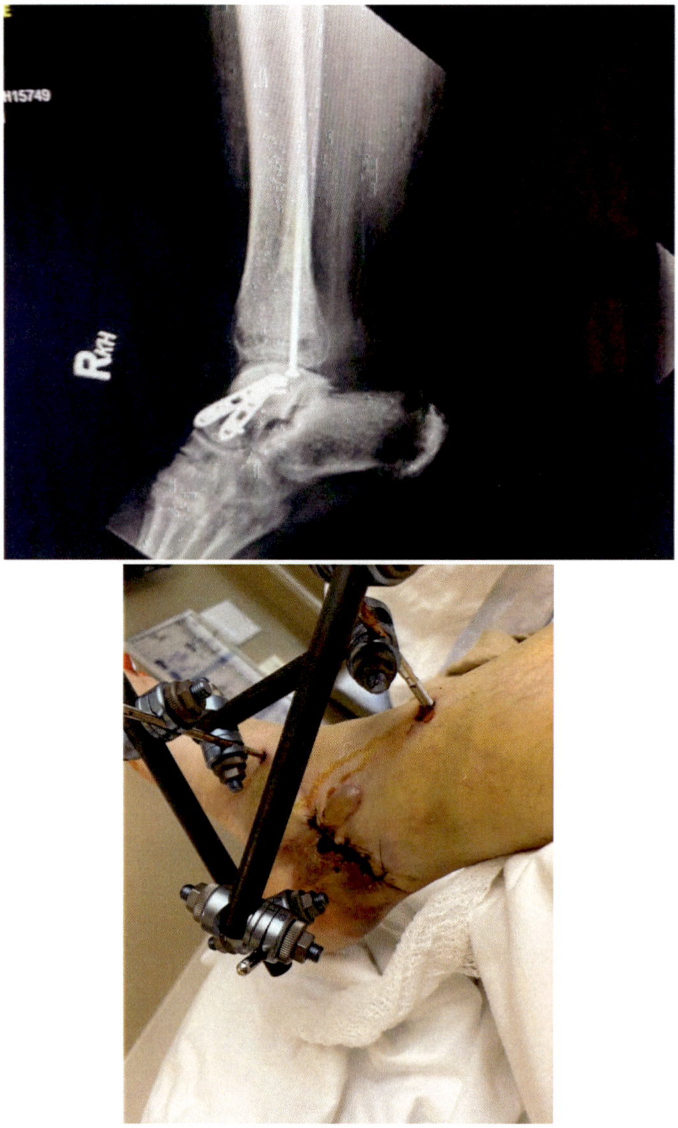

*X-rays of surgical hardware and external fixator*

## Summary of Expenses and Medical Bills

This section is a summary or ledger of all providers and what they billed (do *not* include what was paid by any collateral source). I also include costs of pharmacy medications, OTC drugs, and any transportation they paid out of pocket to attend medical appointments.

## Additional "Heat"

I save this section for the purposes of assuming a human being on the opposing side is reading it and not just some adjuster that simply keys variables into an algorithm. This section is intended to be a value driver. Any conduct by the Defendant that warrants punitive damages (i.e., like DUI or Hit and Run), this is the section to mention it. If I'm throwing the kitchen sink at a case, I might include a close family or a friend's before and after affidavits, detailing what the client was like before this incident and how this event decreased their quality of life. As stated earlier, punitive damages in Georgia are capped at $250,000. If the Plaintiff can show that the Defendant's actions, or failure to act was done with the specific intent to cause harm or while under the influence of drugs or alcohol then the punitive damages are uncapped.[33] I will include photos of any conviction paperwork or proof of a criminal accusation or indictment in this section.

**The Court enters the following judgment:**

| Count | Charge (as indicted or accused) | Disposition (Guilty, Not Guilty,etc) | Sentence | Fine | Concurrent/ Consecutive/etc |
|---|---|---|---|---|---|
| 1 | **Serious Injury by Vehicle** | **Guilty** | **10 years** | **1000** | |
| 2 | **Serious Injury by Vehicle** | **Guilty** | | | **Merge into Ct. 1** |

The Defendant is adjudged guilty ~~or sentenced under First Offender/Conditional Discharge~~ for

*Judge's sentencing order on a reckless driving/serious injury by vehicle case*

## Previous Verdicts and Settlements

This section feels like overkill and only fulfills the purpose of showing the other side that you know exactly what your case is worth. Whether it's cases that I personally know of or it is one I find with similar variables through the Case-Metrix database, I'll include a table of recent results that has the characteristics my case.

| Attorney / Firm | Date | Re$olution | Medical$ | Policy Limits | Carrier | Settled or Filed |
|---|---|---|---|---|---|---|
| Pete Law | 1/15/15 | $72,960,000 | $226,396 | Not Released | Not Released | Jury Verdict |
| Tim Hall | 2/5/2007 | $5,000,000 | $500,000 | $5,000,000 | Not Released | Filed/Settled |
| Andrew Lynch* | 12/20/2016 | $4,000,000 | ? | ? | Self Insured | Jury Verdict |
| Shiver / Hamilton | 9/3/2015 | $29,250,000 | $0/fatality | $21,000,000 | American/Companion | Jury Verdict |

## Client's Current Condition and Demand for Payment with Conditions

The conditions of payment and responses by the insurance companies are the areas subject to most of the recent bad faith legislation. It's helpful to find other cases that

[33] O.C.G.A. §51-12-5.1(f)

have resolved pre-litigation, suit filed, or via jury verdict. The best database for variable-based case values is Case-Metrix.com. My recommendation is to utilize their search function and create a table of cases with similar injuries and facts and what they resolved for. While this may not help pre-litigation, it's a great way to demonstrate preparedness (and to show how high your standards are).

Most cases will start with a demand for the policy limits unless treatment costs are so low that it would be laughable to do so. In this section, I detail the medical special damages, demand specific policy limits for payment, the type of release demanded (i.e., general or limited liability), the conditions and time frame for payment, and when the offer will expire. Under the statute listed above, the recipient has 30 days from the date of receipt to accept. I also like to include relevant case law that notifies them that they are potentially exposing their insured to the consequences of an excess judgment if they do not comply.

Remember, the demand must be sent by certified mail or statutory overnight delivery, return receipt requested, and shall specifically reference O.C.G.A. § 9-11-67.1.

Compiling an effective demand letter may indeed feel time-consuming, but the resulting clarity and strength of a client's argument is invaluable. Over my years of practice, I've found that a basic template offers a great starting point. This will ensure that all necessary components are included, as well as help save time when crafting demand letters for clients.

The included appendix has numerous types of demand templates I've previously used. These include but are not limited to auto liability, auto uninsured motorist, homeowner's, daycare negligence, and a trip and fall demand. Many of these demands and forms can also be found in the appendix of this book or on my website at paisleylaw.com.

## General vs. Limited Liability Release

In cases where the liability carrier should tender their maximum limits, a limited liability release must be demanded and given if any other insurance coverage is sought (e.g. underinsured motorist coverage). Furthermore, 100 percent of the liability limits must be tendered before any underinsured motorist or excess coverage can be available. In a case where there are serious injuries with low policy limits, it is malpractice to accept anything less than a full tender of limits with a limited liability release. I personally know a novice injury lawyer that thought he was giving defense counsel a break by accepting $48,000 of a $50,000 policy, but was then barred from making a UIM claim because the full limits were not tendered. He had to have his malpractice carrier cover the remaining value of the claim.

## Comprehensive Detailed Demand vs. Short and Simple Demand

I work with dozens of law firms and see a broad spectrum of stylistic preferences. One association that I've noticed frequently is that the level of detail seems to be inversely proportional to the volume of cases a firm might have; in other words, a higher volume of cases in a practice means less detail in their demands. One explanation is that a detailed demand wastes time and resources, making it sufficient to send a simple one- or two-page demand for policy limits supplemented by records and bills. I emphatically disagree.

If I write a comprehensive and detailed demand (as shown in the appendix), and an insurance company refuses to pay the limits when they should settle within the limits, I will have stronger grounds to build a bad faith or abusive litigation claim later. Conversely, if I omit details or undermine my client's treatment and injuries, this could hinder a claim for attorney's fees or a future bad faith claim.

Of course, there are exceptions. In a $1.5 million case with $250,000 policy limits, a lawyer certainly doesn't need to go above and beyond in a demand. The facts and injuries in those cases usually speak for themselves. A comprehensive, detailed Holt Demand not only serves the client well in the present moment, but it also sets the groundwork for an effective bad faith claim should the insurance company refuse to pay.

At the conclusion of a catastrophic injury or death case demand I will include a Cc section with the names of two well known trial lawyers that have obtained large bad faith verdicts against insurance companies. This does two things. First, it informs those bad faith lawyers of the intricate details of my meritorious case. Second, if the demand is sent to insurance defense counsel to review then there is little doubt they will notice those names and hopefully take the demand more seriously. On a pre-litigation death case I had that had some poor facts for us, opposing counsel called me up and asked me why I included those two lawyer's names in the Cc section. I explained my reasoning and he actually agreed it was effective for him. They tendered the high limits in that case.

## CHAPTER 12

# What's Next?

In a perfect world, with a case that is clearly worth more than the policy limits, the insurance company would have done the right thing and paid the policy limits with a limited liability release.

But let's say that the insurance company did not follow through on their duty and pay the liability limits. What's next? The best thing to do is file suit and hold them accountable. We could proceed with getting a negotiated settlement in excess of the limits or a judgment and attorney's fees.

Keep in mind that sending a demand letter doesn't always work the way that it is intended to, or it's entirely pointless (i.e., in medical malpractice cases). Or sometimes you must file suit immediately after intake on a case because of the potential spoliation of evidence. In cases against trucking cases or in commercial premises liability cases, it is important to review pertinent evidence (videos, internal emails, driver logbooks, etc) that is likely to be only in the Defendant's possession. Without filing suit there's no way the opposing party would voluntarily give us this damning evidence.

If a demand letter is sent and the insurance company's response does not meet expectations of the case's value, there are several options to explore.

## If the Liability Carrier Pays the Maximum Policy Limits

If the liability carrier pays out the max and they rightfully give us a limited liability release that meets our conditions, we can now pursue our client's

Underinsured Motorist (UM/UIM) coverage or any other party that may be liable. Sometimes the excess liability value is so obvious that I will submit both the third party demand and the UIM demand at the same time, and not let either carrier out until they both agree to tender what they should. This could be useful if the Defendant engaged in punitive conduct like a DUI. If a release is signed by the Plaintiff for the third party, a judge will not allow the inflammatory evidence of DUI to be presented against the UIM carrier alone. If possible, it's best to keep the Defendant in the case if we have good facts against them. If everyone pays their fair value of the case, it's time to begin the closing process of the case. If not, then we proceed accordingly.

As stated in the previous chapter, if the UM or UIM carrier refuses to pay when they clearly should, there is limited recourse for a bad faith action. The award to the client would be capped based on reasonable attorney's fees and the policy limits.

## Option 1: File Suit Immediately

If it's obvious the pre-litigation value will never be met, the best course of action is to go ahead and file suit. Or perhaps it's a case that is easily worth in excess of the policy limits and the insurance company rejects the demand. At that point, a good injury lawyer should file to hold them accountable for their bad faith.

> To Whom It May Concern:
>
> We received your June 9, 2020 time limit demand for your client, . We have concluded the evaluation of your client's claim resulting from this loss. Based on the documentation provided, State Farm® is willing to settle your client's claim for $5,879.44 .
>
> This settlement is inclusive of all damages, known and unknown, and any liens, assignments or statutory rights of recovery.
>
> Please contact us once you have had an opportunity to review this offer.
>
> Sincerely,

*Letter from insurer devaluing our client's injuries.*

If a demand is rejected, I will file suit if there is no hope for a pre-suit settlement. I'll do the same if the case is easily worth in excess of the policy and the insurance company chose not to evaluate the case properly.

Rules can be different for commercial adjusters. Before filing, I'll hear them out on whether they really have intentions to settle a case pre-suit. My firm had a case settle recently where my client was hit by a commercial truck. She suffered a brain bleed and memory loss, and although she recovered very well, her family members all commented on how she was different. She was now more irritable, she would easily slip into a rage, and had become increasingly forgetful. The trucking company's initial offer was extraordinarily low, so I called the adjuster and told her we were going to file suit. She begged me not to and insisted she had good money on the table for discussion. After a few months, we closed and settled the case for 90 percent of what we would've expected to get in litigation.

## Option 2: Send a Counter-Demand

A counteroffer (i.e., a counterdemand) can be effective in some cases. My typical process is to send an original demand followed by two counteroffers; then, I'll get on the phone with the adjuster and gauge what their pre-suit number really is. I have heard in the industry that their original offer is generally 75 percent of their maximum number on smaller cases.

A commercial trucking insurance company might be interested in a pre-suit mediation. This could present a valuable opportunity, because the costs of a legal defense could be massive.

### The Last Counter-Demand

As mentioned above, the initial offer from an insurance company pre-suit is often approximately 75 percent of their intended pre-suit settlement value. In addition to sending one last counter-demand, you can get creative to show them how serious you are. I will often preemptively write a complaint alleging all facts, liability, damages, and a section threatening attorney's fees based on abusive litigation. Sending it to the insurance company puts them on notice: "If my amount isn't paid within X days we will file this at the county courthouse." With some insurance companies like GEICO, this can trigger another adjuster picking up the file for the purposes of triage or damage control. They will sometimes add significant value to their previous number and could help get our case settled.

### Get on the Phone

Although an attorney can call the adjuster and pick their brain at any point in a case, I like to wait until I've sent two counteroffers and I've gotten the adjuster close to their highest pre-litigation authority. Calling them earlier in the negotiations seems pointless. Most of the time, adjusters are plugging variables into an algorithm, and it spits out a number. The adjusters I know for the big insurance companies have very little independent authority on case valuation. They will tell me if they have more room to move on a case, and conversely, they will tell me if they are being handcuffed by a policy that forces them to discount medical bills to Medicare Part B valuations.

Early in my injury practice, I would get frustrated and often audibly angry at adjusters. I learned quickly that this was pointless. An adjuster's role is to communicate a number displayed on a computer screen, created by an algorithm. They don't know the client; they haven't met the family and seen what they had been through; and they certainly cannot feel the pain a client still deals with every day.

In my experience, the best way to help them get to their highest number is to passionately go over all the real-life issues a client is experiencing—and to do so without showing anger. They know almost immediately whether an attorney truly cares about their client. Furthermore, they might even tell an attorney what documentation they need to get the value higher.

Keep in mind that even the best attorneys may not be able to work with an adjuster when the insurance company is, simply put, uninterested in helping their insured. Don't waste weeks of time going back and forth with adjusters who won't work with you—instead, file suit immediately. As of writing this book, I am filing suit immediately after receiving a demand letter response for most of my Progressive, Allstate, State Farm, and Liberty Mutual cases. They appear to value marketing and clever commercials over taking responsibility for their insured.

## What if You're Weighing the Offer but Still Unsure About Case Value?

If the value of a case is obscure or unknown because of certain injuries and damages, there may be two solutions:

1 **Case-metrix.com**. As mentioned in earlier chapters, Case-metrix.com is a valuable resource. Attorneys can start by choosing variables that apply to a given case: body part, soft tissue, surgical, amount of property damage, whether the other party was cited and what for, etc. It will generate a list of case values that similar cases settled for, or amounts reached from a jury verdict.

2 **Join the local trial lawyers association**. Networking and having valuable mentors are extraordinarily valuable. Meet people, meet the experts, and use their ideas as inspiration for your own cases.

# CHAPTER 13

# Litigation

I resisted writing anything in this guide about litigation because this book is intended for pre-litigation strategy and process resolution only. My goal in this chapter is to keep it as short as possible. This is not a litigation or trial manual and was never purported to be one. Many brilliant lawyers have covered civil litigation, trial practice, evidence, and procedure in great depth. This is a basic step-by-step pre-litigation guide that utilizes best practices to maximize value and minimize costs. This chapter is only meant to gloss over the phases of litigation and outline my thoughts on how to maximize the best and quickest resolution if the case must proceed this far.

A competent injury lawyer has to file suit when necessary, which is becoming more and more frequent. As stated in the last chapter, I would guess that a vast majority of my GEICO, Allstate, Progressive, State Farm, Liberty Mutual, and Safeway cases will be filed on without a decent offer for our clients.

## The Attorney Client Litigation Conversation

The decision to file suit is the client's choice alone and I find it important to show the client all of the likely variables including but not limited to length of litigation, likely results, costs of litigation, increased costs of attorney's fees, and strengths and weaknesses in our case that might improve or hurt our result with increased litigation. I'll explain the steps and stages involved and what their involvement will be with discovery, depositions, mediation, and trial prep. I like to provide my client a spreadsheet of likely scenarios and what it takes in litigation just to get back to the number they are offering right now. Sometimes the insurance company's number is so low, analysis is pointless and we just file suit. Other times we look at the numbers, and make a calculated cost-benefit analysis on the best path forward.

A recent case I had involved my client who had a flat tire on a 3-lane interstate highway and pulled over to the left side emergency lane. He felt unsafe changing his tire there, so he drove his car with the flat tire to the right across the 3 lanes of the interstate so he could change his tire in the right emergency lane near the grass. Moving at 5 – 10 mph across the interstate lanes, he was hit at full speed from behind (by a commercially insured sedan) flipping his car. He suffered relatively minor injuries considering he was lucky to be alive. In fact, over the course of his 1 year long treatment cycle none of his MRI's or Xrays showed any objective injuries whatsoever. He was still in pain and treated with a chiropractor, physical therapist, and an orthopedist. He received multiple injections that provided relief. To this day he still occasionally sees his chiropractor. Because of the nature of the impact alone his pain was understandable. Notwithstanding any contributory negligence defenses, I thought his case was worth $300,000-$400,000 in front of a jury. In a pre-suit mediation, opposing counsel's highest offer was $275,000. This is the spreadsheet I showed my client:

| **Stage** | **Pre-Litigation** | **Litigation Before Trial** | **Trial Result A** | **Trial Result B** |
|---|---|---|---|---|
| **Offer/Result** | $ 275,000.00 | $ 325,000.00 | $ 400,000.00 | $ 300,000.00 |
| **Medical Expenses** | $ (50,000.00) | $ (50,000.00) | $ (50,000.00) | $ (50,000.00) |
| **Liens** | $ (20,000.00) | $ (20,000.00) | $ (20,000.00) | $ (20,000.00) |
| **Atty Fees (33.3 or 40 %)** | ($91,666) | $ (130,000.00) | $ (160,000.00) | $ (120,000.00) |
| **Case Expenses** | ($1,500) | $ (7,500.00) | $ (20,000.00) | $ (20,000.00) |
| **NET TO CLIENT** | **$ 111,834.00** | **$ 117,500.00** | **$ 150,000.00** | **$ 90,000.00** |
| ***Resolution Time*** | *Money today* | *$$$ in 12-18 months* | *2 years* | *2 years* |

For a pre-suit resolution I thought this was a no-brainer and he agreed. Yes, we could have done better but there was added risk and time involved that made having control today a priority. He accepted the pre-suit resolution and we closed the case out that day. Of course if they had offered $150,000 then we would have filed suit immediately.

Showing a client on paper the likely amount of time and expense it would take to achieve a likely result helps them decide for themselves what is in their best interest.

## Complaint

The goal in my initial complaint is to create as much leverage as I can to somehow motivate an insurance company to give me a viable number my client can consider. I'll allege all damages, all forms of negligence, punitive damages if applicable, and even set the case up for the clock to start ticking on attorney's fees for stubborn litigiousness under O.C.G.A. §13-6-11.

When I serve my complaints, I will almost always use a private process server. Using the County Marshall has never once worked out for me. I will usually submit my Requests for Production of Documents (RPDs) and my proposed interrogatories along with my complaint. RPDs and proposed interrogatories aren't required to be submitted in this step, but it can work well in an attorney's favor, as it makes them look fully prepared to move forward.

I will always send a copy of my file-stamped complaint to the adjuster. The filing of a complaint might trigger something in their offer algorithm before they send their case to in-house or outside counsel. In some of our filed cases, we will get a call from the adjuster shortly afterward, offering a much more reasonable offer. I'd guess that in 30 percent of our filed cases, we can settle our cases at this point just by filing a complaint. If not, we proceed forward, looking for other ways to apply leverage.

## Answer

When opposing counsel files an answer, they will submit their written discovery with RPDs and Interrogatories. If I have a case that I know should be settled with a reasonable defense counsel and adjuster, I will immediately file an Offer of Judgment under O.C.G.A. § 9-11-68 upon receiving their answer.

In a case where special damages are not that high or under $10,000 or $15,000, this can put the insurance company in a very precarious position. If there is a case with $10,000 in medical special damages, we might send in an offer of $18,000. They probably won't pay it, but if we get a jury verdict for $22,500 or more (1.25 percent higher than the Offer of Judgment), that insurance company will be forced to pay for the verdict plus all reasonable additional attorney's fees and litigation expenses. Adding on attorney's fees, expenses, and sanctions from a court can exponentially add value to even much smaller cases.

## Depositions

After written discovery, both parties will send their notices of depositions. Depositions tend to be pivotal moments in a case. Preparation and appearance for my client is critical. Until now, my client is a number and a name on medical records, bills, and legal documents. For the first time, opposing counsel gets to size up my client, speak to them personally, and form their own opinions on how they answer questions and present.

I always have my clients dress nicely and prepare them to be as calm and collected as possible. Opposing counsel depositions seem to be lasting longer and longer, almost as if they are simply trying to get minimal billing hours recorded. A deposition can be expected to take anywhere between two and four hours. Clients should be prepared for all questions related to medical history, doctor visits, employment history, sources of income, recollection of events and injuries, etc.

For my Defendant depositions, if suspected punitive behavior is involved (such as alcohol or texting and driving), after depositions, I will consider subpoenas for phone and billing history, credit card and bank statements, and even bar receipts.

## Mediation

If ongoing negotiations are in good faith, both parties may consider mediation. I try my best to know for sure whether mediation is even worth it. The cheapest I have recently seen a mediation cost is $1,500 split between the parties. In cases under $50,000, this can get costly for the client. I will ask the opposing counsel whether they are doing this in good faith, and demand the adjuster attend mediation. There are some carriers that will call mediation with no intention of resolving a case and increase their previous offer by less than 10 percent. Their intentions may be to size a lawyer or client up, to arbitrarily add costs to a case, or to catch an attorney playing too much of their hand before trial. When their bad faith intention is clear, I will make it known that we will walk right out of mediation before it gets underway. Their first offer during mediation often speaks volumes on whether they have any intention of settling a case.

Opposing counsel may wait until mediation to share something very damaging to a case. I once had opposing counsel share at mediation that they had extremely prejudicial evidence against my client that related to how he left his last employer. Opposing counsel disclosed the evidence to the mediator in confidence. After hearing the evidence (which was truly awful) upon closing, I was thankful that I didn't hear it in front of a jury for the first time. Mediations can be helpful, and any attorney should certainly know whether they are worthwhile before passing that additional cost to the client.

## Doctor Depositions

If mediation doesn't bring a settlement and it's clear that a case is marching toward an imminent trial, this is where costs start to rise. In lieu of having doctors come to court multiple times, we will take their video deposition and opposing counsel could also have an opportunity to cross-examine them. This video deposition would be played at trial as evidence for the jury.

## Trial

My trial strategy is based on efficiency, honesty, and integrity. I like to be transparent with the negative as soon as possible, during jury selection, and screen for it appropriately. I will not pander to a jury and try to win them over during selection. Instead, I try as much as I can to be myself and treat everyone with respect. In fact, I have even told a jury during jury selection what I think the case is approximately worth to desensitize them from hearing high numbers.

During opening, I'll promise the jury to not waste their time and assure them that my goal is to present my case as effectively as possible. I try not to over-object to opposing counsel or be overly obstructive to the other side. I like to show complete courtesy to the opposing counsel and the judge. In trying over 100 jury trials, I've found that the jury tends to rule in a manner with the side they either respect the most or hate the least. If I have a renegade of an opposing counsel, this is an opportunity for me to let them fall into the trap they've created for themselves: to frustrate and annoy the jury.

The most important traits to have during trial are the same traits that client relationships require credibility and authenticity. I want the jury to respect my client, trust what I give them, and know we are sincere in not wasting their time.

There are countless trial resources out there including books, CLEs, programs like Reptile, and Trial Lawyers College. Personally, I love the opportunity to learn and grow with my colleagues. These resources are all valuable and distinct in their own way, and help fulfill our goal to continuously improve and help our clients more.

# CHAPTER 14

# Resolving Healthcare Liens

Congratulations! You've got your first settlement. But it doesn't end there: there's still plenty of work to be done. Our job as injury lawyers encompasses more than maximizing that settlement or verdict number. We also must minimize what the client must pay out of the settlement to lien holders and medical providers.

Leaving liens or medical debts unresolved is a huge disservice to a client and fails to protect their best interest. Unresolved debts can damage a client's credit, leave them with a mountain of debt, and potentially get the lawyer in financial trouble as well. I have heard from various former clients of the larger high-volume firms that even though they thought they brought home a good number on their case, it meant nothing in the end. In the months and years that followed, they would receive collection notices, harassing calls from creditors, and even lawsuits to collect on debts the lawyer could have resolved—and at a lower cost—when the client had some leverage.

In this chapter, the primary focus is on ERISA health insurance plans and the obligations of paying the health insurer back for their benefits paid. I will briefly touch on paying back independent providers like hospitals, physicians/surgeons, and orthopedic clinics. This a practical guide that is meant as an introduction to the rules and hurdles of resolving injury claims.

This is where an attorney can create the largest margins possible for their client and increase the client's bottom line measurably. Remember, maximizing a settlement or verdict amount is only half the battle; minimizing the amount needed to pay back to health providers and lien holders is almost as important.

## Paying Back a Health Insurance Lien

The cost of health insurance gets more and more out of hand every single year. The plan premiums are astronomical, and many Americans pay a good-sized chunk of their paycheck toward healthcare benefits. So, if the injured person has spent years paying a health insurance premium and receives benefits under that plan, why should they be legally forced to reimburse the health insurance company for benefits paid in the event of a third-party injury or death claim?

I have had hundreds of clients ask me this question, and the answer provides little satisfaction. Federal law and the health insurance company can turn life into a living hell under the right circumstances. Sometimes these health insurers have a legal right to recovery, but sometimes they don't. Knowing how to tell if a plan has a right of reimbursement could be the difference of hundreds of thousands of dollars in a client's pocket.

## ERISA Plans

Most health insurance companies attempt to make subrogation claims under ERISA. Under the Gerald Ford administration, the United States Congress passed The Employee Retirement Income Security Act of 1974 (ERISA). ERISA is federal law that sets minimum standards for most voluntarily established retirement and health plans in the private industry. It also provides protections for these company's rights of reimbursement where there is a third-party payor of compensation to a beneficiary.

## Contrast with the "Made Whole" Doctrine: State vs. Federal

The "Made Whole" doctrine is recognized in most states and under federal common law as well, but state law may provide better protections. In Georgia, the "Made Whole" rule is codified under O.C.G.A. § 33-24-56.1. It states that an insurer can ONLY recover money for benefits paid under their plan if "the amount of the recovery exceeds the sum of all economic and noneconomic losses incurred as a result of the injury…"

In other words, unless the injured person has been made whole through financial compensation, they have no obligation to reimburse the healthcare plan. I don't think I have ever had a client made whole through money alone. Every client I've ever had wouldn't dare go through the injury process again for any compensation. The statute applies to all health insurers, employee benefits plans, disability providers, and even lost wage plans.[34] The best protection of this statute for injured persons is that health insurer plan language cannot conflict with the statute, or it is unenforceable.[35] Georgia is a very friendly made whole jurisdiction and forces the inquiry of how that may conflict with the federal rule.

**Federal common law** is what gives these companies the power to go after someone for a lien collection. Although federal courts recognize the Made Whole doctrine, they allow for these healthcare companies to reject made whole with clear and unambiguous language in their contract with the insured.[36] Since federal law trumps state law, these ERISA self-funded plans must be paid back in most circumstances, subject a few exceptions.

## Which ERISA Plans Must Be Paid Back?

First, let's look at an exception, where a plan does not need to be paid back (or, at least not in full). ERISA specifically excludes government employees, employees of religious institutions, and plans of sole proprietors or partnerships with no employees.[37]

I once represented a man with over $500,000 in medical expenses that BCBS actually paid and asserted their right to reimbursement. A cursory look at the health insurance card revealed the plan was through the county government where the client's wife was employed. My firm responded to the demand for repayment with a flat-out rejection, asserting the Made Whole doctrine. We offered to settle the claim for $1,000 to close it out and have peace of mind for the client. They acquiesced and accepted the $1,000 as full consideration to close the claim. We saved my client over $499,000. It helps to know the law.

For a plan to justify reimbursement, it must be a non-governmental self-funded ERISA healthcare plan that clearly and unambiguously rejects any made whole doctrine and asserts its right to reimbursement.

### Self-Funded

Under ERISA, only companies that self-fund their health insurance benefits program will be entitled to reimbursement. Typically, mid-sized or large corporations can afford to do this. Companies like Delta Airlines, Coca-Cola, and National Cash Register would all most likely self-fund their benefits program. Self-funded

---

[34] **Davis v. Kaiser Found. Health Plan**, 271 Ga 508 (1999)

[35] O.C.G.A. §33-24-56.1(j).

[36] **Cagle v. Brunner**, 112 F.3d 1510, 1522 (11$^{th}$ Cir. 1997).

[37] 29 U.S.C. §1003(b)(1), (b)(2)

means they use their own money to pay health insurance claims but use an outfit like Blue Cross Blue Shield (BCBS) to administer the plan. The bigger the company, the more likely the plan is self-funded, and they have a right to reimbursement.

### Fully Insured

Conversely, there are plans that are funded through the company or employer by paying insurance to fund health insurance claims. These plans are subject to made whole and have no right to reimbursement. These include small company health plans, Obamacare or Affordable Care Act plans, or anything bought on the healthcare exchanges.

## How Can I Tell for Sure Whether it's a Self-Funded Plan?

The only way to know for sure whether a plan is reimbursable is to read the plan language and make sure it specifically rejects made whole and asserts its right to reimbursement. This is hard to do: an attorney must contact the health insurance company asserting its right to recovery and get their hands on a lot of paperwork. Thankfully, I've learned a few tips to speed this process up.

First, I like to start well before settlement. If an ERISA inquiry isn't done until after the case is settled, that can be frustrating for everyone involved. The client wants their money, the attorney wants to close out the case, and neither party has time to sit around and wait. My team makes contact with a health insurer as soon as we learn they have paid benefits.

Second, I like to write a long, detailed letter telling them they are *not* a self-funded plan (even without basis for this assertion). I tell them they have *no* right to recovery, and we are disregarding their claim pursuant to the Made Whole doctrine. Further, if they are a self-funded plan, we request that they provide certain plan documents within 30 days or we will distribute funds to the client.

This seems to light a fire and usually gets us an email or a fax with some proof of a qualifying self-funded plan. To claim rights to reimbursement, the contract should both protect the plan's right to recovery and explicitly reject the Made Whole doctrine. The most important documents that they need to provide are the actual health insurance contract, the Summary Plan Description (SPD), and Form 5500.

The SPD should contain language on how the plan is paid. If it suggests the plan is paid by the company's assets or a trust, it is self-funded. If the SPD suggests any other source, like an insurer, it could be a fully insured plan and not subject to recovery.

Form 5500 is another way to determine whether it is self-funded or fully insured. This form can be found on FreeERISA.com. The critical boxes are 1A and 9A. 1A says whether it is a single employer plan or a multiple-employer plan. Single employer plans most likely mean it is self-funded, whereas multiple employers mean they are exempt from ERISA regulation. 9A lists how the plan is funded. If it says, "general assets," or "trust," then it is likely self-funded. If it checks "insurance" then it's not likely a self-funded plan.

freeERISA.com

**Form 5500**
Department of the Treasury
Internal Revenue Service
Department of Labor
Employee Benefits Security Administration
Pension Benefit Guaranty Corporation

**Annual Return/Report of Employee Benefit Plan**
This form is required to be filed for employee benefit plans under sections 104 and 4065 of the Employee Retirement Income Security Act of 1974 (ERISA) and sections 6047(e), 6057(b), and 6058(a) of the Internal Revenue Code (the Code).

OMB Nos. 1210 - 0110
1210 - 0089
**2019**
**This Form is Open to Public Inspection**

**Complete all entries in accordance with the instructions to the Form 5500.**

**Part I - Annual Report Identification Information**
**For calendar plan year 2019 or fiscal plan year beginning August 01, 2019 , and ending July 31, 2020**

**A** This return/report is for:
☐ a multiemployer plan;
☒ a single-employer plan;
☐ a multiple-employer plan (Filers checking this box must attach a list of participating employer information in accordance with the form instructions.);
☐ a DFE (specify): ______

**B** This return/report is:
☐ the first return/report;
☐ an amended return/report;
☐ the final return/report;
☐ a short plan year return/report (less than 12 months).

**C** If the plan is a collectively-bargained plan, check here ☐

**D** Check box if filing under:
☐ Form 5558;
☐ automatic extension;
☐ the DFVC program;
☐ special extension (enter description)

**Part II - Basic Plan Information** – enter all requested information.

**1a** Name of plan
ALLIED BENEFIT SYSTEMS EMPLOYEE WELFARE PLAN

**1b** Three-digit plan number (PN) 501

**1c** Effective date of plan
August 01, 2006

**2a** Plan sponsor's name (employer, if for a single-employer plan)
Mailing address (include room, apt., suite no. and street, or P.O. Box)
City or town, state or province, country, and ZIP or foreign postal code (if foreign, see instructions)
ALLIED BENEFIT SYSTEMS
200 W. ADAMS, SUITE 500
CHICAGO IL 60606

**2b** Employer Identification Number (EIN)
36-3066057

**2c** Sponsor's telephone number
312-906-8080

**2d** Business code (see instructions)
524290

**Caution: A penalty for the late or incomplete filing of this return/report will be assessed unless reasonable cause is established.**
Under penalties of perjury and other penalties set forth in the instructions, I declare that I have examined this return/report, including accompanying schedules, statements and attachments, as well as the electronic version of this return/report, and to the best of my knowledge and belief, it is true, correct, and complete.

| SIGN HERE | Signature of plan administrator | Date | Enter name of individual signing as plan administrator |
|---|---|---|---|
| SIGN HERE | Signature of employer/plan sponsor | Date | Enter name of individual signing as employer or plan sponsor |

| SIGN HERE | | | |
|---|---|---|---|
| | Signature of DFE | Date | Enter name of individual signing as DFE |

**For Paperwork Reduction Act Notice, see the Instructions for Form 5500.** **Form 5500 (2019)** **v.171027**

**3a** Plan administrator's name and address (if ☐ Same as Plan Sponsor, enter "Same")

**3b** Administrator's EIN

**3c** Administrator's telephone number

**4** If the name and/or EIN of the plan sponsor has changed since the last return/report filed for this plan, enter the name, EIN and the plan number from the last return/report below:

**4b** EIN

**4d** PN

**a** Sponsor's name

**4c** Plan Name

| | | | |
|---|---|---|---|
| 5 | Total number of participants at the beginning of the plan year | 5 | 251 |
| 6 | Number of participants as of the end of the plan year unless otherwise stated (welfare plans only complete lines **6a(1)**, **6a(2)**, **6b**, **6c**, and **6d**) | | |
| a(1) | Total number of active participants at the beginning of the plan year | 6a(1) | 251 |
| a(2) | Total active number of participants at the end of the plan year | 6a(2) | |
| b | Retired or separated participants receiving benefits | 6b | |
| c | Other retired or separated participants entitled to future benefits | 6c | |
| d | Subtotal. Add lines **6a(2)**, **6b**, and **6c** | 6d | 265 |
| e | Deceased participants whose beneficiaries are receiving or are entitled to receive benefits | 6e | |
| f | Total. Add lines **6d** and **6e** | 6f | |
| g | Number of participants with account balances as of the end of the plan year (only defined contribution plans complete this item) | 6g | |
| h | Number of participants that terminated employment during the plan year with accrued benefits that were less than 100% vested | 6h | |
| 7 | Enter the total number of employers obligated to contribute to the plan (only multiemployer plans complete this item) | 7 | 0 |

**8a** If the plan provides pension benefits, enter the applicable pension feature codes from the List of Plan Characteristics Codes in the instructions:

**b** If the plan provides welfare benefits, enter the applicable welfare feature codes from the List of Plan Characteristics Codes in the instructions:

4A 4B 4D 4F 4H

**9a** Plan funding arrangement (check all that apply)
- **(1)** ☒ Insurance
- **(2)** ☐ Section 412(e)(3) insurance contracts
- **(3)** ☐ Trust
- **(4)** ☒ General assets of the sponsor

**9b** Plan benefit arrangement (check all that apply)
- **(1)** ☒ Insurance
- **(2)** ☐ Section 412(e)(3) insurance contracts
- **(3)** ☐ Trust
- **(4)** ☒ General assets of the sponsor

**10** Check all applicable boxes in 10a and 10b to indicate which schedules are attached, and, where indicated, enter the number attached (See instructions)

**a Pension Schedules**
- **(1)** ☐ **R** (Retirement Plan Information)
- **(2)** ☐ **MB** (Multiemployer Defined Benefit Plan and Certain Money Purchase Plan Actuarial Information)- signed by the plan actuary
- **(3)** ☐ **SB** (Single-Employer Defined Benefit Plan Actuarial Information) - signed by the plan actuary

**b General Schedules**
- **(1)** ☐ **H** (Financial Information)
- **(2)** ☐ **I** (Financial Information – Small Plan)
- **(3)** ☒ 5 **A** (Insurance Information)
- **(4)** ☒ **C** (Service Provider Information)
- **(5)** ☐ **D** (DFE/Participating Plan Information)
- **(6)** ☐ **G** (Financial Transaction Schedules)

**Part III Form M-1 Compliance Information (to be completed by welfare benefit plans)**

**11a** If the plan provides welfare benefits, was the plan subject to Form M-1 filing requirements during the plan year? (See instructions and 29 CFR 2520.101-2)..... ☐ Yes ☒ No

If "Yes" is checked, complete lines 11b and 11c.

**11b** Is the plan currently in compliance with M-1 filing requirements? (See instructions and 29 CFR 2520.101-2)..... ☐ Yes ☐ No

*Form 5500 from FreeErisa.com*

To recap: first, look at Form 5500 and the SPD for indications on how the plan is paid and whether it is single employer respectively. If ERISA self-funded is confirmed, review the plan contract to see whether the plan both protects its right to recovery *and* explicitly rejects the Made Whole doctrine. If it's not self-funded, or the plan doesn't reject made whole and assert its right to recovery, the attorney should argue "Made Whole" applies and stand their ground. In this situation, I will offer a nominal amount to close out the claim.

## Negotiating the Health Insurance Lien

Let's say it's been confirmed the plan is self-funded and the contract is airtight. What next? It helps to come up with a reduction request amount before settlement that will encourage a settlement. I will make sure the collecting party knows what that number must be. If the case is already settled, I'll paint a bleak picture of the client and highlight all long-term health issues they now face because of their injuries. I typically see reductions of at least 10 percent, but as high as 33 to 50 percent in lien reductions. There's an inverse trend where it appears that the bigger the number received by the client, the less the collection company is willing to reduce their lien.

Lien resolution companies can take care of all this and do satisfactory work for clients (e.g., Garret Resolution Group or Synergy). I have used them on occasion with our most complex and excessive liens, but we typically choose to resolve in-house for quicker resolution.

## Hospital & Physician Liens

If a client has no health insurance, or the hospital chooses not to bill insurance, there will likely be a hospital and physician's lien on the case.

If a client has health insurance, we do everything we can to encourage the hospital to bill the health insurance company rather than the third-party claim, for obvious reasons. We may alert the hospital or lien filer if liability is not accepted. We inform them if policy limits are miniscule compared to the amount of medical expenses, we demand they bill health insurance or risk not getting paid.

Sometimes, we will go through the health insurance company to back-door the bills through them. We are usually successful. Unfortunately, hospitals may still refuse to bill health insurance, or the client doesn't even have health insurance and we are forced to negotiate the hospital or physician's lien.

Hospital, physician, and nursing home liens are governed by O.C.G.A. § 44-14-470 - 473. Regardless of their respective lien laws, I typically prefer to make sure these liens are paid (or at least accounted for) in the settlement. These are legitimate debts that a client has incurred, albeit involuntarily—but the last thing I want is to destroy a client's credit or get them sued because of something my team could have resolved with simple diligence.

## How Do I Know if There is a Valid Hospital or Physician Lien?

I will first ask my client if they've received notice in the mail of the hospital's intent to file a lien. Even if they haven't, the lien collectors always seem to find the Plaintiff's lawyer. Most of these liens are resolved by collection law firms: The Smith Group, Avectus, RevClaims, etc. These companies handle the pursuit, filing, and collection of hospital liens. Clients should produce anything they have received in the mail regarding their treatment since the day of their wreck. Hospitals usually have their ways of sifting through treatment notes to identify patients that have been injured by a third-party auto wreck. From there, they will likely find an accident report and auto insurance info, and then identify the Plaintiff and the attorney's office.

Second, it's always helpful to check the Superior Court Lien Index (**http://search.gsccca.org**). You can use this website to verify if a lien has been filed, as well as the date of filing. Pursuant to O.C.G.A. § 44-14-471, a hospital must file a lien within 75 days after the patient has been discharged, and a physician's practice has 90 days to file a lien from the patient's first date of service with that practice. This statute also applies to chiropractors, physical therapists, etc. If the hospital waited longer than 75 days to file a lien, this could be leveraged to use during negotiation to further reduce your client's bills. It might make sense to at least threaten distribution unless the providers negotiate fairly.

If liability is disputed at all, the lienholder must know this immediately. They might be more likely to bill Medicaid, Medicare, or health insurance. If the available coverage is low compared to a client's damages, they may also be able to submit an emergency Medicaid application to make sure they get their bill paid.

## Negotiating the Hospital / Physicians Lien

Negotiating with hospitals has become almost impossible. Pursuant to their insurance and Medicare/Medicaid contracts, I will see adjustments of medical bills exceed 95 percent. However, when lawyers ask for a reasonable 40 to 50 percent reduction, we are lucky to see them budge 10 percent off their grossly inflated bill. Furthermore, they typically will not even begin to discuss lien reduction amounts until the case is settled or close to it. They will want to know all medical costs associated with the case, all providers and their reductions, the attorney's fee, and the client's projected bottom line. My experience is that hospitals are much more concerned with getting paid, regardless of price gouging, and even if it appears that a client will receive little or nothing from a case. Therefore, it is important to apply whatever leverage we can.

I typically wait until 90 days has passed since the expenses were incurred and then check if a valid lien exists. If I am unsure of the validity of a lien, I will write the lien filer and tell them a valid lien was never filed and force them to prove otherwise. Again, this usually garners a swift response from the lien holder with proof. If they still won't negotiate, I inform them the case has been settled, hold the lien money in my trust account, and wait. Pursuant to O.C.G.A. § 44-14-473, the statute of limitations on a hospital lien is one year from the date of settlement. If they don't file suit within one year of the case being settled, closed, and released, I will reattempt negotiation with more leverage or distribute the funds to the client. Withholding the bill payment could, however, affect the client's credit—so it's important to bring the client into the negotiation circle and make sure their best interests are being served.

If I have settled a case and the only matter still pending is negotiating hospital or physician liens, I'll distribute funds to them minus the maximum amount of all pending medical lien claims. When those resolve, I will distribute the rest of the money they are entitled to. If the medical liens eat up all the available policy limits in a case, I remind the hospital that the attorney's fee lien is superior to the hospital lien. In this instance, I would be prepared to cut my fee drastically to get the client their fair share.

## Hospital, Physician, or Provider Balance Billing

Balance billing is when a facility or health care provider accepts reduced payments from a health insurance company for services administered and then seeks to recover the unpaid balance from the patient. The contracted adjustment should bring the outstanding balance below the out-of-pocket limits under the contract or even close to zero. Balance billing does not include payments mandated by the health insurance policy that include copays, deductibles, and maximum out of pocket balances.

It is safe to presume that any health insurance contract with an in-network provider has non-recourse language where the provider agrees to accept payment from the insurer for their necessary services, and will not seek the balance of that bill from the insured. Georgia courts have a restrictive definition of what is considered a non-recourse waiver of rights to collect the balance of a bill not paid by insurance.[38] When an in-network facility attempts to balance bill for their services, we reject these bills, and demand to see the contract between the provider and the health insurer. I have not had a case yet where an in-network provider pursued the balance of bills unpaid by the insurance. In a recent trend I have seen hospitals

[38] ***Kight* v. *MCG***, Health, Inc., 769 SE 2d 923 (2015)

balance billing insured patients for bills that were rejected on the basis of being unnecessary or excessive. In these circumstances we will reject the balance bills on the same basis the insurance company did – they were unnecessary.

The balance billing dispute tends to arise when there is an out-of-network provider at an in-network facility. Whether they can balance bill requires asking many questions. The first issue to review is whether federal or state law analyzes the health insurance contract. If a claim is self-funded ERISA, Medicare, or Medicaid, then Georgia case law and statutes will not apply, and federal law most likely governs.

If the plan is not an ERISA, Medicare, Medicaid, or one administered by the federal government, then state law will apply to the analysis of balance billing. Georgia just enacted O.C.G.A § 33-20E that prohibits balance billing in most cases. If the provider is in-network, then balance billing is prohibited. The statute mainly addresses surprise balance billing from an out-of-network provider at an in-network facility. If the treatment was for emergency services, then balance billing by any provider or facility is not allowed regardless of whether client was aware of this and consented to the treatment. If the treatment was non-emergency in nature, then balance billing will be prohibited if administered at an in-network facility by an out of network provider. If the patient properly consents to treatment from the out of network provider (at an in-network facility), then balance billing would be allowed. Balance billing is permitted if non-emergency treatment was administered at an out of network facility.[39]

All federally based health insurance plans will prohibit balance billing for in-network providers. If the plan is administered by Medicaid or Medicare then balance billing is prohibited for almost all providers.[40] Tricare also prohibits balance billing.[41] Federal law now prohibits most balance billing if the plan is a private ERISA self-funded plan. The new federal law is almost identical to the new Georgia law on surprise billing from out of network providers for emergency and non-emergency services.[42] The No Surprises Act will be in effect for all federally administered private plans on January 1, 2022. Out-of-network providers that are not permitted to balance bill must accept the reduced rates that the in-network providers are bound to.

---

[39] O.C.G.A. § 33-20(E)

[40] https://www.aarp.org/content/dam/aarp/ppi/2017-01/medicare-limits-on-balance-billing-and-private-contracting-ppi.pdf (2017).

[41] https://www.tricare-west.com/content/hnfs/home/tw/prov/claims/balance_billing.html (2021)

[42] "No Surprises Act." Consolidated Appropriations Act, 2021, Public Law 116-260 (2020).

## Additional Types of Liens

### Private Ortho/Chiropractor/Physical Therapy/Imaging/Funding Liens

If a client incurred a lien because of their orthopedic treatment, rehab care, or imaging, there should be a client and/or an attorney signature guaranteeing their right to be paid for the funds. I always try to sign a lien directly with a clinic rather than have it funded through a funding company. Removing the middleman typically means my client gets a bigger reduction in the end. Since these provider's bills are almost always just as inflated as a hospital bill, we will ask for 50 to 70 percent off, depending on the case margins (though the ultimate reduction tends to be within the 30 to 50 percent range).

Keep in mind some of these practices treat everyone on a lien and their entire model is heavily risk-based. We keep these providers on a holiday card list and build these relationships constantly. They are such an asset to have for clients that couldn't otherwise afford care or even health insurance. I place a priority on making sure these providers are paid fairly since they are so important to our client's recovery.

### Worker's Compensation Subrogation Liens

Though I don't handle worker's compensation claims, I do come across worker's compensation subrogation liens if a client has dual worker's compensation and third-party liability claims. Let's say they were hurt at work and had a viable worker's comp case but were injured at work by a third-party (i.e., a car wreck). In this scenario, they also have a third-party liability claim against that person and their insurance company. I had a case where my client worked for a residential HVAC company. While at work, he was rear-ended so badly that his work truck flipped over. He made both claims and settled his WC claim within a few months of one another. As part of a worker's compensation (WC) settlement where third-party claims exist, the WC attorney will demand stipulation that any WC lien subrogation be waived. This is usually accomplished in 95 percent of cases. In cases where subrogation to the third-party case is not waived, the WC insurance company may try to collect on their lien.

O.C.G.A. § 34-9-11.1 was enacted because the worker's comp lobby wanted to protect the right of subrogation where benefits were paid back in the event of a dual third-party claim. The legislature appeased them, but pursuant to Georgia's "Made Whole" doctrine, the first concern was whether the injured employee had been made whole. The statute says they must be fully and completely compensated for both economic and non-economic damages. This burden lies solely with the employer asserting its lien; it is a heavy burden to show, and in truth, I have never heard of it being done successfully.

Another problem and barrier with subrogation is that a third-party settlement is never itemized—it's just a lump sum. Some could be for pain and suffering, some could be for punitive damages or lost wages, and another amount could be for medical expenses. Unfortunately, there is no way to tell. The WC lien does not have a lawful claim for non-economic damages like pain and suffering. I encourage any lawyer to fight and stand strong up against any claim for subrogation on a WC lien. I like to highlight how my client is still receiving treatment, is dealing with pain management, and continues to experience limitations due to the wreck. I also like to make sure that the release to the third-party insurance company specifies that they stipulate that my client has not been made whole, yet the settlement is in his/her best interest.

My general opinion is that worker's comp subrogation liens are not worthwhile and rarely sought or enforced because the law is so favorable to the injured person. I might reconsider if there was an award that was itemized extraordinarily high relative to the injuries sustained.

Knowing the law and having confidence to stand up to lien holders is important. The "Made Whole" doctrine in Georgia is very strong and gives lawyers a lot of leverage—but as with any strategy, knowing when and how to deploy it is key.

## CHAPTER 15

# The Closing Table

This is a satisfying moment for the attorney and client if their case went as planned and they have recovered. Sometimes it's bittersweet and the client still have significant limitations, or worse in wrongful death cases, where a parent might have lost a child. It's also a moment we talk about how the case went and their general satisfaction level.

Even when handing clients seven-figure checks, I know for sure they would never go through that process again, no matter how much they received. I don't believe anyone is ever made whole after a serious wreck or injury. This chapter glosses over how my firm handles distribution, balancing, and the releases to finally close a case out. Included in the appendix, you'll find a sample closing statement that includes components discussed below.

## Closing Statement

At the closing table, I will ask my client to sign the insurance company's release. I always try to have the insurance company release mention something to the effect that our client is resolving this case, even though they acknowledge they have not been made whole.

Along with other disclaimers on the closing statement, we are clear that we are not tax lawyers and cannot advise them on whether any of the distribution is taxable or any other tax consequences. A lawyer should also never give financial advice. In high-dollar situations and in cases involving minors, I will recommend one of my contacts in the financial industry for proper planning and protection of settlement money. Some clients will flat-out reject this, but I still have them acknowledge the recommendation in writing.

## The Trust Account

Once a check is received from the insurance company, it is immediately deposited in my trust account. I will move the attorney's fee over to the operating account only after everyone else has been paid.

On the end of the closing statement, I list every payment check that was issued on the case and balance those numbers with the gross amount received. I got into this habit after an administrative error bounced one of our trust account checks and I had to explain myself to the Georgia Bar.

I was winding down my former partnership, and at the same time was opening my new solo law firm, Paisley Law, L.L.C. My client had two different cases: one where he retained me while under the umbrella of the dissolving partnership, and the second case where he retained me after I was solo. The two cases were resolved at the same time and one of my admins paid off a healthcare provider from the wrong trust account. The bar called and we underwent a three-month audit of both trust accounts; thankfully, it was a simple clerical error, and the case was immediately closed. I was so upset that I hired a lawyer to respond to the Bar on my behalf. It was money well spent.

## Paying Healthcare Providers

Healthcare providers are emailed the day we send the check to them. In some situations, there may be a non-lien balance owed to a hospital, and the healthcare provider still has no idea the case involved an auto accident or a lawyer. This predicament arises necessitates calling the hospital and negotiating a discount. Unfortunately, as discussed previously, hospitals are extremely averse to reducing their bills. I like to explicitly, verbally—and in conspicuous writing—advise the client to call the hospital or visit in-person to negotiate a cash discount themselves. I have seen hospitals offer instant 70 percent savings on outstanding bills for payment on the spot. In other cases, the client might choose not to pay the hospital at all (even though we advise against this).

## Case Expenses

I have heard of firms nickel-and-diming expenses to the point of borderline stealing from the client. They will bill for the lawyer to make copies at exorbitant rates or will bill for every bit of mileage driven. In our practice, we will bill for the more obvious expenses: postage, costs of filing suit, service of process fees, deposition costs, record collection costs, etc. If circumstances justify it, we may eat the costs ourselves to give the client a bigger payout.

## Never Keep More than Clients

We will never take a larger attorney's fee than what the client takes home for a net distribution, even if we have to reduce our fee. The second most common complaint people have about those large-volume law firms is that all the money goes to the doctor and lawyers and their clients were left with little or nothing. Although it's true their healthcare was paid for, it feels irrelevant when the client walks away with nothing from the closing table. Making sure the client gets more is not uncommon; it leaves a good feeling in clients and makes them more likely to refer clients to you in the future.

## Keeping in Touch

Most of my clients and I are on hugging terms by the time I hand them their distribution check. When saying our goodbyes, I am sure to let them know they can call or text me anytime. I want to be their first call for any legal question they ever have. I promise them if I don't know the answer, I'll find someone who does. This is also a good time to invite them to leave a review about their experience with my firm (and we'll email or text them the link right away to increase the chances that they will follow through).

Beyond that, I like to keep in touch with former clients. They all get birthday cards, email newsletters, holiday cards, and once a year they will get a phone call from me to check in and say hello. Over the years I have received wedding invitations, bar mitzvah invites, birth notices, graduation notices, and more from former clients. I love getting these; I always wanted a job where I could get to know people and help them in some tangible way. The opportunity to represent personal injury clients is a gift. I include an actual closing statement template in the appendix.

## CONCLUSION

# Parting Words

I didn't grow up wealthy. In fact, my mom scraped together every penny she had just to put food on our table. There were no lawyers or doctors in my family. I had no mentors luring me into the law or any other profession of prestige. At each stage of my life, I just kept on consistently trying to put myself in the best position to get to the next level. With personal injury, I find myself doing the same thing: learning the next thing so I am in a better position to help the next client that needs me. My hope is that this book gives you at least one piece of knowledge or process idea that can regularly help you to crush your injury cases.

Although you may have read this book from start to finish, it is also meant for you to use as a handy reference guide for your pre-litigation cases. Maybe you read this thinking you knew nothing about how to handle these cases. If so, I hope you discovered you knew much more than you thought. Looking back, I realize how much more administrative this practice is, whether it's intake, making sense of medical records, collecting records, or thinking of creative ways to help a client get the care they deserve. Here are a few key takeaways from everything I've written:

## Referral Source Gratitude

I still know lawyers that I will send cases to and hear nothing back from them ever - not even a simple text to say, "thank you". Even when I receive a referral that I ultimately do not accept, I will still reach out to the referral source, say thank you, and tell them why the case was not a good fit for my practice. If a new referral does retain me, I will send a thank you card with a gift card or something more specific to them if I know them well enough. If a lawyer sends me a case, I will ask them if they'd like to co-counsel the case with me and split the attorney's fees before I do anything. Respecting your referral sources is key to longevity and success in the marketplace.

## Get to Know Your Clients

Just keeping in regular contact with clients can keep a lawyer from missing critical details in their case. I would prefer to get to meet every client in person as soon as they sign up, but that doesn't always work for them. As a law firm, our goal is to have our staff reach out to clients at least every two weeks. This helps the attorney build the relationship, keep them informed of the process, avoid lengthy gaps in treatment, and making sure the client's medical needs are being resolved.

## Invest in Paralegal and Admin Staff

Personal injury is heavily administrative, from intake to the initial wave of notices, all the way through medical record collection and then written discovery in litigation. Your admin staff is a critical element of a successful injury practice. I know some solo practitioners that will get bogged down in the minutia of record collection to the point they're rendered ineffective by missing out on other parts of their case. I do my best to pay the admin staff well, and let them know constantly how valuable they are to the clients and the organization. I have several clients that keep in regular contact with my paralegal staff because of the relationship they developed.

## Look Over Intake and Medical Records Several Times

I have recently started reviewing our intake. It has been very helpful to look back over initial symptoms and injury complaints and reviewing those with our clients. If they are complaining about something that was not mentioned in initial records, then we must address it with current providers to establish causation. I also try to avoid situations where there might be an initial diagnosis in one area from a doctor, but the client has other more serious injuries that are being cared for. Making sure the entire client is cared for can avoid gaps and causation issues later.

## Create Processes That Move Cases and Prevent Mistakes

Maintaining established timelines and review periods for every case is critical and helps move them along. When a case sits for too long or is delayed because of administrative hiccups it can quickly sour the attorney client relationship, and lead to countless mistakes. Having full immersion from the entire staff into a cloud-based case management system for all files, and calendars is necessary for optimal efficiency. Tracking cases, former clients, and leads through a Customer Relationship Management (CRM) platform is an ultimate gamechanger. You can follow data, create reports, and track exactly how cases are getting to you so you can optimize rainmaking resources accordingly.

## Put the Client's Needs First Before Your Own

Cases can become personal and adversarial against insurance companies. Our desire to get the highest number possible in front of a jury might be tempting, and many times we are left with no choice. In each case where we are facing litigation or trial, I will review the numbers with my client. With a spreadsheet in hand, I advise clients of the multiple scenarios at play, including if we close the case down with the current offer, or proceed with litigation and compare the increased attorney's fees, likely costs of litigation.

On many occasions, there may not be any choice because the Defense offer is absurd, but the client at least deserves to have all the variables laid out in front of them so both the attorney and client can make the best decision. I once saw a plaintiff's lawyer unilaterally (without consulting their client) reject a high seven figure settlement when their client would've accepted. To make matters worse, that money would've changed the life of their client. Remember, the client is always most important.

## Associate with Lawyers Better Than You – Co-Counsel, Join GTLA, Get Coffee

Jim Rohn once said, "you are the average of the five people you spend the most time with." It's not only necessary to co-counsel with lawyers that bring different tools to the case but it also makes sense to spend time improving your network of lawyers. Joining GTLA and regularly reading and commenting on the listserv is helpful. Getting coffee and networking constantly to widen your ability to help others is invaluable.

## Reach out to Healthcare Providers

If a medical provider is reachable and will pick up the phone or answer emails, I will not hesitate to reach out to them on a case for clarification or to learn more about an injury. If I have concerns about a client, and want to make sure they really focus on one issue, then I will often discuss this matter with them. Sometimes clients don't tell providers everything they need to know, and I won't shy away from managing treatment if it helps the client get the care they deserve.

## Litigate the Good Cases

Injury litigation is much easier than most of us lawyers make it out to be. Most of it is predictable and the relevant issues are mostly known. In a case where property damage is bad, and the injuries are objective, most jurors will use their common sense and be forgiving with small gaps in treatment or even unexplained chronic pain. I find the more I show I believe in my litigated cases, the better result I get.

## Keep in Touch with Former Clients

I'll always tell my clients at the closing table that I am here for them whenever they have any legal issue with which they need help. Even my old speeding ticket clients rarely forget me and call me back years later. When I speak with friends that have used a lawyer in the past for some other legal issue, for fun I'll ask if they remember their lawyer's name. Invariably, they can't remember. It blows my mind how little the lawyer has kept in touch with them, but moreover its fascinating to see my friend forget who they paid all that money too. Use a data-tracking program to record emails and create a monthly newsletter. We send cards, and try to call them once a year. Attorney Chris Simon told me once spending money on legal advertising without first investing in your former clients is throwing money into the wind.

# PARTING THOUGHTS

By reading this book, my greatest hope is that lawyers can grow and better serve their clients. These cases are emotional, and have an infinite list of variables involved. There are many ways to blunder a case. However, my goal is to shorten the learning curve with this quick read. I wish I had this book when I started injury work. I think of the missed chances I had with clients that called and I was unfamiliar with an area of law; I think of the bad cases I took because I didn't know how to recognize them in the first place; I think about the chances I had to call a potential client back but missed the opportunity because I waited too long; or missing that big case because I waited until the next day to sign it up and some runner got to them before I did; I think about when I didn't understand worker's comp liens on my third party case and I unnecessarily made the client wait an extra six months to get their money; and of course, there are countless more missed opportunities and wasted time. Today, I am still learning, but am a remarkably more qualified and experienced lawyer than I was even a few years ago. I know that for sure, and part of the process in writing this book was to help you in the same way that others helped me. I hope you found this helpful and please reach out to me if you ever need anything. Just like I received endless guidance and time from other lawyers, I intend to offer you the same thing in return.

**APPENDIX A**

# INTAKE DOCS

# Advisement Letter - Blank Contract - Limits Affidavit - HIPAA - 4 in 1

**LAW FIRM**
**Law Firm Address**
**Atlanta, GA 55555**
**Firm Telephone**
**Firm Fax**
**Firm Website**

**VIA HAND / EMAIL DELIVERY**

RE: PERSONAL INJURY CLAIM:

***<u>CLIENT ADVISEMENT LETTER</u>***

Dear _______,

Thank you for allowing our firm to represent you in this matter. Our goal in representing you is to maximum the amount we recover for you on your case and to do so an expedited manner, recognizing that we must know the full extent of your injuries before we can begin to recover. Otherwise, we may prejudice your case.

In order to help us maximize your recovery, please be sure to do the following:

1) **Complete the Attached Forms:**
   a. Client Advisement Letter - Just initial each page. That's really just to make sure you everything we need you to do to maximize the value of the case.
   b. Engagement Contract - Read over it and the Client signs the last page. The blanks at the top of the 1st page should be self-explanatory - just print the Client's name and the location of the accident.
   c. Notarized Affidavit - <u>Don't worry about having it notarized or filling in the blanks</u>. Client will sign where the signature line is.
   d. Client Info Paper - Client fills in the applicable blanks to the best of their ability.

   ****Then scan and send everything back to us with a copy of your auto insurance declarations policy page and anything else you think will be helpful.*

2) **Follow Doctors' Orders.** The most important aspect of your claim is the documentation of your personal injuries. It is critical for you to follow the doctor's recommendation and treatment schedule. Be certain to receive treatment for all of your injuries, which may require treatment by more than one or two doctors.

3) **Use Common Sense when Using Social Media**. If you have joined an online social network,(Facebook, Twitter, Linked In, My Space, etc) please keep in mind that insurance companies, their investigators and lawyers will look at your pages. They are

looking for anything which can hurt your case. For example, waterskiing, dancing, or other strenuous, physical, and/or embarrassing activities (ex: alcohol references/pictures, etc.), especially those physical activities occurring after the incident in question. Until your case is resolved, be careful what you put on your page. If you can, make your page private/by invitation only. Even if your page is private, during a lawsuit the insurance company may request court permission to access/view your web-page, so please be careful what you post or say on your site.

4) **Provide Us With Witnesses.** We need to know witnesses who can testify as to the accident and injuries. It is necessary that we know of each and every doctor, eyewitness to the incident, or friend, family member, pastor, etc. that can testify as a "before and after" witness regarding your injuries. Please identify the names, addresses and telephone numbers of any such witnesses so that we can identify them in the case.

5) **Send Us Medical Bills and Records.** All medical bills which you receive should be sent to our office immediately.

6) **Give Us Lost Wage Information.** If you have missed time from work as a result of your accident, be sure to tell our office.

7) **Contact Us With New Information and Questions.** Please contact our office if you have a change in your treatment; your injury gets significantly worse or better or if you have a question regarding your case. Our office will periodically contact you to obtain an update of your treatment schedule and progress. Please be certain to call our office if there are any changes in treatment. If you feel that you are having communication problems with our office, please call and set up an appointment with me personally so we can resolve any problems. Should you wish to have a telephone conference with me, please notify us and leave a date and time when you can be reached.

8) **Provide Us With Releases Before Signing.** In some cases, our clients have incurred damage to their car. If this is the case in your situation, please feel free to deal with the liability adjuster directly. They will come out to the car's location and will write up an estimate. You should be able to take that estimate to a body should of your choice, and have it repaired for the insurance company's price. If there is an issue, please contact the insurer directly, since they will have to discuss the matter with the body shop.
   Please be certain that **you do not sign** any "all claims" releases when you receive the money for your car repair and forward all releases to our office for approval before signing. If you have any questions, do not hesitate to call us regarding any of these issues.

Initial ________ 2

9) **Inform Us of Prior Injuries Or Accidents**. Please tell us if you have had any prior insurance claims or injuries. The insurance companies keep computer records of past claims and can access your nationwide criminal history and driving records.

10) **Inform Us if You Have Recently Filed, or Are in the Midst of a Bankruptcy Proceeding.** Failure to inform us that you are involved in a bankruptcy proceeding could severely jeopardize your case. We can help advise you of your rights concerning your personal injury case even if you are, or do become, involved in a bankruptcy proceeding.

You may have questions as to how much your case is worth. The fact of the matter is there can be no answer to this question until we have completed our investigation in your case. Once we complete our investigation, of course, we can make a determination as to the amount of the defendant's liability, if any, and even with that we will only be at a starting point. After that we must obtain all necessary information consisting of lost wages, your disability, your partial disability, how the injuries have affected you, and what the prognosis is for the future, and any other medical information that is of value to you before we can put a price tag on your case.

You may also have questions as to how long your claim may take to resolve. It is the policy of our firm to not begin steps to resolve the matter until you have completed your medical treatment. This policy protects you in that we will be able to obtain full value for your case since we have complete documentation of your injury. It also prevents you from having your case resolved and then at a later date, developing a more serious condition.

Once you have completed treatment, we will request final medical bills and reports. Once we have received all of this, we will send a demand package which will begin settlement negotiations. On average, we generally will receive and offer within sixty days of sending out the demand letter. Please bear in mind that the insurance company does not have to respond in any set time and that each case is different. Often it is necessary to file a lawsuit and try a case before a jury before we are able to resolve.

In addition, please understand that our assessment of a case may change from time to time as we learn new facts. If at some point our respective valuations of your case are materially different we have the right to withdraw our representation.

We look forward to working with you towards obtaining a resolution for your injuries.

Sincerely yours,

*Law Firm Name*

Attorney Name

Initial ________ 3

**PROFESSIONAL SERVICES CONTRACT**

I, _____________, the undersigned client, do hereby retain and employ **LAW FIRM, LLC** as my attorneys to represent me in my claim against any responsible party, firm or corporation liable therefore, resulting from an auto accident incident occurring on or about _______________________________.

**FEES**

As compensation for their services, I agree to pay my said attorneys **33.33%** of the gross recovery on behalf of the undersigned. If it becomes necessary to file suit, compensation for my attorneys shall be **40%** of the gross recovery. These fees do not cover the handling of any appeals, applications for appellate review or the re-trial of the case should the same be necessary. If an appeal or any post-trial motion is filed by any party at any point of the litigation, the percentage will be **45%**. **As a courtesy we offer to all clients – we will always cut our attorney's fee to the extent the client will net more from any case resolution than we will collect as the attorney's fee.**

Gross recovery is defined as the "gross amount of money recovered" for or on behalf of the undersigned (which term shall include the fair market value of any property which may be recovered). Said fee shall be paid out of the money recovered at the time said money is received or said property is sold. Recovery is further defined as any offer of settlement made, whether actually collected, at any point in the litigation. This representation does not include any workmen's compensation claim or loss of consortium unless indicated otherwise herein.

Client understands that this fee is not negotiable should recovery be made in this case. **NO RECOVERY = NO ATTORNEY'S FEES.** It is agreed and understood that this employment is upon a contingent fee basis, and if no recovery is made, the Client will not owe the Attorney any attorney's fees. Case expenses incurred in the prosecution of these claims will be due and payable by the Client, upon recovery.

**CASE EXPENSES**

I understand that LAW FIRM, LLC may advance legal and cases expenses, which will be deducted from any recovery. **NO RECOVERY = NO CASE EXPENSES OWED BY CLIENT.** Costs and/or case expenses may include, but are not limited to, the costs and expenses normally associated with the litigation or settlement of my claim, such as medical records/bills, medical narratives, investigative fees, service fees, witness fees, deposition costs, transcript costs, expert witness fees, copying costs, postage costs, travel expenses and long distance toll charges. At the end of the case, LAW FIRM, LLC will provide an itemized list of expenses for the undersigned.

It is agreed further that said attorneys may deduct the amount of any unpaid bills for doctors, hospitals, and related items, making disbursement of such funds directly to the entity concerned. At such time as there may be a recovery, the parties agree that LAW FIRM,

Initial ________ 4

LLC will be fully reimbursed for all costs and expenses outstanding or already paid on my behalf, in addition to their fees for professional services. This representation does not include any worker's compensation claim or loss of consortium unless indicated otherwise herein.

**DIVISION OF FEE/CO-COUNSELING**

The parties agree that attorney shall be permitted to divide any fees collected in accordance with the Georgia Rule of Professional Conduct 1.5. In accord with Georgia Rule of Professional Conduct 1.5(e)(2), the client agrees that attorney may divide the fee based solely on his judgment, and the client does not object to the participation of the other lawyer(s), if any, or to the fee splitting with other lawyers, if any. We do not foresee any co-counseling in this case unless it appears there will be lengthy litigation where we see the benefits of putting a bigger trial lawyer team together to maximize value in your case. Bringing on another trial lawyer will have no effect on the fee arrangement for the Client. The fees remain the same regardless of how many attorneys are working on this case.

**TAX ADVICE**

While monies recovered for pain and suffering are non-taxable, elements of a personal injury recovery may have tax consequences. We do not provide tax advice, and where warranted, it may be necessary for the client to consult his or her accountant.

**TERMINATION OF AGREEMENT**

I understand that this litigation can be extremely time-consuming and highly problematical with regard to the chances for success. I further understand that these cases may take many months or years to analyze, gather information and study. For these reasons, I recognize the right of my attorneys to withdraw from the case and to return the file to me at my attorneys' discretion whenever it is their opinion that the chances for success do not justify going forward.

I understand that this Agreement may be terminated at will by, and at any time, by either party upon written notification. I understand that I may dismiss my attorney at any time, for any reason, upon written notice to him and payment of unpaid expenses and services rendered to the date of the receipt of such notice and it is further agreed that attorney may elect, in his sole discretion, to file and enforce a lien at any time after such termination (by either party) the applicable percentage of fee due him under the terms of this agreement of any settlement offers, awards, verdicts, or judgments which have been obtained, made by any adversary or collateral party. In the alternative, if terminated, attorney may in his sole discretion elect payment to be based upon the time devoted to my case at an hourly rate of Four Hundred Dollars ($400.00), whichever method yields the greater amount of attorney fees.

The undersigned authorizes LAW FIRM, LLC to take a lien in the amount of services rendered in the event that he/she decides to terminate the services of the LAW FIRM, LLC.

Initial ________ 5

**POWER OF ATTORNEY AND AUTHORITY TO REPRESENT**

I hereby constitute and appoint LAW FIRM, LLC as my agent and attorney with respect to all matters in connection with their representation of me. This includes but is not limited to signing my name to documents necessary to obtain my health records and converse with my providers, negotiating bills with my health providers, negotiating any and all claims of subrogation, and speaking on my behalf and negotiating my claim with the opposing insurance company and/or attorneys for the insurer and/or other parties involved. I further give LAW FIRM, LLC the authority to execute all receipts and/or releases, endorse all checks, drafts, and/or instruments in my or our name/names necessary to effect settlement, hereby confirming all actions of said attorney or agent.

I agree to permit my attorneys to discard my file materials twelve months after completion of my case. I also authorize my attorneys to file suit at any point, if appropriate. I further authorize my attorneys to talk to any media entity for any purpose. I further acknowledge that attorney is prohibited from loaning or advancing money to me.

The attorney signing below for LAW FIRM, LLC has read and explained this contract to me and I have also personally read this contract and understand the terms stated herein. **I also hereby acknowledge that I have read and understand all of the provisions in the "Client Advisement Letter," and I agree to the recommendations of those provisions.**

Dated this _________ day of ____________________, 201____.

_______________________________________
Signature of Client.
Printed:________________________________

Accepted and approved

By: __________________

This ____ day of

_______________, 201___.

Initial ________ 6

**Insurance Policy Limits Request Affidavit**

Pursuant to **Official Code of Georgia Annotated § 33-3-28**, the Claimant/Our Client,_________________________________, who has executed this request under oath, does hereby request from _______________________________, ("Insurer") the name of each Insured and the limits of coverage of any liability or casualty insurance coverage, including any excess or umbrella insurance, which is or may be liable to pay all or part of any claim resulting from the occurrence described below:

Claimant requests this information as a result of an accident that occurred at _______________________________________________________ in which he/she was involved with _____________________________________ on or about the date of ______________________ and suffered personal injuries as a result of this incident.

In lieu of providing the above-requested information, the Insurer may provide a copy of the declaration page of each such policy.

Please send this information to my attorneys who I have retained to represent me in this matter:

**LAW FIRM, LLC**
**Firm Address**
**Atlanta, GA 55555**
**Firm Telephone**
**Firm Fax**

_________________________________
X. Claimant (PLEASE SIGN HERE)

Sworn to and subscribed before me this ______ day of __________________, 201_

_________________________
Notary Public
My Commission Expires

Initial ________ 7

**AUTHORIZATION FOR USE AND DISCLOSURE OF PROTECTED HEALTH INFORMATION**

**Patient Identification**
Name:______________________________________Date of Birth: ______________________
Address: ______________________________________________________________
Social Security Number:____________________Telephone Number: ____________________

**Information to be Released – Covering the Periods of Health Care**
From (Date)____________________________to (Date) ______________________________
From (Date)____________________________to (Date) ______________________________

**Organization providing the information:** ____________________________________________

**Please check type of information to be released:**

☑ Entire medical records
☑ History and Physical Exam
☑ Laboratory test results/reports
☑ Operative Report
☑ Pathology Report
☑ Consultation Reports
☑ X-ray Reports
☑ Emergency Room Record
☑ Discharge Summary
☑ Progress Notes
☑ X-ray films/images
☑ Itemized Bill

☐ Other (Specify) ________________________________________________________

**Purpose of Request**

☐ Treatment or Consultation ☑ At the Request of the Patient ☐ Billing or Claims Payment

☑ Other (Specify)________Legal_______________________________________________

**Person Authorized to Receive Information**
***LAW FIRM NAME***
***LAW FIRM ADDRESS***
***ATLANTA ,GA 55555***

**Drug and/or Alcohol Abuse, and/or Psychiatric, and/or HIV/Aids Release**
I understand that if my medical or billing record contains information in reference to drug and/or alcohol abuse, psychiatric care, sexually transmitted disease, hepatitis B or C testing, and/or other sensitive information, I agree to its release.

***Check One*** ☑ Yes ☐ No______________(Initials)

I understand that if my medical or billing record contains information in reference to HIV/AIDS (Human Immunodeficiency Virus/Acquired Immunodeficiency Syndrome) testing and/or treatment, I agree to its release.

***Check One*** ☑ Yes ☐ No______________(Initials)

**Time Limit & Right to Revoke Authorization**
Except to the extent that action has already been taken in reliance on this authorization, at any time I can revoke this authorization by submitting a notice in writing to the facility Privacy Officer at the address of the medical provider. Unless revoked, this authorization will expire the earlier of two years from the date of execution below or upon the closing of my legal matter by LAW FIRM, LLC.

**Re-disclosure**
I understand the information disclosed by this authorization may be subject to re-disclosure by the recipient and will no longer be protected by the Health Insurance Portability and Accountability Act of 1996. The facility, its employees, officers and physicians are hereby released from any legal responsibility or liability for disclosure of the above information to the extent indicated and authorized herein.

**Signature of Patient or Personal Representative Who May Request Disclosure**
I understand that the medical provider may not condition my treatment on whether I sign this authorization form unless specified above under Purpose of Request. I can inspect or copy the protected health information to be used or disclosed. I authorize the above named medical provider to use and disclose the protected health information specified above.

**Signature:**________________________________________**Date:** ____________________

Authority to sign if not Patient: ______________________________________________

Identity of Requestor Verified via: ☐ Photo ID ☐ Matching Signature
Other (Specify) ______________________________________________________
Verified by: ________________________________________________________

I hereby acknowledge that the above medical authorization, including my signature below and initials above, will be digitally reproduced by LAW FIRM, LLC for the specific purpose of requesting medical records and/or bills related to medical care that I have received, or will in the future receive, related to my case now being handled by LAW FIRM, LLC. I further acknowledge that my signature and initials below may be digitally transferred to such other authorizations as may be required by the medical providers whom I have seen, or may see in the future, for treatment related to my case now being handled by LAW FIRM, LLC. Such authorizations will be completed by LAW FIRM, LLC. If my signature is digitally transferred from this authorization to another authorization, including a copy of this authorization, the new authorization will be deemed signed on the date my signature is digitally transferred.

Signature of Patient **OR**
Guardian if Patient is a minor:

| | |
|---|---|
| Date Signed: | |
| Initials: | |
| List ALL Names Used (a/k/a) | |
| Printed Name of Guardian: | |
| Authority to sign if NOT Patient / Relationship to Patient: | |

# Letters a Plaintiff Can Use That Never Wants To Hire a Lawyer - Initial Matters

*(letter to the at fault liability carrier)*
***Send via fax, email AND certified US Mail with tracking as required by statute)***
***(delete all the parentheticals and red lines before sending, and see disclaimer at end of these forms)***

Date

**VIA CERTIFIED MAIL**
**AND FACSIMILE**
Insurance Company Name
Address
Address

Re: **Letter of Representation and Request for Policy Limits**
Claim No.: ________________ (call liability insurer and establish claim number)
Injured Claimant: ______________
Responsible Party/Your Insured: ____________________
Date of Loss: ____________________

**Request Pursuant to O.C.G.A. § 33-3-28**

Dear (Insurance Company)

(Injured person's name) suffered personal injuries as a result of an accident on or about (date and location of injury). I have attached the accident report from the (Investigating police agency) regarding this incident for further reference. This is an official notice that we intend to file a liability claim against the driver, ________________. Please direct all future communications regarding this matter to our attention and do not contact our client without our permission.

Pursuant to O.C.G.A. § 33-3-28, we request that you send me a copy of the declarations page for your insured policy and a statement regarding each known policy of insurances issued by your company, including excess or umbrella insurance; the name of the insurer; the name of each insured, and; the limits of coverage for each policy. Policy information can be mailed and emailed to me at:

Home Address

Email address

Thank you in advance for your attention to this matter. We will not discuss the bodily injury claim at this time.

Sincerely,

(Signature)

(Injured Person's Printed Name)

*********This MUST be sent to your UM/UIM carrier ASAP or you will not be able to claim UM benefits under the policy*********** Send via fax, email AND certified US Mail with tracking as required by statute)***

Date

**VIA CERTIFIED MAIL**
**AND FACSIMILE**
Injured Person's UM Insurance Company
Address
Address

Re: **Notice of Uninsured Motorist and Medpay Claim**
Claim No.: ____________________ (call the insurer and open a claim number)
Your Insured: _____________________ (holder of the policy / injured person)
Date of Loss: ______________________

Dear Southern Insurance Company of Virginia:

________________suffered personal injuries as a result of an accident on or about (date and location of incident). I have attached the accident report from (investigating law enforcement agency) regarding this incident for further reference.

This letter is an official notification to your company that incident described above occurred should an uninsured motorist claim need to be filed in the future. Please send all policy coverage information regarding your insured's policy, including but not limited to bodily injury coverage, medical payments coverage, and any umbrella or other policies to our address listed above. If this is a traditional UM/UIM policy then please send over my written waiver of "add-on" coverage. Policy information can be mailed and emailed to me at:

Home Address

Email Address

Thank you for your time and assistance in this regard. Please contact us with any questions to the extent it is required by my policy.

Sincerely,

Signature

Print your Name

**Insurance Policy Limits Request Affidavit for *Pro Se* Claimant**

Pursuant to **Official Code of Georgia Annotated § 33-3-28**, the Claimant, ________________________________, who has executed this request under oath, does hereby request from ______________________________, ("Insurer") the name of each Insured and the limits of coverage of any liability or casualty insurance coverage, including any excess or umbrella insurance, which is or may be liable to pay all or part of any claim resulting from the occurrence described below:

Claimant requests this information as a result of an accident that occurred at ______________________________________________________________ in which he/she was involved with ____________________________________________ on or about the date of ________________________and suffered personal injuries as a result of this incident.

In lieu of providing the above-requested information, the Insurer may provide a copy of the declaration page of each such policy.

Please send this information directly to me:

## (Claimants Address and Email Address)

_________________________________ X.
Claimant (PLEASE SIGN HERE)

Sworn to and subscribed before me this ____ day of _________________, 20__

__________________________
Notary Public
My Commission Expires. ***** *This must be notarized* ********

********Paisley Law disclaims any legal responsibility for these forms and puts whomever that might be using these forms on notice that these forms are no substitute for legal advice and we have not given you any legal advice. No attorney client relationship exists until we have a written agreement in place that has affirmed the course of representation***

# Intake Sheet

**LAW FIRM NAME – Client Intake Form**
FIRM PHONE NUMBER
FIRM EMAIL

| Case type / today's date | |
|---|---|
| REFFERED BY: | |
| CLIENT NAME(S): | |
| DOB: | |
| SSN: | |
| DATE OF LOSS: | |
| SOL Date****** | |
| Venue: | |

Client Information

| Home Address | |
|---|---|
| Occupation / Employer | |
| Phone Number / Email | |
| Auto Insurance / UM Limits | |
| Medpay | |
| Lost Wages/Bankruptcy ongoing? | |
| Type/Area of Injury (Photos?) | |
| Health Insurance Info/ ID# | |
| Medical $pecials | |
| How it Occurred (Photos?) | |
| Property Damage $everity | |
| Resident Relatives for UM | |

Defendant Info

| Name – (Note if Government) | |
|---|---|
| Address/County | |
| Phone Number | |
| Cited? For What? Date of Dispo? | |
| Liability Carrier / Policy No. | |
| Liability Limits: | |
| Aggravating Factors | |
| Last/Highest Offer | |
| Suit Filed? | |

**Treatment Information/Timeline**

| Provider 1 – Bills, notes, etc. | |
|---|---|
| Provider 2 – " | |
| Provider 3 | |
| Provider 4 | |
| Dx/Prognosis/Current Condition | |
| Prior Injuries / Prior Wrecks | |

**Thoughts on the Case** (property damage, impact, objective injuries, client likeability for jury, expectations, heat, etc.)

| Pros | |
|---|---|
| Cons | |

**APPENDIX B**

# NOTICES TO INSURANCE - DEFENDANT - LAW ENFORCEMENT

## LOR and Demand for Def's Limits - Auto - TEMPLATE

# LAW FIRM LOGO

**Mailing Address:**
555 Main St.
Suite 555
Atlanta, GA 30309

**Telephone:** 999-999-9999
Other: 999-999-9999
Facsimile : 999-999-9999

(insert date here)

**VIA CERTIFIED MAIL**
**AND FACSIMILE**
Liability Carrier Insurance
(address here)

Re: **Letter of Representation and Request for Policy Limits**
Claim No.:
Our Client:
Your Driver:
Date of Loss:
**Request Pursuant to O.C.G.A. § 33-3-28**

Dear Liability Carrier Insurance:

Please be advised that _______________ has been retained to represent the interests of _______________, who suffered personal injuries as a result of an accident on or about __________ at the intersection of _______________ and _______________ in _______________, GA. Enclosed, please find the accident report from the _____________ Police Department for further reference concerning said incident. This is an official notice that we intend to file a liability claim against the driver, _______________. Please direct all future communications regarding this matter to our attention and do not contact our client without our permission.

Pursuant to O.C.G.A. § 33-3-28, we request that you send us a copy of the declarations page for your insured policy and a statement regarding each known policy of insurances issued by your company, including excess or umbrella insurance; the name of the insurer; the name of each insured, and; the limits of coverage for each policy. Thank you in advance for your attention to this matter. If you should need anything further from us, please do not hesitate to contact our office.

Sincerely,

Attorney Name
Attorney at Law

Enclosed:
- Affidavit pursuant to O.C.G.A § 33-3-28
- Police Report

**Insurance Policy Limits Request Affidavit**

Pursuant to **Official Code of Georgia Annotated § 33-3-28**, the Claimant/Our Client, ________________________________ , who has executed this request under oath, does hereby request from ________________________________, ("Insurer") the name of each Insured and the limits of coverage of any liability or casualty insurance coverage, including any excess or umbrella insurance, which is or may be liable to pay all or part of any claim resulting from the occurrence described below:

Claimant requests this information as a result of an accident that occurred at ______________________________________________ in which he/she was involved with ________________________________ on or about the date of ________________________ and suffered personal injuries as a result of this incident.

In lieu of providing the above-requested information, the Insurer may provide a copy of the declaration page of each such policy.

Please send this information to my attorneys who I have retained to represent me in this matter:

**LAW FIRM NAME**
**Law Firm Address**

________________________________
______ X. Claimant (PLEASE SIGN HERE)

Sworn to and subscribed before me this ______ day of ________________, 201_

________________________
Notary Public
My Commission Expires

# Letter to Liable Party and Liability Insurance Carrier in Auto Case

January 1, 2021

**VIA CERTIFIED MAIL**
**AND FACSIMILE**
Insurance Company
123 Insurance Street
Atlanta, Georgia 30303

Re: **Letter of Representation and Request for Policy Limits**
Claim No.: 0000000000
Our Client: John Doe
Your Insured: Jane Doe
Date of Loss: December 1, 2020
**Request Pursuant to O.C.G.A. § 33-3-28**

Dear [Defendant] OR [Insurance Company]:

Paisley Law, LLC has been retained to represent the interests of Mr. John Doe, who suffered personal injuries as a result of an accident on or about December 1, 2020 at or near I-75 and 14th Street in Atlanta, Fulton County, Georgia. Enclosed, please find the accident report from the City of Atlanta Police Department for further reference. We hereby give permission to discuss **only matters relating to personal property** with our client, excluding diminished value. We are in the process of investigating and evaluating this claim. It is our understanding that you insure the above-referenced individual who may be liable for payment to our client for this incident.

Pursuant to O.C.G.A. § 33-3-28(a)(1), we request that you provide a statement under oath of a corporate officer or the claims manager stating, with regard to each known policy of insurance issued by it, including, but not limited to, motor vehicle insurance, homeowners insurance, access or umbrella insurance, and the following information: (a) the name of the insurer; (b) the name of each insured; and (c) the limits of coverage. You may provide a copy of the declaration's page of each such policy in lieu of providing the above information in a statement under oath.

The above request is continuing in nature. Upon discovery of any new or changed information, we request that you immediately advise our office.

If my client has given a recorded statement to your company, we hereby request that you provide our office with a copy. Kindly direct all future correspondence regarding this matter to our office. We also request that you confirm receipt of this letter of representation in writing.

Additionally, we would like to ensure that certain evidence is preserved in this case. Your insured's conduct could directly lead to litigation in this case, and all of the evidence we are referring to in this correspondence would be discoverable. **We understand that you may not possess or be directly responsible for maintaining some of these items/documents, so we**

**request that you forward a copy of this correspondence to your insured/the responsible party as soon as possible.**

To the extent that you are responsible (i.e. approving automobile repairs), we request that you take all reasonable steps to ensure to that relevant evidence is preserved.

We specifically request that the following evidence be maintained and preserved and note be destroyed, modified, altered, repaired, or changed in any manner:

1. The vehicle involved in the subject incident;
2. The defendant's cellphone and all data contained therein;
3. Any reports or forms submitted to your insurance company;
4. Maintenance, inspection, and repair records or work orders on the defendant's vehicle for the (6) month period preceding the subject incident;
5. Any pictures of the involved vehicles;
6. The defendant's social media profiles (including profiles on Facebook, Instagram, and Twitter);
7. Any data or printout from the on-board recording device from your insured's vehicle, including, but not limited to the ECM (electronic control module), airbag deployment unit, any on-board computer, tachograph, trip monitor, trip recorder, trip master, or other recording device for the day of the accident and six-month period preceding the accident;
8. Any post-accident maintenance, inspection, or repair records or invoices in regard to your insured's vehicle;
9. Any e-mails, electronic messages, letters, memos, or other documents concerning the subject incident; and
10. Any downloadable computer data from your insured's onboard computer system.

As stated before, this letter shall provide you (and your insured) notice of contemplated litigation for personal injuries resulting from this wreck. Please notify your insured of this situation as quickly as possible.

Thank you in advance for your prompt attention to this matter. If you have any questions, please do not hesitate to contact our office.

Sincerely,
Attorney at Law

# LOR and Notice of UM Medpay Claim - Auto - TEMPLATE

**Mailing Address:**
555 Main St.
Suite 555
Atlanta, GA 30309

**Telephone:** 999-999-9999
Other: 999-999-9999
Facsimile : 999-999-9999

(insert date here)

**VIA CERTIFIED MAIL**
**AND FACSIMILE**
Uninsured Motorist Insurance
(address here)

Re: **Notice of Uninsured Motorist and Medpay Claim**
Claim No.:
Our Client/Your Insured:
Date of Loss:

Dear Uninsured Motorist Insurance:

Please be advised that ______________ has been retained to represent the interests of _________ ______who suffered personal injuries as a result of an auto accident on or about _______ at or near the intersection of______________ and ________________, in _________, GA. Enclosed, please find a copy of the accident report from the __________ Police Department for further reference concerning said incident.

This letter is an official notification to your company that incident described above occurred should an uninsured motorist claim need to be filed in the future. Please send all policy coverage information regarding ________'s insured's policy, including but not limited to bodily injury coverage, medical payments coverage, and any umbrella or other policies to our address listed above. Thank you for your time and assistance in this regard. Please contact us with any questions you may have.

Sincerely,

Attorney Name
Attorney at Law

Enclosed: Accident Report

# LOR and Notice of Resident Relative UM Medpay Claim

LETTER HEAD

**Mailing Address:**
XXXXXXXXXXX
XXXXXXXXXXX
XXXXXXXXXXX

**Telephone:** 999-999-9999
Other: 777-777-7777
Facsimile : 888-888-8888

June 19, 2020

**VIA CERTIFIED MAIL**
**AND FACSIMILE**
__________ Insurance
__________
__________

Re: **Notice of Resident Relative Uninsured Motorist and Medpay Claim**
Claim No.: 000000000
Our Injured Client: ______________
Your Resident Relative Policyholder: ______________
Date of Loss: ________________

Dear ___________ Insurance:

Please be advised that Paisley Law, LLC has been retained to represent the interests of ____________, who suffered personal injuries as a result of an accident on or about _________________ at the intersection of _________________________ in _____________County, GA. I have attached the accident report from the Georgia State Patrol regarding this incident for further reference.

Your insured, ____________________ is a resident relative (mother/father/spouse/partner/sibling/in-law/grandparent) of our client, ____________________ and lives at home with him/her at ____________________________. Per O.C.G.A. § 33-7-11, uninsured motorist coverage is available to the named insured in a UM policy as well as their relatives and spouse when they live in the same household. Your insured's policy therefore covers my client's bodily injury claim.

This letter is an official notification to your company that incident described above occurred should an uninsured motorist claim need to be filed in the future. Please send all policy coverage information regarding Ms. Blalock's insured's policy, including but not limited to bodily injury coverage, medical payments coverage, and any umbrella or other policies to our address listed above. Thank you for your time and assistance in this regard. Please contact us with any questions you may have.

Sincerely,

Attorney at Law

--

# Open Records Request to Law Enforcement - Auto Wreck

***[Open Records Request to Law Enforcement]***

Date

**VIA FAX, EMAIL, and CERTIFIED MAIL**
Georgia State Patrol/Other Agency
Attn: Open Records

RE: ___________________________ (our client) (DOB 1/XX/YYYY)
Crash Report No.: D00000000000-00
OPEN RECORDS REQUEST

Dear Georgia State Patrol,

Please be advised that Law, LLC represents Ms. ________________________ regarding an auto accident that occurred on 6/XX/20 at or near the intersection of ________________________________________, in _______________ County, Georgia. Pursuant to O.C.G.A. 50-18-70, we respectfully request a copy of any/all incident reports and dashcam/bodycam footage, 911 recordings, CAD reports, witness statements, and any other relevant materials associated with this incident.

If you have any questions or require pre-payment for the records, please do not hesitate to contact our office at 404-_____________. Thank you for your time and assistance in this matter.

Sincerely,

Attorney at Law

# Commercial Trucking Spoliation Letter

*Spoliation Notice In a Commercial Trucking Case*

May 1, 2021

**VIA CERTIFIED MAIL**
Progressive Insurance
747 Alpha Drive
Highland Heights, OH 44143

S&J Courier, Inc. (also send to driver personally)
555 Old Town Road
Big City, GA 30228

**RE:** Claim No.: 21-34343434
Our Client: Martin Smith
Date of Loss: April 28, 2021

**NOTICE OF REPRESENTATION**
**AND DEMAND FOR PRESERVATION OF EVIDENCE**

Dear Progressive Insurance/S&J Courier, Inc.

Please be advised that _______________ Law, LLC has been retained to represent the legal interests of Mr. Martin Smith. as a result of injuries sustained from a collision with a Freightliner Truck which occurred on or about April 28, 2021 on or near the intersection of __________ Blvd. and _______________ Rd. in Big City, Big Co., GA. Enclosed, please find a copy of the police report drafted by the Big City Police Department concerning the incident at hand involving your driver, Mr. Bad Driver. In light of a potential legal matter involving S&J Courier and/or Mr. Driver, we ask that S&J Courier (hereafter S&J), Mr. Driver, and their insurance company preserve any and all records noted below as evidence in this case.

This letter is to formally demand the preservation of certain evidence related to this collision. If you fail to properly secure and preserve these important pieces of evidence, it may give rise to the legal presumption that the evidence would have been harmful to your side of the case, also known as spoliation of evidence. It is necessary to preserve all of the evidence below in order for our client to be able to make a determination about the culpability and punitive exposure of any party to this action. We are not allowed to serve discovery in this matter since there has been no lawsuit filed and thus, must rely on this correspondence to you to preserve evidence in this case. We specifically request that the following evidence be maintained and preserved, and not be destroyed, modified, altered, repaired, or changed in any manner, and further that you immediately put any third party vendor that has or controls this information, material, or documentation, on notice to maintain and preserve without change:

1. Bills of lading for any shipments transported by the driver and/or co-driver, for the day of the collision and the thirty (30) day period preceding the collision.

2. Any oversized permits or other applicable permits or licenses covering the vehicle or load on the day of the collision.

3. The driver's complete driver qualification file, as required by 49 C.F.R.391.51, including but not limited to:

    a) Application for employment
    b) CDL License
    c) Driver's certification of prior traffic violations
    d) Driver's certification of prior collisions
    e) Driver's employment history
    f) Pre-employment MVR
    g) Annual MVR
    h) Annual review of driver history
    i) Certification of road test
    j) Medical examiner's certificate
    k) HAZMAT or other training documents

In addition, please also preserve:

    l) All drug and alcohol testing records of the driver
    m) All inquiries and responses concerning the driver's employment history

4. The driver's post-collision alcohol and drug testing results.

5. The accident register, or similar documentation and records, maintained by the motor carrier as required by federal law for one (1) year period preceding this collision. (FMCSR 390.15)

6. All OmniTRAC, Qualcomm, MVPC, QTRACS, OmniExpress, TruckMail, TrailerTRACS, SensorTRACS, JTRACS, and other similar system date for the six (6) months prior to the collision and the day of the collision, for the driver, truck, and trailer.

7. Cargo pickup or delivery orders prepared by motor carries, brokers, shippers, receivers, driver, or other persons, or organizations for thirty (30) days prior to the date of the collision as well as the day of the collision.

8. Accounting records, cargo transportation bills and subsequent or other records indicating billings for transportation or subsequent payment for the transportation of cargo, with both the front and back of cancelled checks for cargo transported by the driver and/or truck involved in the collision for thirty (30) days prior to the date of the collision as well as the day of the collision.

9. The entire personnel file of the driver involved in this collision.

10. All letters, reports, and written material from a government entity involving safety, and safety ratings for the company and driver to include, but not limited to, Department of Transportation audits by the state or federal government, the Federal Motor Safety administration, or material generated on your company or driver pursuant to SAFERSYS or CSA 2010. The request is limited to one (1) year prior to the wreck and

any subsequent document, report, letter, or other material (to include electronically transmitted information) that includes the date of the wreck or driver.

11. The front and back of the driver's daily logs and his co-driver's logs (if any) for the day of the collision, and the six month period preceding the collision, together with all material required by 49 C.F.R. 395.15 for the driver(s) involved in the above matter together with the results of any computer program used to check logs as well as all results of any audit of the logs by your company or a third party. This specifically includes any electric on board computers (AOBRD's EOBR's etc....) and the audit trail for those entries. We require you to put any vendor which stores or audits this information on notice of the need to preserve this data.

12. All existing driver vehicle inspection reports required under 49 C.F.R. 396.11 for the vehicle involved in the above collision.

13. All existing maintenance, inspection and repair records or work orders on the tractor and trailer involved in the above collision.

14. All annual inspection reports for the tractor trailer involved in the above collision, covering the date of the collision.

15. Photographs, video, computer generated media, or other recordings of the interior and exterior of vehicles involved in this collision, the collision scene, the occurrence, or relating to any equipment or things originally located at or near the site of the occurrence.

16. Any lease contracts or agreements covering the driver or the tractor or trailer involved in this collision.

17. Any interchange agreements regarding the tractor or trailer involved in this collision.

18. Any computer data from the tractor or trailer to include but not limited to: any data and printout from on-board recording devices, including but not limited to the ECM (electronic control module), any on-board computer, tachograph, trip monitor, trip recorder, trip master, Hours of Service (HOS) or other recording or tracking device for the day of the collision and six (6) month period preceding the collision for the equipment involved in the collision.

19. Any post-collision maintenance, inspection, or repair records or invoices in regard to the tractor and trailer involved in the above collision.

20. Any weight tickets, fuel receipts, hotel bills, tolls, or other records of expenses, to include expense sheets and settlement sheets regardless of type (to specifically include Comdata or similar vendor reports), for the truck driver pertaining to trips taken for the day of the collision and thirty (30) days prior to the collision.

21. Any trip reports, dispatch records, trip envelopes regarding the driver or the tractor or trailer involved in this collision for the day of the collision and the thirty (30) day period preceding this collision.

22. Any e-mails, electronics messages, letters, memos, or other documents concerning this collision.

23. Any driver's manuals, guidelines, rules or regulations given to drivers such as the one involved in this collision.

24. Any reports, memos, notes, logs, or other documents evidencing complaints about the driver in the above collision at any time.

25. Any DOT or PSC reports, memos, notes or correspondence concerning the driver or the tractor or trailer involved in this collision.

26. Any and all communications via CB radio, mobile or satellite communications systems, email, cellular phone, pager or other in cab communication device to include the bills for the devices for the day before, the day of, and the two days after the collision.

27. Any and all computer, electronic, or e-mail messages created in the first forty eight hours immediately after the incident, by and between the defendant and any agents or third parties relating to the facts, circumstances, or actual investigation of the incident as well as any computer messages which relate to this particular incident, whether generated or received.

28. If not previously listed, all documents required by Federal Motor Carrier Safety Regulation 395.8, specifically those items identified in the Department of Transportation's interpretation of the regulation in its Answer to Question 10, a copy of which is attached.

29. Any other items associated in any way with the wreck, documents, database, or other piece of evidence concerning or reflecting upon the driver, the collision, the truck, or the trailer.

30. All correspondence and documents regarding any safety issue for the driver to include but not limited to the initiation, investigation and final conclusion of any:
    (1) Warning letters,
    (2) Targeted roadside inspections
    (3) Any documents that stated the driver was unfit.

31. Any document that found the driver or the company deficient in any BASIC (Behavior Analysis and Safety Improvement Categories) category.

32. The BASIC measurements for the trucking company and driver for the three years prior to the collision.

33. Any correspondence regarding the company or the driver to, or asking for a correction of, any BASIC measurements or FMCSA intervention.

34. The Pre-Employment Screening Program (PSP) report on the driver for each month for the three years prior to the collision.

35. Any documents showing inquiry by the trucking company for any PSP reports of the driver for the three years to the collision.

36. Copy of the carrier profile maintained by MCMIS ( Motor Carrier Management Information System) for the three years prior to the collision.

37. All logs of activity (both in paper and electronic formats) on computer systems and networks that have or may have been used to process or store electronic data containing information about or related to safety and safety policies, the collision, the driver (s), the truck, the trailer, witness to the collision, the plaintiff(s), the load, the facts of the collision, preventability determinations, GPS data, Hours of Service (HOS) data, dispatcher data for this driver(s), this truck, and this trailer.

38. All e-mails, and information about e-mails (including message contents, header information and logs of e-mail system usage) sent or received by the driver and co-driver involved in the collision for period of time involving the collision and the seven (7) days before and after the collision.

39. All other e-mail and information about e-mail (including message contents, header information and logs of e-mail system usage) containing information about or related to company safety and safety policies, the collision, the driver(s), the truck, the trailer, witness to the collision, the plaintiff(s), the load, the facts of the collision, preventability determinations, GPS data, dispatcher data for this driver(s), this truck, and this trailer.
40. All databases (including all records and fields and structural information in such databases), containing and reference to and/or information about or related to company safety and safety policies, the collision, the driver(s), the truck, the trailer, witnesses to the collision, the plaintiff(s), the load, the facts of the collision, preventability determinations, GPS data, dispatcher data for this driver(s), this truck, and this trailer.

40. All electronic documents and the storage media on which they reside which contain relevant, discoverable information beyond that which may be found in printed documents. Therefore, even where a paper copy exists, we will seek all documents in their electronic form along with information about those documents contained on the media. We also will seek paper printouts of only those documents that contain unique information after they were printed out (such as paper documents containing handwriting, signatures, marginalia, drawing, annotations, highlighting and redactions) along with any paper documents for which no corresponding electronic files exist.

41. Our discovery requests will ask for certain data on the hard disks, floppy disks and backup media used in your computers, some of which data are not readily available to an ordinary computer user, such as "deleted" files and "file fragments." As you may know, although a user may "erase" or "delete" a file all that is really erased is a

> reference to that file in a table on the hard disk; unless overwritten with new data, a "deleted" file can be as intact on the disk as nay "active" file you would see in a directory listing.

In order to assure that your obligation to preserve documents and things is met, please immediately forward a copy of this letter to all persons and entities with custodial responsibility for the items referred to in this letter, to specifically include third parties and vendors. If you have any questions, please do not hesitate to contact our office at 404-618-0960. Thank you for your time and assistance in this matter.

Very truly yours,

Attorney at Law

## Letter of Rep and Spoliation to Homeowner and Their Insurer

# LETTER HEAD

TRIAL LAWYERS

Law Firm Contact Info

May 10, 20__

**VIA FAX AND CERTIFIED MAIL/ RETURN RECEIPT REQUESTED**

**RE: Spoliation Letter / Request for Insurance Policy Information / Letter of Representation**

| | |
|---|---|
| Client: | |
| Date of Incident: | December 11, 20__ |
| Location: | |
| Time: | Unknown |
| Policy/Claim No. | |

Dear [Homeowner] **AND** ________________ Insurance,

My law firm represents your friend, ______________ in regards to personal injuries resulting from an incident on December _______, 20________ at your residence located at ________________________________ in which [our client] suffered serious injuries not limited to ______________________________________________________________________________________________________________________________. We know this was an accident and _________________ has conveyed to us how important it is that you two remain close friends. I know he sincerely appreciates how forthcoming you both have been with insurance policy information and concern for his health. That brings me to the purpose of this letter.

There are 2 purposes for reaching out with this letter:

a. Pursuant to O.C.G.A. § 33-3-28, please provide us with a sworn statement identifying the name of the insurer, the name of each insured and the limits of coverage for each policy issued for your family (including primary, excess and umbrella policies) which may provide coverage for the incident in question. We look forward to receiving this information at the below address in a timely fashion according to Georgia law.

b. The secondary purpose of this letter is to request the preservation of certain evidence related to this accident. Georgia law states if evidence is not maintained or preserved per the statute, then there is a variety of sanctions allowed under the law. R.A. Siegel Co. v. Bowen, 246 Ga. 177, 539 S.E.2d 873 (2000). We specifically request that the following evidence be maintained and preserved and not be destroyed, modified, altered, repaired or changed in any manner:

1. Any record of repairs and receipts for the ________________________ in question in this incident for the past three years;
2. The equipment, the furniture, hardware, walkway, stairs, carpet, flooring, product, itself as well as any accessories used with it on ___________________ – including but not limited to the [parts, pieces, other accessories, etc.).
3. Investigative reports, memoranda, notes, pictures, and statements concerning this incident;
4. Witness statements concerning the incident;
5. Any surveillance videotapes from ________________;
6. All incidents, notes, notations, pictures, or reports having anything to do with any property damage or burns suffered in the past from the propane heater used in this incident.
7. (Anything else relevant)_____________________________________________.

Furthermore, although it appears you have homeowner's coverage to cover any attorney's fees or bodily injury claims to Mr. __________________, we do advise you that you also have the right to seek independent counsel to answer any questions you may have regarding this case. If you have any questions, please do not hesitate to call me on my cell phone anytime 770.265.4630.

Sincerely,

Attorney at Law

# Letter of Rep and Spoliation to Store - Premises Injury

**Mailing Address:**
XXXXXXX
XXXXXXX
XXXXXXX

**Telephone:** 404-000-0000
Other: 770-000-0000
Facsimile : 888-000-0000

Date, __, 202_

**VIA CERTIFIED MAIL**
Defendant Owner/Management of Premises
Address

RE: Our Client: ________________
Date of Incident: ________________

**NOTICE OF REPRESENTATION AND DEMAND FOR PRESERVATION OF EVIDENCE**

Dear __________________,

Our firm has been retained to represent the interests of _________________ with regard to serious bodily injuries that occurred as a result of an incident where [the cause of injury]on ____________________ at ____________________________ located at ________________________ Please direct all future communication to our office regarding this case. I look forward to working with you toward the prompt and amicable resolution of this matter. Additionally, please do not contact our client directly without the express permission of this firm.

I cannot offer you any legal advice, but I do suggest that you notify your liability insurance company now and immediately confer with an independent attorney of your own, who is not paid by the insurance company, and who is experienced in insurance law in Georgia.

As you know, on or about ______________________(date and time) , ________________ was shopping at your store …
________________________________________________________________________________
(describe very brief facts and injuries). We contend that it was the negligence of your store that resulted in these injuries.

This letter formally notifies you herein of our intent to make a claim and, if necessary, pursue litigation. In the event of litigation, of course, I would be obligated to probe more deeply into the circumstances surrounding this case.

This letter is further intended to formally demand preservation of certain evidence relevant to this incident. If you fail to properly secure and preserve those important pieces of evidence, it will give rise to a legal presumption that the evidence would have been harmful to your side of the case. The destruction, alteration, or loss of any of the relevant evidence, may constitute spoliation under applicable law. If you fail to preserve and maintain this evidence, we will seek sanctions available under law. We specifically request that the following evidence be maintained and preserved and not be destroyed, modified, altered, repaired or changed in any manner:

(a) All indoor video camera footage of your store from _________________ to _____________________ (the day before the incident to 2 days after the incident – or whatever is a more appropriate time span)

(b) All outdoor video camera footage of your store and the property surrounding your store from ____________________ to ___________________________;

(c) All emails, reports, documents, photos, electronic communications, recorded communications of any kind and papers in any form related to this incident involving _____________________ on or about ____________________, including photos, witness statements, letters, emails, intranet messages and memorandum;

(d) All photographs and/or videos of the scene of this incident on ___________________ involving ____________________;

(e) All photographs and/or videos of injuries, cuts, bruises, or lacerations of ______________________ taken on or about _______________________;

(f) All reports, documents, photographs or papers of any kind relating to any prior accidents occurring on your store property, either inside the store or outside the store, within a 5 year period prior to ________________________;

(g) Any and all prior complaints by anyone related to the safety of your store premises, either inside or outside, within 5 years prior to _____________________.

Please forward a copy of this letter to your attorney, corporate legal department and your liability insurance company. If you should have any questions or feel the need to discuss this matter further, please do not hesitate to give me a call at ____________________.

I look forward to hearing from you soon.

Sincerely,

Lawyer Name
Attorney at Law

# Apartment Building Spoliation

***Spoliation Notice to Property Management or Owner in Suspected Negligent Security Case***

January 1, 2019

**VIA CERTIFIED MAIL**

Property Management, Inc.
Attn: Manager
9999 Old Town Road, Suite 100
Big City, Georgia 30010

| Re: | Our Client: | James Smith |
|---|---|---|
| | Date of Incident: | December 31, 2018 |
| | Location: | Big City Apartments<br>1111 Metro Avenue<br>Big City, Georgia 30010 |

Dear Representative:

This firm represents the family and heirs of James Smith, who was a tenant and resident of Big City Apartments. He was shot and killed at the complex on or about December 31, 2018. We have been asked to investigate the incident, including potential civil negligent security claims. Please place your insurance carrier(s) on notice of this incident, if you have not already done so. This also gives you further, and formal, notice of contemplated litigation. Accordingly, please preserve all relevant evidence of any kind. Without limitation, that would include:

1. Employee files;
2. Tenant files;
3. Crime notice letters;
4. Any documents reflecting knowledge, notice, or investigation into criminal activity on or around the premises;
5. Any emails pertaining to security, criminal activity, deterrence, resident complaints/concerns, James Smith, or the subject incident;
6. Any evidence reflecting or relating to communications with law enforcement regarding the premises, crime, criminal activity or security; or
7. Any other relevant evidence, including videos, notes, emails or other documentary, physical or electronic evidence pertaining in any way to this incident, crime or safety/security of the premises.

8. Any posts about the incident on any social media platform including but not limited to Facebook, Instagram, Twitter, LinkedIn, or any other digital public platform.

Failure to preserve relevant evidence may lead to sanctions for spoliation.

We would welcome the opportunity to discuss the matter with you or your attorney, and would certainly appreciate any materials you have in this regard. Please feel free to call us at your earliest convenience, and please accept this as a request for all insurance information, including primary and excess policies, pursuant O.C.G.A § 33-3-28.

Sincerely,

Attorney at Law

# Ante Litem - County

***[Ante Litem Notice***
*******Statutes and case law Change – Go read the statute 10 times and make sure the content of your ante-litem is sufficient and appropriate depending on whether the Defendant is a county, state, or municipality. This one was for a county.**********]***

Date

**VIA CERTIFIED MAIL AND FACSIMILE**

________ County Board of Commissioners
Mr. Peter ________. BOC Chairman
____________ County [Department]
P.O. Box 7777777
Big City, Georgia 39999

Billy __________., Esq.
County Attorney -___________ County, Georgia
P.O. Box 444
Big City, GA 39818

____________ Insurance Group
P.O. Box 55555
York, PA 17405

VVVVVVV Insurance
P.O. Box 222
Littleville, AL 36266

Re: **Ante Litem Notice /Letter of Representation and Request for Policy Limits Pursuant to O.C.G.A. § 33-3-28 / Spoliation Notice**
Claim No.: GA- 010101010____________________
Our Client: ______________________ (DOB 2/1/__)
Your Insured: _____________ County [Department]
Date of Loss: ________________
Location of Loss: ______________ County, Georgia

To Whom it May Concern:

This letter shall serve as notice pursuant to O.C.G.A § 36-11-1 and any and all other applicable Georgia legislative statutes, administrative rules and regulations, common law, and/or local court rules, that my client, __________________, is pursuing a claim for bodily injury damages and economic losses against the government entities identified within this letter. All future communications should be sent to our office.

**BRIEF STATEMENT OF FACTS**

On July _______, ________ at approximately 12:00 PM, Investigator ___________ of the __________________ Public Safety Department was responding to a house fire in conjunction with _____________ County Fire and Rescue at or near __________ Drive in Big City, Georgia. At the scene, _______________ County Fire and Rescue Engine No. __________ hit and subsequently ran over Mr. ____________, severely injuring _____________. Mr. ___________ was in the line of duty retrieving an item from a fire apparatus when suddenly and out of nowhere Engine _______ hit Mr. ________________ from behind and subsequently pulling his legs under the truck and crushing them. The negligent actions on the part of the ______________ County Fire and Rescue truck driver, ______________________, caused said injuries to occur. Mr. _________________ did not contribute in any way to the cause of this loss as he was unable to use any evasive maneuvers to avoid the collision happening suddenly and unannounced behind him. EMS personnel at the scene tended to Mr. ____________________ upon noticing said incident and transported him immediately to Big City Memorial Hospital where he underwent multiple surgeries over the next few days. Accordingly, under the ante litem statute, we are pursuing a claim for bodily injury damages and economic losses on behalf of Mr. ______________ against any and all entities that were responsible for said losses. For a diagram of the incident and further statements, please refer to the attached reports and audio recordings by ____________Grady 911, ______________ County Fire and Rescue, and the Georgia State Patrol. Furthermore, please be advised that there is at least one independent witness of said incident listed in the GSP report as well – Mr. -- ___________ of Big City, GA; who can be reached at 777-777-7777.

**ADDITIONAL INFORMATION PERTINENT TO THESE CLAIMS**

A. **Name of Government Entity/Entities:** ____________ County, ____________ County Board of Commissioners – Chairman ______________, ______________ County Fire and Rescue, ________________ Insurance Group, AND/OR ______________ Insurance

B. **Date and time of the transaction or occurrence out of which the loss arose:** Friday, July ____, ____________ @ 12:00PM.

C. **The place of the transaction or occurrence:** 1111 ___________ Drive, approximately 500 ft. east of Hwy 110 in Big City, _____________ County, Georgia.

D. **The nature of the loss suffered:** Personal injuries, past and future medical expenses, temporary and permanent disability, physical and mental pain and suffering and other non-economic damages. Said injuries include, but are not limited to broken fibia, tibia in both legs requiring multiple surgeries, as well multiple neck and back injuries. As treatment progresses, we will learn the full extent. We have no knowledge of the current medical expenses but we predict the billed amounts will easily exceed $200,000. The current medical expenses are ongoing an increasing.

E. **The amount of the loss claimed and demanded is <u>$5,000,000.00</u>**

F. **The acts or omissions which caused the loss:** All entities named above were negligent in the execution of their ministerial duties in multiple ways. Said negligent execution of their ministerial duties includes, but is not limited to, the following: 1) failing to yield to a pedestrian, 2) failing to maintain lane, 3) negligently supervising operations; and 3) committing other negligent acts as may be discovered through litigation.

**OFFER TO COMPROMISE CLAIM**

The purpose of an ante-litem notice such as this is to afford a government entity the opportunity to investigate a claim, ascertain the evidence, and avoid unnecessary litigation. *See* Stelling v. Richmond County, 81 Ga. App. 571 (1950). Accordingly, please consider this letter as an opportunity to amicably resolve this claim. We ask that you pass along this letter to any other proper parties. If this offer of compromise is denied, our office intends to pursue all litigation. If you have any questions or need further clarification on this important matter, please feel free to contact our office at 404-________________. In addition, we invite the opportunity to further discuss the underlying incident and would appreciate any related documentation you can provide.

**<u>***SPOLIATION NOTICE ***</u>**

This letter is also a formal demand for the preservation of certain evidence related to the subject incident. If you fail to properly secure and preserve these important pieces of evidence it will give rise to the legal presumption that the evidence would have been harmful to your side of the case. Furthermore, if you fail to preserve and maintain this evidence, we will seek all sanctions available under the law. Please see: *Court of Appeals of Georgia v. Bailey Brothers Realty, Inc., 2010 WL 2652453 (Ga. App. June 6, 2010).* The destruction, alteration, or loss of any of the below constitutes a spoliation of evidence under Georgia law. We specifically request that the following evidence be maintained and preserved and not be destroyed, modified, altered, repaired, or changed in any manner:

1. All logs referencing or related to the subject incident;
1. All video or audio recordings of the subject incident;
2. Any e-mails, phone calls, audio recordings, electronic messages, letters, memos or other documents concerning the subject incident;
3. Any manuals, guidelines, policies, procedure rules or regulations pertaining to handling calls for and dispatching emergency medical care;
4. A list of all employees involved in the subject incident; and
5. The entire personnel file of all employees involved in the subject incident.

In order to assure that your obligation to preserve documents and things is met, please immediately forward a copy of this letter to all persons and entities with custodial responsibility for the items referred to in this letter.

Lastly, Pursuant to O.C.G.A. § 33-3-28, we request that you send us a copy of the declarations page for your insured policy and a statement regarding each known policy of insurances issued by your company, including excess or umbrella insurance; the name of the insurer; the name of each insured, and; the limits of coverage for each policy.

**Further, in the event that you feel this ANTE LITEM NOTICE does not satisfy the statutory requirements, in any way, please notify our office immediately**. Thank you for your cooperation, and please feel free to call us with any questions at 404-618-0000.

Sincerely,
Attorney at Law

## APPENDIX C

# DEMAND

# Basic Auto Wreck Rear End Demand

***[Basic Rear-End Auto Demand Template]***

(Date)

**VIA CERTIFIED MAIL**
**RETURN-RECEIPT REQUESTED**
XXX Insurance
1949 East Sunshine St.
Springfield, MO 65899

Re: Claim No.: xxx
Our Client: xxx
Your Insured: xxx
Date of Loss: July 4, 2018

**Time-Limited Holt Demand for Settlement of Claim**

Dear XXX Insurance:

Please review the following settlement demand package for my client, XXX:

**Facts of Loss and Determination of Liability**

Ms. XXX's claim for bodily injury damages arises out of a collision caused by your insured, Mr. YYY. The following material, including medical reports, bills, receipts, analysis, evaluations, and other documents, has been compiled to evaluate the liability of your insured, the nature of Ms. XXX's injuries, and the extent of damages sustained by Ms. XXX as a result of the automobile accident occurring on or about INSERT DATE HERE. Ms. XXX seeks redress for injuries and damages sustained in this loss, the facts of which follow below. Liability for this loss lies solely with Mr. YYY as he caused the crash at hand to occur by following too closely and slamming in to the back of our client's vehicle. Ms. XXX did not contribute in any way to the cause of this loss as she was a passenger and unable to use any evasive maneuvers to avoid the collision.

This material is being submitted to you for purposes of settlement negotiations only. Your review of this information is under the condition that information contained herein shall not constitute an admission by Ms. XXX and that nothing contained herein shall be admissible against Ms. XXX at any future hearing or trial. We are submitting this material and communicating the information contained herein in a good faith attempt to reach a compromise settlement and for no other purpose.

*Summary of Loss*

On July 4, 2018 at approximately 2:00pm, Ms. XXX was driving her 2018 Lamborghini Aventador Coupe on I-85 in Atlanta, Georgia and came to a stop for traffic ahead. Your insured was driving behind our client, followed too closely, and struck her vehicle from behind. For more details and a diagram of the incident, please refer to the attached police report and photos below.

INSERT REALLY BAD CRASH PHOTOS HERE

After the collision occurred, the police were called and Officer _________ of the ____________ Police Department responded to the scene. Upon investigating the scene and interviewing the drivers, Officer ___________ issued your insured a citation for "following too closely" in violation of O.C.G.A. §40-6-49 and drafted the police report attached. So, but for, your insured's negligent actions as stated above, this collision would not have occurred. This sequence of events, with no intervening or superseding actions, indisputably led to the damages and injuries suffered by Ms. XXX outlined below. Your insured's negligence is therefore the proximate cause of the Ms. XXX's losses.

Our client is entitled to fair compensation for her physical, emotional, mental, and financial injuries sustained as a result of this loss. XXX Insurance has prepared a thorough investigation and concluded that your insured is at fault. We are prepared to file suit to obtain a proper recovery for Ms. XXX; however, in a good faith gesture of professional courtesy, my client and I are making a one-time pre-trial settlement demand to resolve this claim amicably and efficiently before litigation. I think it would be in your insured's best interest if you considered our client's generous offer of pre-trial settlement, and failure to tender your insured's policy limit may result in additional exposure for XXX Insurance as an excess verdict is almost certain. This issue is further discussed below with the applicable statutes and case cites.

**Bodily Injuries and Pain and Suffering**

In the days following the collision, Ms. XXX began to feel pain in her neck, shoulders, arms, back, left knee, and hips. She attempted to rest and take over the counter medication in anticipation that her pain would go away; however, her pain worsened to the point that she felt compelled to seek evaluation/treatment at DOCTOR'S OFFICE 1 on July 10, 2018.

*Doctor's Office 1*

At DOCTOR'S OFFICE 1, Ms. XXX was given a physical exam and x-rays by Dr. John Doe (D.C). It was noted that Ms. XXX was exhibiting pain and stiffness in her shoulders, chest, neck, back and left knee. A loss of lordosis in the lumbar and thoracic regions was discovered via the x-rays taken. In response to these findings, Dr. Doe diagnosed Ms. XXX with the following:

- **Sprain of ligaments of cervical spine, initial encounter (S13.4XXA)**
- **Cervicalgia (M54.2)**
- **Sprain of ligaments of lumbar spine, initial encounter (S33.5XXA)**
- **Low back pain (M54.5)**
- **Sprain of ligaments of thoracic spine, initial encounter (S23.3XXA)**

- **Pain in thoracic spine (M54.6)**
- **Segmental and somatic dysfunction of cervical region (M99.01)**
- **Segmental and somatic dysfunction of lumbar region (M99.03)**
- **Segmental and somatic dysfunction of thoracic region (M99.02)**
-

Ms. XXX was given a back brace to stabilize her lumbar spine and an ice pack to promote healing at said visit. On the next day, July 11, 2018, Ms. XXX visited Dr. Doc again and a conservative treatment plan was developed which consisted of various modalities and therapies including, but not limited to electric muscle stimulation, heat/ice therapy, chiropractic manipulation, manual therapy and therapeutic exercises. Ms. XXX treated at DOCTORS OFFICE 1 for a total of 36 visits between the dates of July 10, 2018 and January 11, 2019.

*INSERT SUBSEQUENT PLACES OF TREATMENT AND SUMMARY OF DIAGNOSES/TREATMENT HERE*

*Treatment to date*

To date, Ms. XXX has benefited greatly from conservative treatment at Doctor's Office 1, slowly tapering her treatment as time has progressed. She is currently treating at the rate of once a month to address flare-ups that occur every now and then – especially in situations where she has to sit or stand for long periods at her job.

**Summary of Special Damages to Date**

| | |
|---|---|
| **DOCTOR'S OFFICE 1** | **$6,875.00** |
| **TOTAL:** | **$6,875.00** |

*Please note this amount is subject to increase as more records become available – including but not limited to medical mileage records and/or additional doctor visit records

**Demand for Payment**

As we set out in great detail above, **our client's current special damages are $6,875.00.** I have received a certified copy of the policy for your insured, which carries limits of $50,000 per person/$100,000 per accident for liability coverage. In an effort to compromise prior to filing suit, we hereby make a one-time demand and opportunity on your company for tender of FULL POLICY LIMITS (**$50,000.00**) in exchange for my client signing a LIMITED RELEASE of claims against YOUR INSURED. This is a time limited demand that will expire if tender is not received on or before **March 19, 2019. Please note that this demand is being made pursuant to Southern General Insurance Company v. Holt, 200 Ga. App. 759 (1991).**

This settlement demand letter contains all of the material terms in compliance with O.C.G.A. § 9-11-67.1. This is a courtesy, one time offer for XXX Insurance to avoid a bad faith claim. We intend to move swiftly in filing suit on this matter if necessary. Once suit is filed, all prior demands and offers to settle are withdrawn. **Therefore, if $50,000.00 for the injuries to Ms. XXX are not tendered by 12-noon on March 19, 2019,** it would potentially expose your insured to an excess verdict and your company to a claim for bad faith. See Cotton States Mut. Ins. Co. v. Brightman, 256 Ga. App. 451; 568 S.E. 2d 498 (2002), aff'd., 278 Ga. 683, 580 S.E.

2d 519 (2003). Accordingly, if the tender is not made, you may wish to advise your insured to allow them time to seek independent counsel. Please also accept this letter as my written notice to you and your insured, in care of you, by certified mail for unliquidated damages in the amount aforementioned in conformity with O.C.G.A. § 51-12-14 which provides for the assessment of prejudgment interests as allowed by the code section commencing on the 30th day following mailing of such written notice until the date judgment is rendered in an ensuing lawsuit. If the demand is met within (30) days, no interest can or will be assessed.

If you should have any questions or feel the need to discuss this matter further, please do not hesitate to give me a call at 770-265-4630.

Sincerely,

ATTORNEY NAME HERE
Attorney for Ms. XXX

Cc: Ms. XXX

Enclosed:
1. Accident Report
2. Doctor Office 1 bill and records
3. Photos of the crash

# Scientific Studies Language for Low Impact Demands

***[Demand Insert Language for Low Impact/Low Property Damage Case. Note – Credit to a great professional, Lisa Lewis who compiled all of this.]***

**THERE ARE EIGHT *SERIOUS AND ABSOLUTE FACTS* IMPACTING AND REGARDING THAT WHICH IS TODAY IDENTIFIED AS A "WHIPLASH" INJURY:**

**1**. The "Threshold" for cervical spine soft tissue injury becomes a reality at 5 MPH.
**2.** Most injuries occur at speeds ***below*** 12 MPH.
**3**. Crashed cars can often withstand collision speeds of 15 MPH (some even more) ***without*** sustaining damage.
**4.** A delay in the onset of symptoms has been found to be the "Norm" rather than the "Exception".
**5.** Mild traumatic brain injury can be the result of a Whiplash -Type injury. (These symptoms are often referred to as "Post-Concussion Syndrome").
**6.** Up to 10% of victims of "Whiplash" become **totally disabled.**
**7.** Of the 31 important whiplash studies since 1956 (19 of them executed since 1990) regarding patients from all vectors of motor vehicle accident collision impacts (be they rear, frontal, or side) it was found "***over 60% of them***" needed long-term medical follow-up.
**8.** In 2003 several million Americans suffered a "Whiplash-Type" injury. This figure increases each and every day at an alarming rate.

**TIME NEEDED TO RECOVER**

Studies have proven 45% of the victims remained symptomatic at 12 weeks and 25% remained symptomatic at 6 months. The minimum time needed to initially stabilize the victim ***in moderate cases*** took 17 weeks. Thus, the notion that whiplash injuries heal in a short period of time is just not true.

**THREE SOLID "INJURY-CRASH-FACTS"**
**1.** Most injuries occur at speeds below 12 MPH.
**2.** Rear-end impacts of 6 MPH to 12 MPH cause the most injuries.
**3.** Between 1 and 2 years post-injury, 22% of patient's conditions have ***not*** returned to "Normal".

**SEVEN ABSOLUTELY CORRECT WHIPLASH "RISK-FACTORS"**

**1. DEGENERATIVE DISEASE**: Headaches and/or neck injury pain (for whatever reasons) ***prior*** to the crash.
**2. PRE-EXISTING HEALTH PROBLEMS**: These can positively lead to even greater pain. (For example: An arthritic situation will ***always*** lead to the severity of the injury and the pain).
**3. VEHICLE SIZE**: Even if both are about the same size an 8 MPH impact produces two times the force of gravity. If one is greater than the size of another the "Gravity-Force" becomes monumental.
**4. HEADREST POSITION**: The injury becomes ***much worse*** if it's too far away. It must be close enough to catch the head in time -- or about 2 inches. (Over 98% of headrests are ***more than*** 2 inches from the victim's head).
**5. POSITION OF HEAD AT IMPACT**: If not positively straight (***it rarely is***) all the G-forces are localized to one side of the spine, substantially increasing the severity of injuries.
**6. AGE:** How old one is plays a ***crucial role*** regarding a "whiplash-type" injury. Why? Because

as the body becomes older, ligaments become less pliable, muscles are weaker and less flexible plus there's a decreased range of motion.
**7. WOMEN AND CHILDREN:** They injure ***more seriously*** than men because they have smaller necks. They may also be too close to the steering wheel, airbag and/or are wearing an improper fitting shoulder harness. [1]

## EMPIRICAL STUDIES

Studies conducted by White and Panjabe indicate that an 8 (eight) mph rear-end collision may result in a 2 (two) g-force acceleration of the impacted vehicle and a 5 (five) g-force acceleration acting on the occupant's head within 250 milliseconds of impact. (One"g" equals an acceleration of approximately 32 feet per second.) Car crashes happen in literally one/two eye blinks. The point is that the **head and neck experience more g-forces than the car in low-speed impacts.** [2]

Kenna and Murtaghsay state: "It is wrong to assume maximum neck injury occurs in a high-speed collision; **it is the slow or moderate collision that causes maximum hyperextension of the cervical spine**. High-speed collisions often break the back of the seat, thus minimizing the force of hyperextension."[3]

A major dilemma exists for the auto manufacturer, insurance companies and the consumer of automobiles. Each would like the vehicle to provide the maximum protection for the occupant with the minimum material damage to the vehicle during a collision. Stiffer cars with spring-like rear bumpers that increase the rebound have less damage costs; however, there is an inverse consequence in that the occupant experiences an increased neck snap and the potential for greater injury. When a car gets struck from the rear by another vehicle, the very first thing that happens is that the struck car is accelerated. The occupant of the struck car experiences higher speeds as it (the occupant's body) attempts to "catch up" with the car.[4]

Navin and Romilly state: "This relative movement of the head to the shoulder during the rebound is the likely cause of neck injuries as this is the point at which dynamic loading of the neck will be maximum." They conclude: "Of major concern to researchers is the lack of structural damage present below impact speeds of 15 mph. This indicates the bumper system is the predominant system of energy absorption between the impact and the occupant. It was also observed that deflection of the seatback tends to pitch the occupant forward, with the shoulder displacement leading the head. This relative head- to- shoulder motion is the likely source of whiplash injury." [5]

Research has shown that **high impact forces are transmitted directly to the occupant in low-speed impacts though the vehicle does not begin to crush until impact speed exceeds**

---

[1] Daniel G. Baldyga (2004)
[2] White AA, Panjabi MM. Clinical Biomechanics of the Spine, New York, JB Lippencott, 1978, pp 153-158.
[3] Kenna C, Murtagh J. Whiplash, Australian Family Physician, June, 1987; 16:6.
[4] Navin FP, Romilly DP. An investigation into vehicle and occupancy response subjected to low-speed rear impacts. Proceedings of the Multidisciplinary Road Safety Conference VI, June 5-7, 1989, Fredericton, New Brunswick.
[5] Id.

**15 or 20 mph.** [6]
Severy demonstrated a 10 mph impact produced total collapse of only 2 1/2 inches in the rear structures of the impacted vehicles. **Therefore, minor property damage does not equate to minor injury**. The most important question is not, "What is the damage to the vehicle?" but, **"What was the acceleration to the vehicle that you were in?"** Injury will occur because of the acceleration differences between the different inertial parts of the occupant's body, especially from the person's head versus trunk inertial acceleration differences. [7]

**Thus, the low/moderate property damage – minor injury theory is not at all sustained by current research and has no semblance of validity as bumpers are made to withstand impacts of up to 15-20 miles per hour without sustaining major damage. This does not mean, however, that the vehicle occupants do not sustain significant injury.**

**You will note that with any impact, even ones as low as 5 mph, the velocity and accompanying force have to be transferred somewhere; and if it was not transferred to the vehicle via property damage, *it was transferred to the occupant(s) via injury.***

**Motor vehicles are built to withstand impacts; human bodies are not.**

In all. We have provided you with sufficient information. evidence and empirical case studies in light of which you can now adjust our client's claim in good faith. In that regard we ask you not to summarily dismiss this claim and our clients' injuries as low-impact. If you claim any of the medical treatment was unnecessary or any of the bills were unreasonable, please identify in writing which bills you dispute and the factual basis for disputing. If you dispute them with a qualified expert opinion from a doctor willing to testify then please provide me with a copy of his report. If not then please confirm in writing that you dispute the bills as an adjuster and not a qualified medical professional. If you do not respond in writing to this request. I will assume you do not dispute the amount of medical bills, which we believe are more than reasonable.

---

[6] Severy DM, Mathewson JH, Bechtol CO. Controlled automobile rear- end collisions, an investigation of related engineering and medical phenomena. Can Serv Med J, 1995;11:727; States JD, Korn MW, Masengill JB. The enigma of whiplash injuries. Proceedings of the 13th Annual Conference of the Amer. Assoc. for Auto. Med., 1969.

[7] Severy DM, Mathewson JH, Bechtol CO. Controlled automobile rear- end collisions, an investigation of related engineering and medical phenomena. Can Serv Med J, 1995;11:727.

# Counter Offer Demand

***[Template for a counter-offer letter/demand]***

October 1, 2019

**VIA FACSIMILE**
Mutual Insurance
PO Box 51111111
Los Angeles, CA 90000

Re: Claim No.: LA000-0393393939
Our Client: Seth Smith
Date of Loss: February 2, 2019

Dear Mutual Insurance:

We are in receipt of your latest offer via telephone on October 2, 2019 to settle our client's claim in the amount of $________________. After discussing your offer with our client, we respectfully decline the offer.

To begin, an offer of $______________ still doesn't even cover the amount of my client's medical bills – let alone any pain and suffering. My client's case is worth more than what is being offered and we tried to demonstrate that via objective settlement figures of cases involving similar injuries, venue, and amount of medical specials cited in our last correspondence. Furthermore, the $780,000.00 jury verdict that we recently obtained involving a case with only disc bulges and NO SURGERY additionally attests to the fact that there is much more value to this case and that we are prepared to litigate if necessary.

**My client is articulate, likeable, knowledgeable in medicine as a Medical Doctor working in the ICU of Big City Hospital**, and I am certain that a Big County jury (very favorable Plaintiff's venue) would sympathize with him, his ongoing ordeal, and award him a just compensation for his injuries far higher than what has been offered to date. Also, if we should resort to litigation, I will seek for attorney's fees to be paid as well due to litigiousness on the part of Mutual. It is bad enough that my client was hit by a person without insurance, but for his own insurer to cause further hassle to my client is troubling.

Second, my client needs to be compensated for the repercussions of his injuries that he will have to deal with after this accident. An offer of $__________ simply undervalues the pain and suffering he will have to endure in an eggshell state. Bulges and protrusions do not just go away; in many cases, they get worse with age and/or subsequent trauma and eventually develop into herniations/protrusions. My client already has to do home exercises and routine chiropractic visits just to stay mobile and this inevitably creates more value for his case above the current amount of his medical bills.

What about pain and suffering? Over 20 doctor and rehab visits, and you devalue his entire claim at least $5,000 under his medical expenses? Nobody goes to a doctor over 20 times if they are not in extraordinary pain. Your valuation must account for this.

Moreover, I disagree with Mutual's position on my client's bills being excessive as well. We have consulted with various healthcare billing experts and re-reviewed our client's bills in an effort to understand Mutual's position, but the bills are in line with standard prices for the same care/treatment. If you disagree, please let us know which expert you relied on for that opinion.

- Mr. Smith did not treat for a lengthy period of time, thus incurring an unreasonably large bill.
- His physician/specialist visits are well within the market of billing practices (under $700).
- His MRIs came back positive and were warranted given his complaints. The billed amount for his MRI was vastly cheaper than what any hospital would charge.
- You said PT gouged this bill because it was an injury case – this is simply not true and if it was, it would be insurance fraud! You have no data to support this assertion and to say that is reckless.
- His physical therapy bill is not substantially high given the type of injuries he sustained.
- We are familiar with billing experts being called the last few years as defense witnesses, and I've routinely seen their opinions fall on deaf ears with the jury. Juries understand that medical expenses everywhere are high and sticking an accident victim with a large corporate health bill is unconscionable. I've yet to see a billing expert work favorably for the Defense.
- Lastly – our claim really isn't based on his medical expenses anyway. It's based on **OBJECTIVE INJURIES** that he will deal with the rest of his life. This impact was severe, caused a bulging disc, and an annular tear on a thecal sac. Those both are acute conditions caused by trauma. **Consider our $780,000 verdict** last year in the super conservative venue of Forsyth County (verdict form attached) where we literally told the jury that the $40,000 of medical expenses was irrelevant and that her non-surgical case was worth high 6 figures because of the injuries alone (2 bulging discs with 3 injections). **This present case is valued because of his injuries sustained and NOT a billing department's subjective appraisal of spinal treatment.**

Our client's final offer to settle this claim in good faith is for **$25,000.00**. If we cannot reach a reasonable before **October 11, 2019** then we will have no choice but to proceed with filling the attached lawsuit and seeking attorney's fees for bad faith/litigiousness on the part of Liberty Mutual.

I'll be elated if you actually read this entire letter. If you would like to further discuss please do not hesitate to call me at 770-265-4630 or fax me at 888.815.0480 as well. Thank you and I look forward to talking with you soon.

Sincerely,
Attorney at Law…

# Punitive Damages Demand - TEMPLATE

***[DUI/Punitive Conduct Section Insert into a Demand]***

**Punitive Damages**

Personal injury suits involving defendants that were driving under the influence are subject to punitive damages. The following facts would be relevant in allowing a jury to assess punitive damages:

- YOUR INSURED was driving erratically on__________________.
- YOUR INSURED recklessly left his lane to merge into oncoming traffic and hit Ms. XXX.
- YOUR INSURED was clearly impaired by alcohol to the extent that he had no idea that he was doing anything unsafe.
- YOUR INSURED was observed to have physical manifestations of alcohol impairment by Ms. XXX and Officer Adams at the scene.

Georgia law allows for punitive damages when a tortfeasor's conduct is reckless, willful and wanton or shows a conscious disregard for the consequences of his actions. O.C.G.A. § 51-12-5.1. When a driver causes an accident while intoxicated, the issue of punitive damages for his conduct is always for the jury to decide. Craig v. Holsey, 264 Ga. App. 344, 590 S.E.2d 742 (2003). Under Georgia law, punitive damages are covered by any insurance policy issued to a person within this state. Lunceford v. Peachtree Cas. Ins. Co., 230 Ga. App 4, 495 S.E.2d 88 (1997).

***[Punitive Damages Insert Language for Reckless Driving Case]***

...On top of that, punitive damages are applicable in this case. YOUR INSURED_____________, did not simply violate a rules of the road. If he was merely talking on his cell phone, failing to maintain his lane, or just ran a red light, there would be no claim for punitive damages. However, he violated numerous rules of the road in treacherous traffic and weather conditions, which displayed a pattern and policy of dangerous driving that was even more dangerous than drinking and driving. (Exhibits 1 – 5).

Recovering punitive damages requires a showing that the collision resulted from "a pattern or policy of dangerous driving, such as driving while intoxicated or **speeding excessively**." Brooks v. Gray, 262 Ga.App. 232, 233(1), 585 S.E.2d 188 (2003). Furthermore, in awarding punitive damages, the trier of fact may consider several factors, including the egregiousness of the defendant's conduct, potential or prior criminal sanctions against the defendant based upon the same wrongful acts, and any other pertinent circumstances. Hospital Authority of Gwinnett County v. Jones, 259 Ga. 759, 764 n. 13, 386 S.E.2d 120 (1989).

Your insured, Mr. _________________, did far more than excessively speed (which alone would be enough to get punitive damages). He sped at least 24 miles per hour over the speed limit in the rain, through dense fog, during the dark of early morning, around a curve, weaving in and out of lanes, traveling downhill in light to moderate traffic, all after he was severely sleep deprived from staying up all night. This pattern and policy of dangerous driving was a recipe for the disaster Mr. Smith created, and certainly meets the criteria to impose punitive damages against your insured. The dangerous driving wasn't even the most disturbing part of these facts. Consider Mr. Smith's further display of callousness immediately following the accident when his injured "friend" was screaming, begging for help, and almost bleeding out. All Mr. ___________ could do was ignore his friend and vocally show his anger only about the damage to his precious and mangled Ford Mustang. Moreover. Mr. ___________ could not accept responsibility for his recklessness and fabricated facts in his statement to police in a failed attempt to pin blame on another driver.

_______________ was initially cited with speeding, reckless driving, failure to maintain lane, and serious injury by vehicle, which is a felony offense. **On November 1, 2019, _______________ pled guilty to one felony count of "serious injury by vehicle"** (Exhibit 4). The conduct associated with that offense incorporates all the tickets he was cited for. He did not enter a plea under Georgia's First Offender Act but accepted the felony conviction. The plea, judgment, and sentence would be fully admissible in a jury trial against your insured.

# UIM Policy Demand Template

***[UIM Policy Limit Demand for Auto Wreck Case]***

November 1, 2018

**VIA CERTIFIED MAIL**
**RETURN RECEIPT REQUESTED**
GEICO
One GEICO Center
Middle City, GA 31295-0001

Re: **UIM DEMAND**
Claim No: 048048048048
Our Client/Your Insured: Kim Brown
Responsible Party: Vinnie Vincent (USAA Ins.)
Date of Loss: March 1, 2018

**UIM POLICY LIMIT DEMAND**

Dear GEICO Insurance,

**This letter is made for the purpose of attempting to compromise disputed claims. It is subject to the privileges attached to proposals to compromise, including but not limited to O.C.G.A. §§ 24-4-408, 51-12-14(d) and Federal Rules of Evidence 408.**

As you are aware, this law firm has been entrusted with the responsibility of assuring that our client and your insured has the financial resources to both medically treat her injuries and to be fairly compensated for the other damages flowing there from.

Recognizing that GEICO as UIM carrier shares in this responsibility as the driver of the vehicle which caused this collision was woefully underinsured (he only carried $25,000 per person/$50,000 per accident in insurance); the enclosures are intended to document our client's injuries and to provide GEICO Insurance the opportunity to resolve all claims within our client's policies of insurance and without need for further litigation and/or mediation.

We have been advised that Ms. Kim Brown (your policyholder) has one (1) add-on policy of UM/UIM insurance with limits of $30,000 per person/$60,000 per accident. **Based on the foregoing, my client has authorized me to settle the following UIM claim against GEICO Insurance for the full policy limits of $30,000.00.**

**LIABILITY – AUTO ACCIDENT OF MARCH 14, 2018**

On March 1, 2018 at approximately 7:00 A.M., Ms. Brown was driving a 2008 Acura RSX heading eastbound with the right-of-way on High Rd at its intersection with Creek Place in

Large City, GA. As Ms. Brown was proceeding straight (eastbound) on High Rd, Mr. Vincent failed to yield while turning left, jetted in front of our client's vehicle, and caused the accident at hand to occur. (see the attached accident report for a more detailed diagram of the incident) According to the police report, it was noted that our client's vehicle sustained **severe damage** as a result of this accident. Furthermore, at the time of the impact, Ms. Brown's head hit the driver's side window and she eventually had to be removed forcefully from the vehicle as well since her door was unable to open.

Immediately following the crash, the police were called and Officer D. Baker of the GA Dept. of Public Safety responded to the scene. Upon investigating the scene and interviewing the drivers, Officer Baker issued Mr. Vincent a citation for "failure to yield turning left" in violation of O.C.G.A. §40-2-71. So, but for, Mr. Vincent's negligent actions as stated above, this collision would not have occurred. This sequence of events, with no intervening or superseding actions, indisputably led to the damages and injuries suffered by Ms. Brown outlined below. Mr. Vincent's negligence is therefore the proximate cause of our clients' losses.

Our client entitled to fair compensation for her physical, emotional, mental, and financial injuries sustained as a result of this loss. USAA prepared a thorough investigation and concluded that their insured was at fault. Our client has signed a LIMITED LIABILITY RELEASE TO DATE (see attached) and we are now looking to GEICO as UIM carrier in this matter to supplement compensation for our client due to the fact that Mr. Vincent was underinsured in comparison to our client's damages outlined below.

We are prepared to file suit to obtain a proper recovery for Ms. Brown; however, in a good faith gesture of professional courtesy, my client is making a one-time pre-trial settlement demand to resolve this claim amicably and efficiently before litigation. I think it would be in GEICO's best interest if you considered our client's generous offer pre-trial settlement, and failure to tender policy limits may result in additional exposure GEICO Insurance as an excess verdict is almost certain. (our client still complains of ongoing pain to date)

**BODILY INJURIES & PAIN AND SUFFERING**

At the accident scene, Ms. Brown complained of severe pain to her head, neck, back, face, and jaw and EMS personnel were called to attend to the scene. Ms. Brown was transported to Big City Hospital via AMR ambulance from the accident scene.

*Big City Hospital*

At Big City Hospital, Ms. Brown was evaluated by Dr. Paula Bones (MD) and given x-rays and a physical examination to determine if she needed more invasive treatment. After performing the exams, Dr. Brathwaite ultimately diagnosed Ms. Brown with the following:

**S00.83XA – Contusion of other part of head, initial encounter**
**M. 54.2 - Cervicalgia**

Dr. Bones prescribed Ms. Brown pain medication in order to help alleviate her pain and recommended that she follow up if her pain persisted/worsened in the coming days. Ms. Brown was discharged that same day from Big City Hospital.

*Southern Clinic*

In the weeks following her ER visit, Ms. Brown took her prescribed medication and rested to no avail – her pain continued to worsen. Due to her ongoing pain, Ms. Brown decided to visit Southern Clinic on April 1, 2018 for further evaluation/treatment. At Southern, Ms. Brown was given a physical examination by Dr. June Knee (MD) and ultimately diagnosed with the following:

**G89.11 – Acute pain due to trauma**
**S13.8XXA – Sprain of joints and ligaments of other parts of neck, initial encounter.**
**S33.5XXA – Sprain of ligaments of lumbar spine, initial encounter.**

Ms. Brown was recommended to undergo an MRI of her cervical spine in order to assess if she needed more invasive treatment. Additionally, Dr. Knee referred Ms. Brown for conservative treatment/physical therapy in order to help alleviate her pain. Dr. Knee also recommended that Ms. Knee follow up with a neurologist for further evaluation and treatment regarding her headaches and loss of sleep issues as well.

*Radiology of Georgia*

On April 6, 2018, Ms. Brown underwent an MRI of her cervical spine at Radiology of Georgia. The MRI revealed the following:

1. **Straightening of the cervical lordosis**
2. **C5-C6: Disc bulge compressing on thecal sac**

*Big City Orthopaedics*

On May 3, 2018, Ms. Brown visited Big City Orthopaedics for further evaluation regarding ongoing neck and back pain. At Orthopaedics, Ms. Brown was seen by Dr. Scott Bigcity (MD) and was recommended to undergo a lumbar MRI to further explore her back pain issue. Due to health insurance and scheduling issues, Ms. Brown was unable to get the MRI done until the next month at the recommendation of Dr. Joseph. In the interim, Ms. Brown continued to treat with conservative treatment at Southern.

*Center City Neurology, P.C.*

While still undergoing conservative treatment at Southern, Ms. Brown visited Dr. Joseph at Center City Neurology on June 1, 2018 at the recommendation of Dr. Knee. Ms. Brown was feeling severe daily headaches up to this point and felt that her symptoms were not getting any better. At Center, Dr. Joseph performed a physical examination upon Ms. Brown and noted that she had neck range of motion issues as well as jaw clicking issues as well. After reviewing prior MRIs and analyzing Ms. Brown's complaints, Dr. Joseph ultimately diagnosed Ms. Brown with the following:

**F07.81 – Postconcussional syndrome**
**G43.009 – Migraine without aura, not intractable, without status mirainosus**
**M54.17 – Radiculopathy, lumbosacral region**

Dr. Joseph recommended that Ms. Brown continue with chiropractic treatment, take over the counter migraine medication (because she couldn't afford to pay for prescription grade medication at the time), and be referred to an oral surgeon for further evaluation regarding the jaw clicking issues. A TENS unit was provided to her to help alleviate her pain as well and an MRI was recommened of the brain and lower back in order to further evaluate her issues. Lastly, according to Dr. Joseph, "**migraines are chronic and usually a LIFELONG condition that requires usually chronic and lifelong treatment…like other chronic illnesses (such as diabetes for example) it can be controlled but it can not be cured.**"

*North City Hospital*

On July 9, 2018, Ms. Brown visited North Hospital at the recommendation of Dr. Joseph to undergo MRIs of her brain and lower back. The lumbar MRI revealed the following:

1. **L4-5: Mild diffuse disc bulge. Bilateral facet arthropathy. Otherwise normal.**
2. **L5-S1: Minimal disc bulge. Otherwise normal.**

Additionally, the brain MRI revealed the following:

1. **No acute infarct. No brain parenchymal signal abnormalities. NO intracranial hemorrhage.**
2. **Mildly low-lying cerebellar tonsils, which do not meet criteria for a Chiari I malformation.**

*Center Neurology, P.C.*

Ms. Brown followed up post-MRI with Dr. Joseph on July 21, 2018 to go over her results and for further evaluation/treatment. After reviewing the MRI results and conducting a physical exam, Dr. Joseph ultimately diagnosed Ms. Brown with the following:

1. **Grade 1 concussion.**
2. **Sinusitis.**
3. **Post-concussive syndrome, recovering.**
4. **Post traumatic migranes, unimproved.**

Dr. Joseph prescribed Ms. Brown ___________ to help her alleviate the pain of her migraines and advised that she continue to use her TENS unit. Additionally, Dr. Joseoh recommended that Ms. Brown visit an oral surgeon for evaluation when she was able to afford the consultation as well.

*Southern Clinic*

On July 22, 2018, Ms. Brown visited Southern Clinic for her last visit regarding her physical therapy/conservative treatment. Ms. Brown's treatments at Southern Clinic for the most part consisted of electric muscle stimulation, ultrasound therapy, manual therapy, mechanical traction, and chiropractic adjustments for the most part. Ms. Brown treated for 20 visits at Southern Clinic between the dates of 4/1/18 to 8/1/18.

## FUTURE MEDICAL EXPENSES

To date, Ms. Brown continues to experience migraines as well as pain in her neck, back, and left jaw. As demonstrated by the MRI reports, Ms. Brown currently has to deal with **FIVE** bulges in her spine (three of which are in her neck and two in her back). She currently does not have health insurance and is having a hard time finding a provider that will treat her on a lien basis. Once she is able to find an orthopedist/oral surgeon that is able to treat her, she will get an evaluation for surgery regarding her neck/back pain and jaw clicking issues. It is very probable that this accident caused these issues because it is on her left side, which is the same side that hit the window violently during the crash that she sustained the brunt of the impact. If surgery or injections in her neck/back are warranted in the future, then this will definitely cause Ms. Brown's medical expenses to increase substantially. Furthermore, as noted in Dr. Jospeh's records, migraines are a chronic condition and there is no definite cure for this. As you are aware, injuries usually tend to worsen over time so she will have to deal with this problem for a long time to come. (and she will also need be compensated accordingly to be able to manage these issues)

## SUMMARY OF SPECIAL DAMAGES TO DATE

| | |
|---|---|
| **EMR Ambulance** | **$2,144.00** |
| **Big Greedy Hospital** | **$1,796.20** |
| **Emerg Phys, LLC** | **$719.00** |
| **South Imaging** | **$46.00** |
| **Southern Clinic** | **$5,587.00** |
| **Radiology (Cervical MRI)** | **$1,950.00** |
| **Big City Orthopaedics** | **$1,649.16** |
| **North Hospital (2 MRIs)** | **$8,582.00** |
| **North Radiology Assoc** | **$673.00** |
| **Center Neurology P.C.** | **$1,861.00** |
| **TOTAL:** | **$25,007.36** |

*Please note that this amount will continue to increase as more records become available – including, but not limited to additional radiology bills, prescription bills, medical mileage receipts, and orthopaedic/urgent care bills for follow up visits.

**SETTLEMENT**

Our client is entitled to recover an amount of damages for her physical and mental pain and suffering - past, present and future. We are confident that a Folsom County jury would award her a fair amount of pain and suffering, specials, and permanent injury should this case proceed to trial. Ms. Brown is a very sympathetic figure and we know without a shadow of a doubt that a jury will like her and be able to relate to her and her on-going ordeal.

As stated earlier, **my client has authorized me to settle all claims against GEICO Insurance Company as UIM carrier for full policy limits of $30,000.00**. These claims include compensatory damages for pain and suffering, any special damages and medical expenses (past, present and future). This demand to GEICO Insurance is made pursuant to *Smoot v. State Farm Mutual Automobile Ins. Co.*, 299 F. 2d 525 (5th Cir. 1962) and 381 F. 2d 331 (5th Cir. 1967), and the Georgia Unliquidated Damages Act (O.C.G.A. § 51-21-14), which entitles our client to interest at the rate of 3% above prime as determined by the Federal Reserve on the amount of this demand if it is not paid within sixty (60) days.

§ O.C.G.A. 33-7-11(j) reads in part the following:

"If the insurer shall refuse to pay any insured any loss covered by this Code section within 60 days after a demand has been made by the insured and a finding has been made that such refusal was made in bad faith, the insurer shall be liable to the insured in addition to any recovery under this Code section for not more than **25 percent ("or $25,000… whichever is greater…" with the new GA UM law) of the recovery and all reasonable attorney's fees for the prosecution of the case under this Code section**. The question of bad faith, the amount of the penalty, if any, and the reasonable attorney's fees, if any, shall be determined in a separate action filed by the insured against the insurer after a judgment has been rendered against the uninsured motorist in the original tort action."

If you have any questions regarding this matter, please do not hesitate to contact me directly at 770-265-0000. Thank you for your attention to this matter and I look forward to working on a swift and reasonable resolution in the coming days with you.

Very truly yours,
Attorney at Law

CC & Enclosures…

# UIM Demand with Resident Relatives UIM

***UIM Demand for Resident Relative Policy. For Simple UM/UM Claims the Resident Relative Language Can Be Discarded... Disclaimer: Just a guide and not intended to be used without specific demand language for that particular case and client. Names changed for confidentiality***

September 1, 2020

**VIA CERTIFIED MAIL**
**RETURN-RECEIPT REQUESTED**
Allgood Insurance
PO Box 660636
Dallas, TX 75266

Re: Claim No.: 05959595959 AAA
Our Client/Your Insured: SUSAN SMITH
At Fault Party: Karen Jones (Bristol West Ins)
Date of Loss: June 1, 2020

**UIM Resident Relative Demand for Settlement of Claim**

Dear Allgood Insurance:

**This letter is made for the purpose of attempting to compromise disputed claims. It is subject to the privileges attached to proposals to compromise, including but not limited to O.C.G.A. §§ 24-4-408, 51-12-14(d) and Federal Rules of Evidence 408.**

As you are aware, this law firm has been entrusted with the responsibility of assuring that our client and your insured has the financial resources to both medically treat her injuries and to be fairly compensated for the other damages flowing there from. Recognizing that Allstate Insurance as UIM carrier shares in this responsibility as the driver of the vehicle which caused this collision was woefully underinsured (she had only $25,000 per person/$50,000 per accident available in liability insurance), the enclosures are intended to document our client's injuries and provide Allstate Insurance the opportunity to resolve all claims within our client's policies of insurance and without need for further litigation and/or mediation. Now that the liability limits have been tendered, we are looking to Allstate Insurance as resident-relative UIM carrier to compensate our client for the remainder of her damages pursuant to O.C.G.A. § 33-7-11, *et. seq.*

**Ms. Bonnie Smith daughter and resident relative of Ms. Susan Smith**, has one (1) *reduced-by* liability bodily injury UIM policy with policy limits of $250,000 per person/500,000 per accident with Allstate Insurance.

**Our reasonable demand to settle this RESIDENT RELATIVE UIM claim against Allstate Insurance (based on the demand package submitted) is for FULL UIM POLICY LIMITS of $250,000.00. This demand is highly comprehensive and intended to help make this a simple decision to tender $250,000.00.**

Ms. Smith is a resident relative (mother) of Ms. Bonnie Smith and resides with her at 11 Timber Way, Big City, GA 30111. Ms. Smith has her own *reduced-by* liability bodily injury UIM policy with Hartford Insurance with limits of $250,000 per person/$500,000 per accident. A UIM demand was sent to Hartford today as well. Thus, based on the underinsured status of the at-fault party combined with the resident relative relationship between Ms. Smith and Ms.

Bonnie Smith, **<u>Allstate is obligated to provide additional coverage in this UIM claim</u>** for a total a gross recovery of $500,000 from all insurance companies involved. (Bristol West for liability, Hartford and Allstate for UIM respectively)

Additionally, a demand for $25,000.00 maximum liability policy limits in exchange for Ms. Smith signing a LIMITED LIABILITY RELEASE was sent to Bristol West Insurance (aka Coast National Insurance) on August 1, 2020. Once the policy limits are tendered and the LIMITED LIABILITY RELEASE is executed, we will supplement accordingly.

Lastly, pursuant to the *Premium Test* outlined in <u>Georgia Farm Bureau Mut. Ins. Co. v. State Farm Mut. Auto. Ins. Co.</u>, 255 Ga. 166 (1985), Hartford Insurance, the UM carrier that receives premium payments from Ms. Smith, would be entitled to a UM set off before Allstate. **Allstate is not entitled to an offset because Brandy's UIM coverage is a "reduced by liability" policy.**

*Summary of Loss*

On or about June 1, 2020 at approximately 3:20pm, Ms. Smith was driving 2019 Honda Accord at or near the intersection of Lilly Ln. and Rose Rd. in Big County, GA. As Ms. Smith was stopped for traffic ahead, Ms. Karen Jones followed too closely and struck Ms. Smith's vehicle from behind. For a diagram of the accident, please refer to the images below and on the attached accident report:

**<u>[INSERT ACCIDENT PHOTOS AND DIAGRAM HERE]</u>**

Immediately following the crash, the police were called and Trooper J. Saul of the Georgia State Patrol responded to the scene. Upon investigating the scene and interviewing the drivers. **Trooper Saul issued Ms. Jones a citation for "following too closely" in violation of O.C.G.A. §40-6-49**. So, but for, Ms. Jones's negligent actions as stated above, this collision would not have occurred. This sequence of events, with no intervening or superseding actions, indisputably led to the damages and injuries suffered by Ms. Smith outlined below. Ms. Jones's negligence is therefore the proximate cause of the Ms. Smith's losses.

Our client is entitled to fair compensation for her physical, emotional, mental, and financial injuries sustained as a result of this loss. We are prepared to file suit to obtain a proper recovery for Ms. Smith; however, in a good faith gesture of professional courtesy, my client and I are making a one-time pre-trial settlement demand to resolve this claim amicably and efficiently before litigation. I think it would be in your insured's best interest if you considered our client's generous offer of pre-trial settlement, and failure to tender your insured's policy limit may result in additional exposure for Allstate Insurance as an excess verdict is almost certain. This issue is further discussed below with the applicable statutes and case cites.

**<u>Bodily Injuries and Pain and Suffering</u>**

Ms. Smith was transported by EMS to Wellstar Hospital due to sustaining severe injuries at the scene of the crash.

*Wellstar Hospital*

At Wellstar Hospital, Ms. Smith underwent a comprehensive evaluation including a physical exam and multiple imaging exams (including CT scans and X-rays) and was diagnosed with the following (non-exhaustive list):

**S92.121B – Displaced fracture of body of right talus**
**S25.00XA – Unspecified injury of thoracic aorta**
**S22.080A – Wedge compression fracture of T11-T12 vertebra**
**S80.12XA** – Contusion of left lower leg
**S80.812A** - Abrasion, left lower leg
**S92.131B – Displaced fracture of posterior process of right talus**

Ms. Smith was admitted to the hospital's critical care department upon initial evaluation to undergo emergency surgery on her severely deformed right ankle. An external fixator was placed on her ankle and she also was evaluated by a neurosurgeon concerning her thoracic spine fractures. Ms. Smith remained under intensive care/supervision at Wellstar for a total of 7 days from June 1, 2020 to June 8, 2020.

Additionally, Ms. Smith underwent a second right ankle surgery on July 1, 2020 to further stabilize her ankle. The records for this visit are still pending; however, the bill for this surgery is accounted for in Ms. Smith's special damages below.

[INSERT INJURY/SURGICAL PHOTOS HERE]

*Treatment to date*

Many of Ms. Smith's bills/records are still forthcoming; however, they will be supplemented accordingly if necessary. The amount of her two ER bills alone surpass $160,000.00; thus, even without the subsequent numerous therapy, drug, doctor visit, and specialist bills, it is evident that Ms. Smith's loss is substantial and warrants a full policy limit tenders from Allstate (UM), Hartford (UM), and Bristol West Insurance respectively. Ms. Smith's special damages substantiated by bills received to date are as follow (again, this is only a very small portion and the beginning of a plethora of medical bills and lost wages/pain and suffering/future damages forthcoming):

**SPECIAL DAMAGES TO DATE**

| | | |
|---|---|---|
| **Big County EMS** | | **$1,200.00** |
| **Wellstar Hospital** | | **$160,799.03** |
| **ER Physician (6/1/20 only)** | | **$3,800.00** |
| **ER Radiology** | | **$2,300.00** |
| **Anesthesiology (7/1/20 only)** | | **$1,600.64** |
| **Orthopedics (until 9/23/20)** | | **$18,300.01** |
| **Physical Therapy** | | **STBD** |
| **Wellstar Medical Group** | | **STBD** |
| **Future Medical Expenses** | | **STBD** |
| **Future Lost Wages** | | **STBD** |
| | **MEDICAL EXPENSES:** | **$193,000.68*** |
| | **LOST WAGES:** | **$19,240.65** |
| | **TOTAL:** | **$212,300.33** |

*this amount WILL increase as more records become available – including but not limited to medical mileage records, additional treatment records, future treatment, surgeries, therapy, prescription records, etc.

**Susan Smith's Current Condition**

In every gruesome and catastrophic injury case I have, it's my hope that my client makes a full recovery with no lingering serious issues like deformity, loss of function, or worse - unrelenting pain that is unmanageable. Unfortunately for Susan, although her bones have healed up well post-surgery, she has hot shooting electrical pains hundreds of times per day into her ankle that doesn't seem to be improving. The doctors have increased her Neurontin dosage but that has its own set of debilitating side effects. It is unknown at this point if this will improve with time or will require more surgical intervention, but what we do know now is that our client is living in hell with this pain every day. Susan was a full time nurse, and very active in the community as well as her young grand-children. Her daughter/caregiver Bonnie Smith has reiterated to me numerous times now that her mother is a different person and that she has "aged 20 years overnight." This is a serious case with serious injuries and a jury would very likely return a 7-figure verdict if this case went to trial.

***[INSERT CURRENT CONDITION PHOTOS HERE]***

**Future Medical Specials**

After two surgeries, Ms. Smith's ankle is currently held in place by metal hardware. It is not likely that she will be able to reach a level of flexibility and stability that she experienced prior to this crash. Additionally, it is unknown whether the surgery will be successful in the long run or if Ms. Smith will require future surgery to repair/replace the current hardware she has installed. Lastly, **Ms. Smith's doctors still need to address/treat her FRACTURED VERTEBRE in her thoracic spine– which will also lead to more future damages and/or surgical procedures.** Thus, Ms. Smith has a very long road of recovery ahead and that she will inevitably incur the more medical expenses with time including, but not limited to some of the following treatment types:

- **FUTURE MRI'S AND CT SCANS**
- **CONTINUING MEDICAL TREATMENT**
- **OCCUPATIONAL THERAPY**
- **PHYSIAL THERAPY**
- **FUTURE LOST WAGES / INABILITY TO WORK**
- **COUNSELING**

**Elements of Damages**

- **PAST MEDICAL BILLS**
- **PAIN & SUFFERING (PRESENT, PAST AND FUTURE)**
- **PERMANENT INJURY**
- **EMOTIONAL PAIN & SUFFERING (GARDEN VARIETY)**
- **FUTURE MEDICALS**
- **LOST EARNINGS (PRESENT, PAST AND FUTURE)**
- **LOSS OF EARNING CAPACITY**
- **DISABILITY**
- **LOSS OF CAPACITY TO ENJOY LIFE**
- **CONSEQUENTIAL DAMAGES**

**Demand for Payment**

As we have set out in great detail, **Ms. Smith's current special damages are $212,300.33 without accounting for a plethora of forthcoming bills, future medical expenses, or future lost wages.**

Also, as you rightfully stated in your email from November 1, 2020, Allstate is entitled to a set off of the liability carrier's policy limits of $25,000.00 because Allstate is the excess UM insurer in this case. Thus, considering that Ms. Smith's damages are catastrophic and justifiably warrant a full policy limit tender on the part of all insurers, her global recovery should be as follows:

1) $25,000.00 from Coast National Insurance (tendered to date)
2) $250,000.00 from the Hartford (primary UM insurer);
3) **$225,000.00 from Allstate (excess UM insurer – entitled to set off of liability carrier's limits of $25,000.00)**

**TOTAL RECOVERY FOR MS. SMITH: $500,000.00**

Based upon the foregoing, **my client has authorized me to settle all claims against Allstate Insurance as UM carrier for $225,000.00 in exchange for my client signing a LIMITED LIABILITY RELEASE OF CLAIMS.** These claims include compensatory damages for pain and suffering, any special damages and medical expenses (past, present and future).

Our records indicate that Allstate received (via return receipt) our initial UM demand dated September 25, 2020 on October 12, 2020. My client's offer to settle for full policy limits (minus entitled set off to Allstate as excess insurer – i.e. $225,000.00 from Allstate) has not changed and thus, **Allstate has until the 60th day after October 9, 2020 (December 11, 2020) to tender $225,000.00 to avoid a bad faith UM action.**

§ O.C.G.A. 33-7-11(j) reads in part the following:

"If the insurer shall refuse to pay any insured any loss covered by this Code section within 60 days after a demand has been made by the insured and a finding has been made that such refusal was made in bad faith, the insurer shall be liable to the insured in addition to any recovery under this Code section for not more than **25 percent ("or $25,000... whichever is greater..." with the new GA UM law) of the recovery and all reasonable attorney's fees for the prosecution of the case under this Code section**. The question of bad faith, the amount of the penalty, if any, and the reasonable attorney's fees, if any, shall be determined in a separate action filed by the insured against the insurer after a judgment has been rendered against the uninsured motorist in the original tort action."

Furthermore, this demand to Allstate Insurance is made pursuant to Smoot v. State Farm Mutual Automobile Ins. Co., 299 F. 2d 525 (5th Cir. 1962) and 381 F. 2d 331 (5th Cir. 1967), and the Georgia Unliquidated Damages Act (O.C.G.A. § 51-21-14), which entitles our client to interest at the rate of 3% above prime as determined by the Federal Reserve on the amount of this demand if it is not paid within sixty (60) days.

**<u>PLEASE MAKE YOUR TENDER PAYABLE AS FOLLOWS:</u>**

**"Law Firm, LLC in trust for Susan Smith".**

**<u>PLEASE MAIL YOUR TENDER TO THE FOLLOWING ADDRESS:</u>**

**Law Firm, LLC at 1010 Peachtree St. Suite 111 Atlanta, GA 30300**

If you have any questions regarding this matter, please do not hesitate to contact our firm at 404-618-0000. Thank you for your attention to this matter and I look forward to bringing this matter to resolution over the next 60 days.

Sincerely,
Attorney for Susan Smith

Cc: Susan Smith

Enclosed:

… All the Exhibits of bills, records, evidence, reports, photos, etc.

# Homeowners Demand

***[Comprehensive Homeowner's Demand.***
***A similar case we had but names and circumstances have all been changed]***

October 1, 2020

**VIA CERTIFIED MAIL**
**RETURN RECEIPT REQUESTED**
Georgia Insurance Company
PO Box 7777
Middle City, GA 31277-7777

RE: Claim No.: 2018005106
Date of Loss: December 1, 2019
Your Insureds: Charlie Smith
Our Client: John Doe

**HOLT DEMAND FOR HOMEOWNER'S POLICY LIMITS**

Dear Mr. Adjuster:

As you know, we represent John Doe in the above-referenced claim. The following material, including medical reports, bills, receipts, analysis, evaluations, and other documents, has been compiled to evaluate the liability of your insured, the nature of John Doe's injuries, and the extent of damages sustained by John as a result of fire accident occurring on or about December 1, 2019 at the residence and home of Carol Smith.

This material is being submitted to you for purposes of settlement negotiations only. Your review of this information is under the condition that information contained herein shall not constitute an admission by John Doe and that nothing contained herein shall be admissible against him at any future hearing or trial. We are submitting this material and communicating the information contained herein in a good faith attempt to reach a compromise settlement and for no other purpose. **This demand is for your insured's total homeowner's liability and policy limits of $1,000,000.00 for** John Doe's **injuries.**

**Biographical and Personal Information on John Doe**

John Doe is a good man. At the time of his catastrophic burns he was 40 years old. John is a dad of 2 children: John Jr. who is 21 years old, and his daughter, Jenny who is 11 years old. They mean everything to John Doe. Many of the John Doe's everyday activities have been forever altered because of this fire. His upper body mobility has been severely limited, in the summer he overheats much faster than he used to and is prone to heat related illnesses. Furthermore, his permanent scarring is so severe, widespread, and visually haunting, that this has and will continue to have a lifelong devastating psychological impact on John Doe. [Remainder is cut out for confidentiality reasons]

**Facts of Loss and Determination of Liability**

Settlement Proposal – Claim No.: 11-43434343

This claim for bodily injuries arises out of a fire caused by a Coleman commercial grade 50,000 BTU propane heater owned by your insured, where Charlie chose to put a powerful commercial grade heater within 18 inches of Mr. John Doe while he slept and then left him unattended indoors for approximately 30 minutes. His actions defied logic, reasonable safety guidelines, common sense, AND the explicit warning label itself. Furthermore, contrary to the warning label and basic common sense when dealing with a heater this powerful, there were countless flammable items well within the 6 foot radius the warning label cautions against.

**Bell Consulting (Fire & Explosion) Report**

Despite Mr. Smith's negligence being plainly obvious in this case, my office felt it was proper diligence to have experts evaluate all the evidence we had. My office consulted **Bell Consulting- Fire & Explosion**. Our expert analysis was completed by **Robert K. Bell, IAAI-CFI, NAFI-CFEI II**, and **Frank E. Hagan, P. E.** (See attached report/Exhibit). Their conclusions were very straightforward and unequivocal:

1. John Doe's burn injuries are consistent with the operating Coleman propane heater being placed too close to his body by Mr. Smith.
2. The Coleman propane heater was likely within 18" of Mr. John Doe's left side based on burn research.
3. Similar heat output radiant heaters fueled by propane have clearance to combustible requirements equal to or greater than 36".
4. Open flame damage to items inside the garage are likely the result of the towel and/or shirt Mr. Smith placed on Mr. Doe coming into at or near direct contact with the Coleman propane heater.

***[INSERT PHOTOS OF AREA OF INJURY]***

*Police Photos by Officer Butts of BCPS – **Chair incinerated** - Isolated burn with very little else burned in the vicinity. 2nd photo is likely general area where heater was placed.

Although in the attached video, you hear Mr. Smith defend himself and claim the heater was set far from where John Doe was sitting, that is simply not what the evidence shows and concludes. Charlie claims John must have gotten up on his own, walked over to the heater, walked too close and caught himself on fire, but this is highly unlikely. Consider the following: John Doe was admittedly asleep just outside the garage. Your insured tried to awake him, and even kicked him and told him to "get [his] ass up." Mr. Doe didn't move. Charlie then picked John up, and then put him in directly in front of the 50,000 BTU commercial grade propane heater and left him unattended for approximately 30 minutes. Being on fire is literally the only thing that could've awoken Mr. Doe in his state that Mr. Smith left him in. John Doe was asleep in the chair when he was burned.

If you look at the pictures attached and the expert analysis, one would obviously conclude that the nature of isolation of the items that were burned in the garage are highly inconsistent with John getting to his feet, walking over to the heater, slowly catching himself on fire, panicking, and falling back into the chair only for it and a couple other items to be consumed by a fire. That simply doesn't make sense. This was an isolated fire that was put out immediately upon Mr. Doe waking up. He jumped to his feet took his t-shirt and overalls off and threw them on the burning chair.

Furthermore, consider the analysis of R. K. Bell Consulting:

2

Settlement Proposal – Claim No.: 11-43434343

"Fire patterns on items inside the garage post-fire are inconsistent with Mr. Smith's statements as to their pre-fire location. Further, Mr. Doe's burns are inconsistent with open flame damage… Mr. Doe's burn injuries are radial in nature and decrease in severity (e.g. 3rd degree to 2nd degree) when moving from the left side of his torso towards the center of his chest. The burns are consistent with a point heat source (i.e., the propane radiant heater) being too close to Mr. Doe. Radial burn demarcation lines and the direction of heat source application have been denoted on the photograph of Mr. Doe's burn injuries seen in EXHIBIT 1. Heat from the radiant heat source would conduct through any likely fabric items to Mr. Doe's skin. The location and severity of burns as determined by the attending physician corroborate our testing and analysis."

It is therefore scientifically concluded based on the scene of the fire, the power of the heater, the origin of the fire being John Doe, the severity and nature of his burn patterns, and circumstances known to us that Charlie more than likely negligently left a 50,000 BTU commercial grade heater within 18" of proximity to John Doe and left him unattended while John slept.

John never consented to being left in the garage next to the commercial heater while he was incapacitated. By falling asleep outside, he deserved whatever might happen outside of the garage but he was absolutely defenseless against a heater that powerful while he was asleep and never knew it was there or turned on. The bottom line is the negligence occurred when Charlie without John's knowledge, turned that heater on and left John unattended for 30 minutes.

**Our Claim of Negligence**

Charlie had a legally mandated duty to protect John from dangerous conditions as John was a guest on his premises. O.C.G.A § 51-3-1 states that where an owner or occupier of land, by express or implied invitation, induces or leads others to come upon his premises for any lawful purpose, he is liable in damages to such persons for injuries caused by his failure to exercise ordinary care in keeping the premises and approaches safe. The facts establish that Charlie picked John up and removed him from where he was resting outside and, without John's knowledge or consent, placed him in a chair in the garage. Mr. Smith, who had also been drinking alcohol, then took an old, dangerous propane heater and placed it in close proximity to Mr. Doe. Mr. Smith turned the heater on and left John alone and unattended. Charlie's actions were not that of a sober, careful property owner.

It's pretty obvious that putting a large commercial grade propane heater within close proximity to countless flammable items, and then leaving John completely unattended, exceeds this standard for proving negligence. Mr. Smith knew that John had consumed alcohol that evening and placed him within close proximity of a flammable, dangerous heater without his knowledge. Charlie had a legally imposed duty to keep John safe and not subject him to any dangerous conditions. In this case Mr. Smith clearly failed to do so.

**Possible Defense of Contributory Negligence and Assumption of Risk**

The key response to any attempt by Charlie to assert any affirmative defense is that John had absolutely no opportunity to avoid the harm caused by Mr. Smith's negligence and John did not voluntarily subject himself to the potential harm. Contributory negligence applies where negligence on the part of the injured party contributed to the injuries. Likewise, assumption of the risk in Georgia bars recovery where an injured party, through ordinary care, could have avoided the cause of injury. Moreover, "A

3

defendant asserting an assumption of the risk defense must establish that the plaintiff (1) had actual knowledge of the danger; (2) understood and appreciated the risks associated with such danger; and (3) voluntarily exposed himself to those risks." Findley v. Griffin, 292 Ga. App. 807, 809 (2) (666 SE2d 79) (2008) (citations omitted)."Knowledge of the risk is the watchword of assumption of risk, and means both actual and subjective knowledge on the plaintiff's part." Kroger Co. v. Williams, 257 Ga. App. 833, 835 (572 SE2d 316) (2002).

Here, John Doe was completely unaware that he was being placed inside a small, confined area with a commercial grade propane heater around other flammable objects. John Doe did not voluntarily subject himself to this dangerous environment and had no opportunity to remove himself from it. Instead, Charlie made the decision to remove John from the area where he was resting and place him inside what was nothing short of a torture chamber with knowledge of John's intoxicated state and left him unattended. It's also noteworthy that Charlie provided John with most of his alcohol consumed that night and knew John was intoxicated and kept serving him more. Certainly, the argument could be made that John assumed the risk of any known hazards outside of the garage by choosing to fall asleep outdoors, but John never voluntarily chose to enter the garage and sit in close proximity to an old beat up, commercial grade propane heater. In short, John had no knowledge of the risk that ultimately caused his injury and had no opportunity to choose another course of action.

In addition, Georgia appellate courts have recognized that contributory negligence and assumption of risk should not generally be the basis for granting summary judgment and should, instead, be submitted to a jury. Turner v. Sumter Self Storage Co., 215 Ga. App. 92, 94 (3) (449 SE2d 618) (1994). Therefore, by relying on these defenses, your company would be subjecting Charlie to the risk that a jury of 12 persons from the community would see things differently than your company and find Mr. Smith negligent. As you know, if the jury determines that Mr. Smith is either completely negligent or bares the majority of the responsibility for John's injuries, the value of this case will easily exceed Mr. Smith's policy limits, especially since the medical bills alone are in excess of one million dollars. We specifically request that you notify your insured of this risk if you chose not to accept our demand offered herein.

**Possible Assertion of Coverage Defenses From Georgia Insurance Company**

My office contacted ______________________ on or about May 1, 20120 and there had been no claim number created under this policy. That lead us to believe GFB might assert a coverage defense for the homeowner failing to disclose this event in writing. Asserting this defense would fail based on the current case law in Georgia.

Mr. Smith's policy with GIC specifically states the following:

> "In case of an occurrence, you or another insured will perform the following duties that apply. We have no duty to provide coverage under this policy if failure to comply with the following duties **is prejudicial to us**:
>
> a. Give written notice to us or our agent **as soon as practical** which sets forth…"

When possible, insurance policies are construed to provide coverage, so as to advance the benefits intended to be accomplished by such policies. Plantation Pipe Line Co. v. Stonewall Ins. *Co.*, 335 Ga.App. 302, 310, 780 S.E.2d 501 (2015). Where a notice provision is NOT expressly made a condition

4

precedent to coverage of the insurance contract, an insured's failure to comply with the notice provision will result in a forfeiture of coverage only if the insurer demonstrates that it was prejudiced by the insured's failure." Id. at 311(2),780 S.E.2d 501. This policy condition written above is at best a vague general provision. A general provision that no action will lie against the insurer unless the insured has fully complied with the terms of the policy admittedly can suffice to create a condition precedent. Lankford v. State Farm Mut. Auto. Ins. Co. , 307 Ga.App. 12, 14, 703 S.E.2d 436 (2010). In cases in which a policy's notice provision gives no specific time frame, there is no bright-line rule on how much delay is too much. Progressive Mountain Insurance Co. v. Bishop, 790 S.E.2d 91 (Ga. App. 2016). In many cases 11 months to 2 years is routinely held by a factfinder to be either not excessive as a matter of law or a question for the factfinder. The purpose of the notice provision in an insurance policy is to enable an insurer to investigate promptly the facts surrounding the occurrence while they are still fresh and the witnesses are still available, to prepare for a defense of the action, and, in a proper case, to determine the feasibility of settlement of the claim. Bituminous Cas. Corp. v. J. B. Forrest etc., Inc., 132 Ga.App. 714, 209 S.E.2d 6 (Ga. App. 1974).

The written notification of this occurrence was given 5 months after the fire at your insured's residence. Upon being retained on this case, we immediately contacted your insured to obtain homeowner's insurance details. he provided those to my office, and we immediately sent letters of representation to your claims department on May 1, 2019. Before this, Mr. Smith had no inclination that Mr. Doe would make a claim or if this type occurrence was something even covered under his policy. Nobody had ever advised him to call his insurance company, or consult legal counsel, and John Doe had not once intimated that he would make a claim on your insured's homeowner's policy. Under the language of your policy with your insured, Mr. Smith complied via my office sending notification of the occurrence "as soon as practical," or as soon as he realized a claim on his policy was occurring. Furthermore, Mr. Smith told me himself that he verbally in person notified his GFB agent only days after the accident. Although that doesn't comply with the written notice requirement, it surely shows there was knowledge of the incident by GFB and therefore dissolves a prejudice defense.

At best the vague condition set forth in this policy is a condition precedent to coverage BUT, where the law is unclear, the policy language specifically articulates that GIC must make a showing they were prejudiced by this delay. Showing prejudice in this case is absolutely unattainable. All police investigation pictures and videos my experts have used to render their analysis on this case have been available to GIC though open records and GIC could've obtained them just as easy as my firm did. Furthermore, in the attachments we have provided everything our experts used to investigate this matter, which they had no trouble doing. Since the incident, GIC has had access to their insured's property for the purposes of photographs, witness statements, etc. All witnesses are still alive and live locally in Big City, GA. Through our investigation of this incident, even 5 months after it occurred, we were able to establish the cause and origin of the fire, and the vicinity burned as well as how it burned – all pointing to the negligence of Mr. Smith.

## Injuries and Loss Related Medical Treatment

### Length of Treatment

| | | |
|---|---|---|
| First Treatment Date: | 12/10/2017 | 0 days from |
| Last Treatment Date: | Still Treating | 300+ and counting |

5

Settlement Proposal – Claim No.: 11-43434343

## Medical Providers

***John's Good Samaritan Ride to the Hospital***

According to my brief conversation with your insured, approximately 30 minutes after your insured left JOHN alone with the heater, your insured and one of his friends/tenants, Jane Walker walked up to the garage and saw black smoke billowing out. John Doe was in a different chair with most of his clothing removed, and his finger was twitching. Charlie and his friend realized John had been burned, so they put John in Jane's car and she drove him to Memorial Hospital.

***Big City Memorial Hospital (12/1/2019 – 12/11/2019)***

**[INSERT PICTURES AT HOSPITAL]**

Upon arriving in the Memorial ER just after midnight on 12/1/2017, John was given immediate emergency medical attention. The hospital staff and doctors assessed his burns, the burn patterns, and notified immediate family. After assessing the severity of the burns, the hospital staff quickly realized they did not have the means or the facilities to give John's burns the medical attention they deserved. They notified the Be Well Burn Center in Away City of the patient's condition and the 2 medical facilities arranged for a "life flight" from Big City to Away City in the coming hours.

***Life Flight from Big City to the Be Well Burn Center in Away City, GA (12/1/2019)***

At approximately 6:00 A.M. on 12/1/2019, John Doe was loaded onto the medical life flight helicopter in Bainbridge and flown over 233 miles to Augusta where he would spend the next month of his life enduring multiple surgeries and recovering from these tragic burns.

***Be Well Burn Center (12/1/2019 until 1/12/2020)***

[INSERT PICTURES AT BURN CENTER]

For the purposes of understanding and quantifying John Doe's pain and suffering while in the burn center, it is helpful to understand generally what occurs in skin grafting surgeries.

**Allograft, cadaver skin or homograft** is human cadaver skin donated for medical use. Cadaver skin is used as a temporary covering for excised (cleaned) wound surfaces before autograft (permanent) placement. Cadaver skin is put over the excised wound and stapled in place. After surgery, the cadaver skin may be covered with a dressing. This temporary covering is removed before permanent autografting. It appears from the records John Doe **had 5 of these cadaver skin surgeries**.

**The final autografting** is skin taken from the person burned, which is used to cover wounds permanently. Because the skin is a major organ in the body, **an autograft is essentially an organ transplant.** Autograft is surgically removed using a dermatome (a tool with a sharp razor blade). Only the top layer of skin is used for donor skin. The site the skin is taken from will heal on its own. There are two types of autografts used for permanent wound coverage:

6

Settlement Proposal – Claim No.: 11-43434343

1. **Sheet graft** is piece of donor skin harvested from an unburned area of the body. The size of the donor skin is about the same size as the burn wounds. The donor sheet is laid over the cleaned wound and stapled in place. The donor skin used in sheet grafts does not stretch; it takes a slightly larger size of donor skin to cover the same burn area because there is slight shrinkage after harvesting. When the body surface area of the burn is large, sheet grafts are saved for the face, neck and hands, making the most visible parts of the body appear less scarred. When a burn is small and there is plenty of donor skin available, a sheet graft can be used to cover the entire burned area. There was not much sheet grafting in John Doe's case because so much of his body was burned, they needed to cover a large area via "meshing."

2. **Meshed skin grafts** - very large areas of open wounds are difficult to cover because there might not be enough unburned donor skin available. It is necessary to enlarge donor skin to cover a larger body surface area. Meshing involves running the donor skin through a machine that makes small slits that allow expansion similar to fish netting. In a meshed skin graft, the skin from the donor site is stretched to allow it to cover an area larger than itself. Healing occurs as the spaces between the mesh fill in with new skin growth. The disadvantages of meshing are that it is less than a sheet graft and that the larger the mesh, the greater the permanent scarring. Meshing allows blood and body fluids to drain from under the skin grafts, preventing graft loss, and it allows the donor skin to cover a greater burned area because it is expanded. John Doe underwent this surgery on December 27, 2019.

Below is a detailed list directly from John Doe's records of his numerous surgeries and skin grafts he endured at the burn center: (*Out of courtesy, I will spare you the operation photos*)

1. **12/12/2017**: "Start date: 12/2/19 Start time: 1126. Pre-procedure diagnosis: total burn TBSA (20%) Post-procedure diagnosis: same, total burn TBSA (20% (18% TBSA FT)) Procedure(s) performed: surgical prep/excise cadaver; epiburn. Devitalized tissue was in initially removed in tangential fashion with a Norsen and then a Goulian knife down to a level of viable tissue. Level of excision included subcutaneous tissue in spotty areas. Overall the deepest area of excised was deep dermis. Once the excision was complete, larger bleeding points were cauterized using bovie cautery, and the wound was covered with epinephrine soaks and spray thrombin. Once satisfactory hemostasis was obtained, the wound was covered with cadaver, which was applied carefully, tailored as necessary, and secured with surgical staples. The cadaver skin was mesh 2:1. Once the skin substitute was placed, it was covered with conformant and exalt as well as sterile Kerlix dressing. Attention was then directed to the face. Blunt debridement was performed with a sterile lap pad. Further an adison and forceps was used to trim away loose epithelium. Epiburn was applied in proper orientation and hydrated with normal saline. It was tailored as necessary. Conformant and Kerlix gauze dressing was subsequently applied."
2. **12/13/2018:** John Doe underwent a quick local procedure to put a pic line in his upper right arm with a catheter in to his heart for administration of life saving medications.
3. **12/19/2013**: "Start date: 12/ 19/19 Start time: 1340. Pre-procedure diagnosis: burn 2nd degree, burn 3rd degree (20% with 18% full-thickness). Post-procedure diagnosis: same. Procedure(s) performed: Surgical prep and application of cadaver to the back 44 x 29, anterior torso 55 x 27, left arm 29 x 20, left forearm 13 x 9 right ankle 9 x 12, 3 x 4 Excision including subcu / Third-degree. Soaks. General anesthesia"

7

Settlement Proposal – Claim No.: 11-43434343

4. **12/24/2017:** "Start date: 12/24/17 Start time: 1505 Pre-procedure diagnosis: 20% TBSA (18% FT) Post-procedure diagnosis: same. Procedure(s) performed: Devitalized tissue was in itially removed in tangential fashion with a Norsen and then a Goulian knife down to a level of viable tissue. Level of excision included subcutaneous tissue. Once the excision was complete, larger bleeding points were cauterized using bovie cautery, and the wound was covered with epinephrine soaks and spray thrombin. Once satisfactory hemostasis was obtained, the wound was covered with cadaver, which was applied carefully, tailored as necessary, and secured with surgical staples. Once the skin substitute was placed, it was covered with bridal veil as well as sterile Kerlix dressing. "
5. **12/27/2017**: Start date: 12/27/17 Start time: 0927 Pre-procedure diagnosis: burn 2nd degree, burn 3rd degree (20% with 17% ft ). Post-procedure diagnosis: same. Procedure(s) performed / notes: Autografting: ..."The devitalized tissue was excised in tangential fashion using a Goulian knife including subcutaneous tissue. Here is a recent picture of the skin grafting harvest site:

   [INSERT POST SKIN GRAFT PHOTO]

   Then, it was covered with epinephrine soaked laparotomy pad. The larger bleeding points were cauterized using both the cautery. Then we brought to our attention to the area from where the split-thickness skin graft was harvested using a Zimmer dermatome at a depth of 10 thousandths of an inch from the bilateral thighs. This graft was then meshed and applied carefully, tailored as necessary and secured using medical glue and or surgical staples."

6. **12/30/2017**: "Start date: 12/30/17 Start time: 1033 Pre-procedure diagnosis: total burn TBSA (20%). Post-procedure diagnosis: same. Procedure(s) performed: dressing change and staple removal. General anesthesia. Attention was directed to the torso left upper extremity right lower extremity and bilateral thighs .. A sterile soaked gauze and Norsen was used to remove non-viable tissue. After adequate debridement, the surface was irrigated with saline. Staples were removed. Dressings of cuticerin and silver nitrate soaks were applied, as well as sterile Kirlex. The thighs were placed in Silvadene cream. And the left 5th digit was placed in conformant and exalt. The patient tolerated the procedure well and was taken to the post-anesthesia care unit for post-operative recovery in stable condition."

**Follow up Medical Care**

On January 11, 2020, John Doe was released from the burn center and taken home by a family member from Away City to Big City, GA. Since his release from the burn center, John Doe immediately has significant blood sugar issues related to his diabetes and took multiple emergency trips to Memorial to control his type 1 diabetes. These issues were no doubt exacerbated by his traumatic burns. Although for the purposes of this demand we are not submitting his bills for Memorial after his release from the Burn Center because the treatment was focused primarily on his diabetes, and not John's burns – it bears noting here as it relates to complications and further pain and suffering from our client.

***Georgia Medical Center – Georgia City, GA – 2/7/2020 – Present***

John has been seen numerous times at Georgia Medical Center for the purposes of follow up care and

8

physical therapy to make sure his skin is stretched out properly to promote healing and maximum mobility as his skin heals. He will likely be treating here every month or so for the foreseeable future. Based on the records we have John treated there on 1/24/2018, 2/7/2018, and 2/28/2018. He has been seen there since but we do not have those records.

[RECOVERY PHOTOS]

**SPECIAL DAMAGES**

MEDICAL EXPENSES:

| | | |
|---|---|---|
| 1. | Medical Consultants | $2,659.71 |
| 2. | Memorial Hospital | $6,917.80 |
| 3. | City Emergency Physicians – ER doctors | $701.00 |
| 4. | MED Trans – Emergency Life Flight | $51,033.66 |
| 5. | Be Well Burn Center | $1,035,488.45 |
| 6. | Lab Path Services | $192.00 |
| 7. | Georgia Medical Center – Big City, GA | $4,641.78 |
| 8. | | |

**TOTAL MEDICAL EXPENSES** (not including diabetes treatment) **$1,102,528.31**

**Other Recent Settlements and Verdicts**

These settlements and verdicts below are taken from our Case-Metrix database as well as attorneys that we are very familiar with and mutually depend on each other for ideas, guidance, and possible case association given their knowledge of 3rd party insurance bad faith law. All of these cases are similar to Mr. Doe's case because they represent life threatening injuries and burns, surgical procedures, with massive amounts of medical expenses from their respective catastrophic burns/incidents.

| Attorney / Firm | Date | Re$olution | Medical$ | Policy Limits | Carrier | Settled or Filed |
|---|---|---|---|---|---|---|
| Pete Law | 1/15/15 | $72,960,000 | $226,396 | Not Released | Not Released | Jury Verdict |
| Tim Hall | 2/5/2007 | $5,000,000 | $500,000 | $5,000,000 | Not Released | Filed/Settled |
| Andrew Lynch* | 12/20/2016 | $4,000,000 | ? | ? | Self Insured | Jury Verdict |
| Shiver / Hamilton | 9/3/2015 | $29,250,000 | $0/fatality | $21,000,000 | American/Companion | Jury Verdict |

* This case tried by Andrew Lynch was not a burn case, but is relevant because it involves a highly intoxicated man who fell over a defective balcony railing at his apartment.

**Impact on Daily Life**

Because of these catastrophic burns John has suffered, he is a shadow of the man he once was. He wakes up many mornings in a panic because of the nightmares of being on fire. He is in chronic pain because of the way his scars have healed and lack mobility. He is prone to heat exhaustion because his skin does not sweat and cool his body the way it should. His physical activities with his kids and lack of mobility have strained his ability to be a good father. His labor demands of being a contractor and handy man are torturous with his injuries and pain with mobility.

[INSERT CURRENT PHOTOS OF DEFORMITIES]

**Demand**

It is without hesitation that we make this unliquidated damages demand pursuant to O.C.GA. § 51-12-14 in the amount of $1,000,000.00. This offer to settle will remain open for 32 days of your certified receipt of this demand and, thereafter, will no longer be available for your acceptance. This amount represents the full amount of YOUR INSUREDS' liability and umbrella policy limits. This demand is made pursuant to Southern General v. Holt, 262 Ga. 267, 416 S.E.2d 274 (1992). Failure to settle this claim for policy limits after this notice of our willingness to accept this amount (which is within your insurance limits) may result in your company being liable for the full amount of any judgment obtained, even if it is in excess of the limits of the policy. *See* GEICO v. Gingold, 249 Ga. 156 (1982); Shaw v. Caldwell, 229 Ga. 87 (1972); Smoot v. State Farm Mutual Auto Insurance Co., 299 F. 2d 525 (5th Cir. 1962.) I hope we will be able to come to terms quickly and resolve the case. Please forward a copy of this demand to YOUR INSURED and encourage them to obtain private, independent counsel to represent their interests in this case.

As we set out in great detail above, our client's current special damages are at least **$1,102,528.31**, and still increasing daily. Your company provided us with a statement under oath pursuant to O.C.G.A. § 33-3-28 indicating you maintained $1,000,000.00 of liability coverage for YOUR INSUREDS. Not tendering policy limits as requested in this Holt demand would be the action of an unreasonable, imprudent and bad faith insurer because:

1. There is a strong likelihood, given the liability facts of this claim, that a verdict will be returned against your insured.
2. There is an equally strong likelihood the verdict will be for a sum greater than its insurance coverage such that your client's personal assets and finances are exposed;
3. It is apparent that our client's medical treatment was not unreasonable or unnecessary, or that costs were not fair and reasonable;

We will not accept a tender of your companies limits once this demand expires. We specifically request that you notify your insured of this attempt to resolve this case within his policy limits and advise him of his right to independent counsel. Please notify your insured that if your company does not accept this offer to settle within his policy limits we will seek a judgment against him personally in this case. Please suggest to your insured that he set aside a *minimum* of $30 million dollars of his own personal funds to pay any future judgment in this case.

Please note that this Holt demand is being made subject to the following terms in accordance and satisfaction with O.C.G.A § 9-11-67.1 . and although that statute applies only to motor vehicle cases, the appellate courts in Georgia are recently applying these same guidelines to homeowners and non-motor vehicle cases:

1. As previously stated this offer to settle must be accepted by your company in writing within 32 days of

Settlement Proposal – Claim No.: 11-43434343

your receipt of this demand. Note that this demand will be withdrawn automatically if not accepted in writing within this specified timeframe;

2. Upon our receipt of your written acceptance of this offer within the specified timeframe, our firm and John Doe will execute a limited release of YOUR INSURED's, Carol and Charlie. This limited release will apply to any and all claims of any kind arising from the fire incident of December 1, 2019, including but not limited to present, past and future medical expenses, lost wages, lost earning capacity, present, past and future pain and suffering and punitive damages;

3. If you should need additional information to evaluate this claim, please contact us immediately. In addition to the phone numbers listed above, you may reach key members of this law firm on their personal cell phones 24/7 to assist you with anything you need regarding this case as follows:

   (a) Lawyer Jim – Partner – 770-265-0000
   (b) Paul the Case Manager – Paralegal – 404-618-0000
   Please understand that Mr. Doe's pain, suffering, and future medical expenses only increase with time. As such, we urge you to avoid unnecessary delay;

4. Should you choose to send a settlement draft instead of accepting this offer in writing please issue the draft directly to this firm and John Doe. You should physically deliver he draft to 1111 Peachtree Street NW, Suite 111, Atlanta, Georgia 30303. Our firm's federal taxpayer ID is ____________. Should you chose to accept this offer in writing, payment must be physically received by this office no later than 10 days after your acceptance, as contemplated by O.C.G.A. § 9-11-67.1(g).

We look forward to hearing from you soon.

Sincerely,
Attorney at Law

Enclosures: See Attached CD

Cc. *[NOTE: I like to list a bunch of heavy hitter trial lawyer names in this Cc section. Names of lawyers that have rocked insurance companies for big bad faith verdicts. Why not? In a big enough case, there will be defense lawyers involved that will know you might refer this to a well-known attorney]*

11

# Slip and Fall Demand

***[Slip and Fall Demand on a Commercial Big Box Defendant]***

August 1, 2018

**VIA CERTIFIED MAIL RETURN RECEIPT REQUESTED**
First Insurance CorporationAddress…

| | |
|---|---|
| RE: Claim Number: | 0201802180218 |
| Date of Loss: | January 1, 2018 |
| Your Insured: | Holdings, Inc. |
| Our Client: | Alexander Alex |

Dear First Insurance Corp.,

Please review the following settlement demand package for our client, Mr. Alexander Alex:

1. Barbour Orthopaedics bills and records
2. American Imaging bills and records;
3. Dr. Rich bills and records.

As you are aware, we represent the above-referenced client, Mr. Alexander Alex who sustained a slip and fall injury at Cinema 17 (123 Cinema Pkwy. Big City, GA 30315) on or about January 1, 2018. We have evaluated the above referenced matter and are prepared to enter into a good faith effort to resolve the above-referenced claim on Mr. Alex's behalf with Holdings, Inc. and its insurer for the amount of **$50,000.00** in exchange for a general release.

This letter summarizes Cinema's liability, the extensive damages our client has suffered and continues to suffer as a result, and the financial exposure your client will face should First Insurance Corp. fail to resolve this claim on Cinema's behalf. Please be advised that this letter is sent for the purposes of negotiating settlement, and thus any statements contained herein or attached exhibits are inadmissible at any trial of this case per O.C.G.A. § 24-4-408.

**Facts and Liability**

On January 22, 2018, Mr. Alex was a customer lawfully on the premises of Cinema, owned by your insured, Holdings, Inc. At the time of the slip and fall incident at hand (approximately 9 or 10 pm that day), the move theater was open for business and Mr. Alex was there to watch a movie. Mr. Alex decided to go to the restroom during this time and as he approached the men's restroom near theater 22, he slipped and fell on a slippery substance located on the tile floor immediately outside of the men's restroom door. During the slip, Mr. Alex's right ankle contorted and his lower back suffered the brunt of his impact with the hard floor. There were no signs in the area to indicate that the floor was wet prior to the incident at hand. Furthermore, a plumbing issue appeared to be happening at the time of Mr. Alex's slip and fall. Shortly after the incident our client noticed that water was leaking from the inside of the bathroom to the outside section where he was located. It is unclear whether Cinema knew about the plumbing issue prior to the incident at hand; however, in any case, it still does not excuse Cinema from in its duty to exercise ordinary care in keeping the premises and approaches safe in accordance with O.C.G.A. § 51-3-1. If anything, proving that Cinema knew about the plumbing issue (and potential repercussions) and yet did nothing to keep their premises safe would aggravate the severity of the tort at hand as well.

Additionally, immediately following the slip and fall, an usher named "Ivan" rushed to help Mr. Alex back to his feet. It is unknown if camera footage recording the incident exists or if a report was filed on Cinema's behalf; however, a letter demanding the preservation of evidence was sent to Cinema shortly after the incident on February 1, 2018.

With all this said, because there were no wet floor signs present at the time of Mr. Alex's slip and fall, it is more likely than not that Cinema was in violation of O.C.G.A. §51-3-1. Georgia law requires that, "[w]here an owner or occupier, by express or implied invitation, induces or leads others to come upon his premises for any lawful purpose, he is liable in damages to such persons for injuries caused by his failure to exercise ordinary care in keeping the premises and approaches safe." O.C.G.A. § 51-3-1.

In addition to O.C.G.A. §51-3-1, the Georgia Supreme Court has also held that by encouraging others to enter the premises to further the owner/occupier's purpose, the owner/occupier makes an implied representation that reasonable care has been exercised to make the place safe for those who come for that purpose, and that representation is ·the basis of the liability of the owner/occupier for an invitee's injuries sustained in a "slip-and-fall." Prosser, Law of Torts (4th ed.), § 61, p. 422; Begin v. Ga. Championship Wrestling, supra, 172 Ga.App. at 294, 322 S.E.2d 737.

An invitee who responds to the owner/occupier's invitation and enters the premises does so pursuant to an implied representation or assurance that the premises have been made ready and safe for the invitee's reception, and the entering invitee is entitled to expect that the owner/occupier has exercised and will continue to exercise reasonable care to make the premises safe. Id. It is in this light that an invitee's exercise of ordinary care for personal safety must be examined.

The owner's duty includes inspecting the premises to discover possible dangerous conditions, and taking reasonable precautions to protect invitees from dangers foreseeable from the arrangement and use of the premises. *Robinson v. Kroger*, 268 Ga. 735, 741 (1997).

All of the previously mentioned facts confirm that your insured (1) failed to inspect, (2) failed to discover, and (3) failed to warn of the dangerous hazard (i.e. wet floor). Additionally, your insured had employees that were on-duty at the premises that day and failed to notice or remove the water puddle from the entrance of the store as well.

**At no point does it appear that any employee inspected the area to attempt to discover or remedy the hazard.** This is significant because the plaintiff has met his burden of establishing actionable negligence on the part of the premises owner. See Mazur v. Food Giant, Inc., 183 Ha.App. 453, 454 (1987); see also Jones v. Krystal Co., 231 Ga.App. 102, 105 (1998). Moreover, an owner's constructive knowledge of a hazard may be inferred where there is evidence that an employee **was in the vicinity of the hazard and could have discovered and removed it by even a simple casual observation**. See Sharpton v. Great Atlantic & Pacific Tea Co., Inc., 112 Ga.App. 283 (1965). In this case, more than one employee was in the area that could have done something about the wet spot on the floor.

It is clear that your insured failed to exercise ordinary care in keeping its premises safe and allowed a dangerous hazard to exist on the floor for an extended period. Additionally, your insured apparently did nothing to discover hazards of this type either; therefore, it let its customers "enter at their own risk."

**Injuries and Loss-Related Medical Treatment**

In the hours following the slip and fall incident, Mr. Alex began to develop severe swelling and pain in his right ankle and lower back. Mr. Alex attempted to ice the affected areas and take over the counter pain relief medication to see if his pain would subside; however, the pain worsened as time passed. Mr. Alex eventually decided to visit Urgent Care in order to further evaluate /treat his ongoing pain despite the medical expenses that he would incur. Records/bills for this provider are currently pending; however, we have been made aware that Mr. Alex received an bandage for his ankle here and was given pain medication as well for his injuries.

**Barbour Orthopaedics – January 20, 2018**

On January 20, 2018 (__ days after the incident), Mr. Alex visited Dr. Sam Barbour in order to further evaluate his pain and to assess whether he would need more invasive treatment. At Barbour Orthopaedics, Dr. Barbour performed a physical exam and took x-rays to further assess Mr. Alex's injuries. After performing said exams, Dr. Barbour ultimately diagnosed Mr. Alex with the following:

**M54.5** - Lumbago
**S93.491A** - Sprain of other ligament of right ankle, initial encounter

Dr. Barbour prescribed Mr. Alex pain relief medication in order to help manage his pain, ordered an MRI to be done for further evaluation of his injuries. and ordered a brace for Mr. Alex to wear on his right ankle to help support him in the interim.

**Health Imaging – February 1, 2018**

On February 1, 2018, Mr. Alex visited Health Imaging to undergo MRIs of his right ankle and lower back at the recommendation of Dr. Barbour.

The right ankle MRI revealed the following:

***[Cut and Paste images from Radiology MRI Readings that have Objective Findings]***

**Barbour Orthopaedics – February 11, 2018**

On February 11, 2018, Mr. Alex followed up with Dr. Barbour to review the MRI findings and further assess/treat his injuries. After reviewing the MRI findings and conducting a follow up physical exam, Dr. Barbour discussed various treatment options including but not limited to epidural injections in his lumbar spine and a cortisone injection in his right ankle to help him manage his pain. Additionally, physical therapy was recommended for the next four weeks as well.

**Dr. Rich – March 1, 2018**

In the weeks following the February 11, 2018 visit to Dr. Barbour, Mr. Alex went back to Tanzania and did as much home-care as he possibly could while he could find a doctor to begin conservative treatment with. Mr. Alex's at home care at this time included rest, ice, stretching, and over the counter medication in order to manage his pain. On March 11, 2018, Mr. Alex was finally able to follow up for treatment with Dr. Rich regarding his injuries. At Dr. Rich's office, Mr. Alex was given an initial evaluation and was diagnosed with the following:

**M51.26 – Other intervertebral disc displacement, lumbar region**
**S33.5XXA – Sprain of ligaments of lumbar spine, initial encounter**
**S93.401A – Sprain of unspecified ligament of right ankle, initial encounter**

Dr. Rich recommended that Mr. Alex undergo various treatments including hot/cold therapy, massage therapy, chiropractic adjustments and extremity adjustments in order to help alleviate his pain. Mr .Alex treated with Dr. Rich for 10 visits between the dates of March 1, 2018 to April 1, 2018.

**Present date treatment**

Since April 3, 2018, Mr. Alex has not been able to find a place to treat because he has relocated from Tanzania to Big City for work. He still complains of lower back and ankle pain; however, is willing to attempt to settle his case now in good faith before he continues to explore much costlier treatment options that are usually associated with a herniated disc (including but not limited to physical therapy, epidural injections, surgery, etc.). As you are probably aware, a herniated disc is not a soft tissue injury that heals over time in most cases and our client will most likely need more invasive procedures done in order to help him heal from his injuries.

**Damages**

To date, Mr. Alex's special damages include but are not limited to the following:

| | |
|---|---|
| 1. Urgent Care | $222.00 |
| 2. Barbour Orthopaedics | $2,642.82 |
| 3. Health Imaging | $4,595.00 |
| 4. Dr. Rich (D.C.) | $2,081.00 |
| **Total:** | **$ 9,318.82*** |

*Please note that his amount is subject to increase as more records become available. This includes amounts from prescription records, medical mileage reimbursements, and additional doctor's visits.

**Demand**

As we set out in great detail above, **our client's current damages are $9,318.82.** In addition to medical expenses, our client is entitled to pain and suffering. Pain and suffering are general damages given to compensate an injured party for all non-pecuniary loss, inconvenience, hardship, pain, discomfort, anxiety, etc. whether mental, physical, or both, experienced as a consequence of a personal injury. The injury does not need to be permanent; temporary injury will permit recovery for physical pain and suffering.

Therefore, **we hereby demand you tender you tender $50,000.00 to settle our clients bodily injury claim in exchange for a general release.** This Demand is being sent pursuant to O.C.G.A. § 9-11-8. If we do not receive your acceptance in writing of your tender of policy limits within 32 days from your receipt of this letter, our offer to settle will automatically withdraw and we will proceed with filing suit.

**Terms**

Finally, experience has taught us that a successful settlement discussion can easily unravel unless we identify some general matters which must be included with the settlement of this claim. Therefore, please consider the offer to compromise this claim *subject to the following terms*:

- The settlement draft will be issued directly to this firm and only in the names of **"Alexander Alex"** and **"Law Firm LLC."** You should deliver the check to 1776 Peachtree St., Suite 333, Atlanta, GA 30303. Our firm's federal taxpayer ID is __________________. Payment must be physically received by this office no later than 10 days after your acceptance, as contemplated by O.C.G.A. § 9-11-8.
- No reductions or withholdings from any settlement amount and no indemnities and hold harmless clauses shall be implied or made unless expressly communicated, in writing, prior to acceptance of a parole settlement offer. Any settlement document will be signed only by our client and shall contain no representations, warranties, seals, or sworn statements.

- We will agree to release Holdings Inc. in consideration of your full tender of the $50,000.00 demand. The release will be in the form a general release pursuant to O.C.G.A. § 33-24-41.1 for all personal injury claims arising out of the subject incident and will only be signed by Mr. Alex.
- Settlement is conditioned upon the agreement that it represents a compromised claim. Therefore, our client is not fully compensated by the very definition of "compromise" and thus will not have been made whole or received full and fair compensation under O.C.G.A. § 33-24-56.1. We will presume our client has not been made whole unless expressly stated in writing and in advance of any parole agreement subsequent to this writing.

We will assume these general terms are accepted and are included as part of any offer either of us may propose even though not expressly restated.

Best regards,
Attorney at Law

Enclosures: a, b, c, d...

cc: Mr. _________________

**APPENDIX D**

# LIENS

# Lien Reduction Request for Orthopedic or Chiropractic Clinic

***[Lien Reduction Request for Chiropractic Clinic or Orthopedic Clinic That Treats on a Lien]***

March 1, 2021

**VIA EMAIL and FAX**
Orthopedics and Sports Medicine, Inc.
1111 Rock Rd. Suite 111
Big City, GA 33333

**Re: Patient: Colleen Smith (DOB 1/1/2000)**

Dear Orthopedics and Sports Medicine, Inc.

As you are aware, our firm represents Ms. Colleen Smith concerning personal injuries sustained in an auto accident on 1/1/19. Based on the circumstances of her case, we need to negotiate a reduction with you concerning her account. The highest offer to date on her case is $55,000.00. The current amount of her medical bills is as follows:

| | |
|---|---|
| **EMR Ambulance** | **$1,689.00** |
| **Bewell Medical Center** | **$37,366.30** |
| ***... Many More Providers*** | **$XX,XXX.00** |
| **ACME Billing Solutions (medication)** | **$18.42** |
| **TOTAL:** | **$82,014.47*** |

*Please note this amount is subject to increase as more records become available – including but not limited to medical mileage records, additional doctor visit records, prescription records, etc.

Allstate has been reluctant to offer anything near the total policy limits of $100,000.00. We do not anticipate settling for much more without pursing litigation at this point. Further, Ms. Smith has expressly indicated to us that she does not want to litigate her case. Since we cannot file suit without Ms. Smith's consent, **we respectfully propose to settle Ms. Smith's account in the amount of $7,030.25 (50% off of your $14,060.50 balance to date)**. Also, even if we filed a lawsuit, your clinic might not see any payment on this account for at least two years if any recovery at all is made. Lastly, if a verdict in excess of policy limits is obtained, the resulting bad faith suit would also prolong the resolution of this matter. If we do litigate I would recommend you contact a local medical funding company and request they buy out your lien. Please call me and we can discuss this. We also want you to know we are also reducing our fee by ______ in order to make the numbers work for the client. We will provide a signed settlement statement when the case closes if the client consents.

If our offer is acceptable, please respond in writing and we will send payment out within 30 days of settlement with AllSnake. Thank you for your time and assistance and please do not hesitate to call us at 404-618-0000 to further discuss.

Sincerely,

Attorney at Law

# Lien Reduction Request to a Hospital

***[Lien Dispute/Reduction Request to a Hospital - Payoff Balance Reduction Request]***

April 1, 2021

**VIA US MAIL**
Wellstar Health System
PO Box 747474
Atlanta, GA 30774-7474

**Re:** **Settlement Offer/Cease and Desist Notice**
**Patient:** Sarah Smith
**Account No's:** 30000000000 and 30000000001
**Dates of service:** 1/11/20 and 2/8/20

Dear Wellstar Hospital:

As you are aware from our letter dated August 1, 2020, ____________ Law, LLC represents Ms. Smith concerning personal injuries sustained in an auto accident that occurred on January 11, 2020. Also, please note that you already have a HIPAA authorization form on file to allow us to discuss Ms. Smith's above-referenced accounts with you.

On April 1, 2021, Ms. Smith notified our office that Wellstar Health Systems mailed her a bill claiming a balance due of $140.000.01. Please cease and desist from contacting Ms. Smith.

Moreover, Wellstar has no reimbursement right to any funds from Ms. Smith's auto accident settlement. As of today, there is no record that Wellstar filed a "hospital lien" pursuant to O.C.G.A. § 44-14-470 within 75 days after discharge. Since Wellstar did not file a lien in time. Wellstar is precluded from asserting a lien on any proceeds collected on Ms. Smith's auto insurance settlement per O.C.G.A. § 44-14-471.

Lastly, Ms. Smith has no assets so sending her account to collections will not expedite any payments to you.

Given the foregoing reasons, **Ms. Smith is willing to offer $6,500.00 in good faith to resolve any and all accounts with Wellstar Health Systems in full.** If this offer is acceptable, please respond in writing and our office will issue payment within the next 30 days. If you have any questions or would like to further discuss, please do not hesitate to contact me at 770-265-0000 or email at james@lawyerjames.com. Thank you in advance for your time and assistance.

Sincerely,

Attorney at Law

# Letter to Health Insurance Requesting Paid Amounts for Subrogation

***[Letter to Health Insurance Subrogation Department Telling them to Send Balance and ERISA Designation Forms if they are an ERISA Helath Plan]***

(insert date here)

**VIA CERTIFIED MAIL**
**AND FACSIMILE**
Health Insurance Subrogation Department
(address…)

Re: **Notice of Representation and**
**Letter of Protection Concerning Subrogation Interests**
Our client/your insured: John Doe (DOB xxx)
Health Insurance Member ID No.123456
Date of Loss:

Dear Health Ins. Co. Name:

Please be advised that LAW FIRM, LLC represents ____________regarding injuries sustained as a result of an automobile accident on or about _____________in___________, GA. It is my belief that your health care insurance program/plan paid or intends to pay benefits for this incident and that you may have a subrogation lien. I am enclosing an executed HIPAA release form signed by ___________ and a copy of the accident report regarding this matter for further reference.

(CLIENT NAME) wishes to move swiftly in resolving this case. As such, please provide my office with a complete and thorough list of all medical expenses paid under the above-referenced plan and a firm total of what you are claiming in subrogation. **Also, please provide my office with a copy of the health insurance contract that you have in place with my client, the Summary Plan Description, and your Form 5500 as well**. All requested items should be mailed to our office address listed above. You can reach our office at ________________or via fax at_____________ if you have any questions or would like to further discuss. Thank you for your time and assistance in advance.

Sincerely,

Attorney Name
Attorney at Law

# Lien Dispute Letter Template - We Deny ERISA but Inquire Further

***[Health Insurance Lien Dispute Letter to Possibly ERISA Exempt Health Insurance Carrier – With Further Inquiry]***

November 1, 20____

**VIA CERTIFIED MAIL**
Anthem Inc.
PO Box 99999
San Antonio, TX 77777

RE: Your Insured/Our Client.: John Doe
Your Client: State Health Benefit Plan of Georgia
Your Member: Jane Doe
Date of Birth: 1/1/1975
Case No: 88888888
Date of incident: 1/1/2019

Dear Anthem Inc. (C/O Blue Cross Blue Shield):

We understand your company has made payments for medical or health-related services arising from the incident at issue, and is asserting a right to reimbursement. This letter serves as written notice that in the present case, **we do not believe there is any legal right to reimbursement** with the policy John Doe was insured under. Under Federal and Georgia State law and public policy, there are 2 scenarios where a health insurer has a right to reimbursement for benefits paid:

1. The member is covered under a **private** self-funded Employment Retirement Income Security Act of 1974 plan (ERISA).

2. Where the person compensated has been made whole or completely compensated for their injuries. Under O.C.G.A. § 33-24-56.1. you are entitled to reimbursement in this case only if "[t]he amount of the recovery exceeds the sum of all economic and noneconomic losses incurred as a result of the injury." (See also *Thurman v. State Farm*, 278 Ga. 162, 598 S.E.2d 448 (2004), which states "an insurer is prohibited from obtaining reimbursement for amounts paid under medical payments coverage unless and until the insured has been completely compensated for her loss").

In addressing the first coverage issue, based on our initial analysis we do not believe John Doe's health insurance plan is a self-funded plan for the purposes of ERISA rights of reimbursement. If you have any reason to believe we are incorrect and this is a protected self-funded plan then please provide my office with a copy of the health insurance contract that you have in place with my client, the Summary Plan Description, and your Form 5500 as well. All requested items should be mailed to our office address listed above.

However, since we don't believe there is a right of reimbursement, the only analysis left to consider is the second issue of whether Mr. Doe has been "made whole" based on settlement proceeds.

As stated above, Under O.C.G.A. § 33-24-56.1, you are entitled to reimbursement in this case only if "[t]he amount of the recovery exceeds the sum of all economic and noneconomic losses incurred as a result of the injury. This rule, which is the public policy in Georgia, is commonly referred to as the "complete compensation" or "made whole" doctrine, and it means that a health insurer is not entitled to reimbursement unless the injured party is completely compensated for his/her injuries. This case against the tortfeasor was settled against the tortfeasor for his homeowner's policy limits.

No amount of money could EVER completely compensate or make John Doe "whole." He has __________________ injuries to the point where much of his life will never be the same. These injuries are permanent, debilitating, and severe. No amount of money in the world could ever fully compensate Mr. Doe for his non-economic damages (pain and suffering, loss of enjoyment of life, etc.).

This aforementioned rule, which is the public policy in Georgia, is commonly referred to as the "complete compensation" or "made whole" doctrine - it trumps any specific policy language in the health insurance policy that covered him and his wife that claims any right of reimbursement or subrogation.

For the foregoing reasons, we will distribute settlement funds on _________________, and have no intention of holding funds in trust for reimbursement to Blue Cross Blue Shield/Anthem.

If you have any questions or dispute this, please do not hesitate to call. You can reach our office at 404-618-0000 or via fax at 888-815-0000. My cell is 770-265-0000.

Sincerely,

.

Attorney at Law

# Lien Dispute Letter Template - We are Erisa exempt

***[Lien Dispute Letter to Health Insurance Who is ERISA Exempt Carrier… This letter will save our clients a lot of money]***

November 1, 20____

**VIA CERTIFIED MAIL**
Anthem Inc.
PO Box 99999
San Antonio, TX 77777

RE: Your Insured/Our Client.: John Doe
Your Client: State Health Benefit Plan of Georgia
Your Member: Jane Doe
Date of Birth: 1/1/1975
Case No: 88888888
Date of incident: 1/1/2019

Dear Anthem Inc. (C/O Blue Cross Blue Shield):

We understand your company has made payments for medical or health-related services arising from the incident at issue, and is asserting a right to reimbursement. This letter serves as written notice that in the present case, **there is no legal right to reimbursement** with the policy John Doe was insured under. Under Federal and Georgia State law and public policy, there are 2 scenarios where a health insurer has a right to reimbursement for benefits paid:

1. The member is covered under a **private** self-funded Employment Retirement Income Security Act of 1974 plan (ERISA).

2. Where the person compensated has been made whole or completely compensated for their injuries. Under O.C.G.A. § 33-24-56.1, you are entitled to reimbursement in this case only if "[t]he amount of the recovery exceeds the sum of all economic and noneconomic losses incurred as a result of the injury." (See also *Thurman v. State Farm*, 278 Ga. 162, 598 S.E.2d 448 (2004), which states "an insurer is prohibited from obtaining reimbursement for amounts paid under medical payments coverage unless and until the insured has been completely compensated for her loss").

In addressing the first coverage issue, Title I of ERISA specifically removes from its coverage any employee benefit plan that qualifies as a government plan. 29 U.S.C. § 1003(b). Under ERISA, a government plan means any plan established or maintained by the federal government, a state government or political subdivision, or by any agency or instrumentality of any of the foregoing. 29 U.S.C. § 1002(32). In this present case, Mr. Doe was covered under his wife's Blue Cross Blue Shield plan that she maintained through her employer, the Fulton County School System – a public government/county/state run organization. Because this health insurance policy is a "government self-funded plan," it is specifically exempt from ERISA's rights to reimbursement. Therefore, the only analysis left to consider is the second issue of whether Mr. Doe has been "made whole" based on settlement proceeds.

As stated above, Under O.C.G.A. § 33-24-56.1, you are entitled to reimbursement in this case only if "[t]he amount of the recovery exceeds the sum of all economic and noneconomic losses incurred as a result of the injury. This rule, which is the public policy in Georgia, is commonly referred to as the "complete compensation" or "made whole" doctrine, and it means that a health insurer is not entitled to reimbursement unless the injured party is completely compensated for his/her injuries. This case against the tortfeasor was settled against the tortfeasor for his homeowner's policy limits.

No amount of money could EVER completely compensate or make John Doe "whole." He has 3rd degree burns scars over 20% of his body to the point where much of his skin more resembles fish scales than that of a person. Because his body cannot perspire the way it should with the skin damage, he cannot maintain a living as a residential and commercial contractor in the summer as he is highly prone to heat related illnesses. These injuries are permanent, debilitating, and severe. His mobility is even severely limited because of the way the scars healed. No amount of money in the world could ever fully compensate Mr. Doe for his non-economic damages (pain and suffering, loss of enjoyment of life, etc.).

This aforementioned rule, which is the public policy in Georgia, is commonly referred to as the "complete compensation" or "made whole" doctrine - it trumps any specific policy language in the health insurance policy that covered him and his wife that claims any right of reimbursement or subrogation.

For the foregoing reasons, we will distribute settlement funds on ________________, and have no intention of holding funds in trust for reimbursement to Blue Cross Blue Shield/Anthem.

If you have any questions or dispute this, please do not hesitate to call. You can reach our office at 404-618-0000 or via fax at 888-815-0000. My cell is 770-265-0000.

Sincerely,

________________, Esq.
Attorney at Law

# Lien Reduction Request for ERISA Protected Health Insurance Lien

***[ERISA Protected Health Insurance Lien Reduction Request – even though I allege in the letter they are not ERISA protected]***

April ___, 2021

**VIA EMAIL**
International Subrogation Management
22222 W. Land Street
Suite 222
Springfield, Ill 60501

Re: **Reduction Request Concerning ERISA Subrogation Lien**
Our Client/Your Participant: Colleen Smith
Group: Georgia OPCO Holdings
Date of Injury: 6/1/2020
Recovery Incident: 55555

Dear Mr. Benefit:

I just wanted to provide you with an update on Ms. Smith's case. To date, Ms. Smith is set to undergo two more surgeries on her ankle and back, respectively. Further, the claim against the liability carrier has settled for maximum policy limits of $25,000.00. The primary UM carrier has also tendered $250,000.00 maximum UIM policy limits as well.

Given that this case involves catastrophic injuries and multiple reconstructive surgeries and therapy, we need to negotiate a reduction with you concerning Benefit Systems' subrogation lien. On January 20, 2021, you sent us a final lien in response to our request noting that Allied's subrogation interest is $29,053.54. **We propose to settle Allied's subrogation lien in the amount of $5,810.70 (80% off).**

The main reason why we are proposing an 80% reduction is based on Allied's Form 5500, effective on the date of Ms. Smith's crash. Per the form, Allied is a "single-employer [welfare] plan" that is both funded by insurance and the general assets of the sponsor. This means that under ERISA, 29 U.S.C. § 1003(a), Allied's plan is not a fully "self-funded" plan and thus the Georgia "made whole doctrine" – O.C.G.A. § 33-24-56.1 -applies. Per the made whole doctrine, an insurer can only recover money for benefits paid if "the amount of recovery exceeds the sum of all economic and noneconomic losses incurred as a result of the injury". Thus, even if we recover a maximum global recovery of $500,000.00, Ms. Smith's economic and non-economic losses would still exceed that amount and Allied's subrogation interest would be curtailed, if not barred completely under Georgia law. For example, Ms. Smith's medical bills and lost wages to date alone (without the forthcoming surgeries) account for over $200,000.00:

| | |
|---|---|
| **Cobb County EMS** | **$1,168.00** |
| **Wellstar Kennestone Hospital** | **$165,790.03** |
| **ER Physician** | **$3,820.00** |
| **ER Radiology** | **$2,344.00** |
| **Anesthesiology** | **$1,628.64** |
| **Resurgens Orthopedics** | **$18,326.01** |

| | |
|---|---|
| **Benchmark Physical Therapy** | **STBD** |
| **Wellstar Medical Group** | **STBD** |
| **Medical mileage/Prescription Medications** | **STBD** |
| **Future Medical Expenses** | **STBD** |
| **Future Lost Wages** | **STBD** |

| | |
|---|---|
| **MEDICAL EXPENSES:** | **$193,076.68** |
| **LOST WAGES:** | **$19,240.65** |
| **TOTAL:** | **$212,317.33** |

Also, the above-referenced damages are only accounted up to November, 2020 and does not include any treatments in 2021 nor the forthcoming two surgeries, therapy appointments, imaging, medical specials, follow up orthopedist visits, lost wages, and ongoing/future pain and suffering.

We hope to swiftly and amicably negotiate a final settlement with Allied concerning its subrogation interest. Since Georgia law would apply in this case, Allied's recovery is limited. Ms. Smith needs to maximize all the recovery that she can obtain given the catastrophic nature of her case. If you have any questions or would like to further discuss, please do not hesitate to contact me at ____________________ or email at ________________________. Thank you for your time and assistance in advance.

Sincerely,

Attorney at Law

**APPENDIX E**

# LITIGATION

# Basic Complaint Template

*[BARE BONES COMPLAINT TEMPLATE]*

**IN THE STATE COURT OF BIG COUNTY**

**STATE OF GEORGIA**

| | |
|---|---|
| Sam Smith<br>Plaintiff,<br>v.<br>Dev Deangelo,<br>Defendant. | CIVIL ACTION<br>FILE NO.:____________________ |

**JURY TRIAL DEMANDED**

**COMPLAINT**

COMES NOW, __________________, plaintiff, and makes and files this complaint against defendant __________________ as follows:

**PARTIES AND JURISDICTION**

1.

Plaintiff ____________ resides at 111 Village Road, Big City, GA 30111, and is subject to the jurisdiction of this court.

2.

Defendant ________________resides at 3 River Run, Unit R, Atlanta, GA 30333 and may be served with a copy of the summons and complaint at this address.

3.

Jurisdiction and venue are proper in this court.

**BACKGROUND**

4.

- 1 -

On or about January 1, 2014, plaintiff was driving her 2005 white Toyota Camry cautiously in the River Run Apartments located in Big City, GA. Her vehicle was traveling north.

5.

Defendant was traveling behind Ms. Smith in the same direction.

6.

Plaintiff noticed an icy patch on the road ahead and slowed for the hazard.

7.

Defendant was following too close did not slow down, and as a direct result hit Plaintiff from the rear causing property damage and physical injury to the Plaintiff, Noor Mohammed.

**COUNT 1**

**NEGLIGENCE**

8.

Plaintiff realleges and incorporates herein the allegations contained in paragraphs 1 through 7 above as if fully restated.

9.

Defendant was negligent in the following manner:

(a) *following too closely to plaintiff's vehicle*; and

(b) *driving too fast for conditions;*

10.

Defendant was negligent in failing to maintain a safe distance from Plaintiff's vehicle and traveling too fast for the weather conditions.

11.

As a result of defendant's negligence, Plaintiff suffered injuries to lumbar spine and lower back and her wrist. These injuries required medical attention and expenses that the Plaintiff could not afford.

12.

Defendant's negligence is the sole and proximate cause of plaintiff's injuries.

- 2 -

WHEREFORE, plaintiff prays that he/she have a trial on all issues and judgment against defendant as follows:

(a) That plaintiff recover the full value of past and future medical expenses in an amount to be proven at trial;

(b) That plaintiff recover for mental and physical pain and suffering and emotional distress in an amount to be determined by the enlightened conscience of the jury;

(c) That plaintiff recover such other and further relief as is just and proper;

(d) That all issues be tried before a jury.

This ________ day of ________________________, 2014.

**LAW FIRM, LLC.**

By: ______________________
Attorney for Plaintiff...

- 3 -

# Litigation Memo for Cases to Refer to Co-Counsel

**Paisley Law, LLC – CLIENT LITIGATION MEMO**
404.618.0960
james@injuredhelp411.com

| Case type / today's date | |
|---|---|
| REFFERED BY: | |
| CLIENT NAME(S): | |
| DOB: | |
| SSN: | |
| DATE OF LOSS: | |
| SOL Date****** | |
| Venue: | |

Client Information`

| Home Address | |
|---|---|
| Occupation / Employer | |
| Phone Number / Email | |
| Auto Insurance / UM Limits | |
| Medpay | |
| Lost Wages | |
| Type/Area of Injury (Photos?) | |
| Health Insurance Info/ ID# | |
| Medical $pecials | |
| How it Occurred (Photos?) | |
| Property Damage $everity | |
| Resident Relatives for UM | |

Defendant Info

| Name – (Note if Government) | |
|---|---|
| Address/County | |
| Phone Number | |
| Cited? For What? Date of Dispo? | |
| Liability Carrier / Policy No. | |
| Liability Limits: | |
| Aggravating Factors | |
| Last/Highest Offer | |
| Suit Filed? | |

**Treatment Information/Timeline**

| Provider 1 – Bills, notes, etc. | |
|---|---|
| Provider 2 – " | |
| Provider 3 | |
| Provider 4 | |
| Dx/Prognosis/Current Condition | |
| Prior Injuries / Prior Wrecks | |

**Thoughts on the Case** (property damage, impact, objective injuries, client likeability for jury, expectations, heat, etc.)

| Pros | |
|---|---|

**Paisley Law, LLC – CLIENT LITIGATION MEMO**

404.618.0960
james@injuredhelp411.com

| Cons | |
|---|---|

# Pl's 1st Interrogatories and RPD to Def - Template

***[PLAINTIFF'S 1ST INTERROGATORIESAND REQUEST FOR PRODUCTION OF DOCUMENTS – BARE BONES TEMPLATE]***

**IN THE STATE COURT OF BIG COUNTY**
**STATE OF GEORGIA**

| | |
|---|---|
| James Jensen<br>Plaintiff,<br><br>v.<br><br>Beatrice Smith<br><br>Defendant. | CIVIL ACTION<br>FILE NO.: 20SV0000p |

**PLAINTIFF'S FIRST INTERROGATORIES AND REQUEST FOR PRODUCTION OF DOCUMENTS TO DEFENDANT**

TO: Defendant, by and through counsel of record.

Plaintiff, pursuant to O.C.G.A. § 9-11-33 and §9-11-34, submits herewith to the Defendant above named for response within 30 days after service hereof, in the form provided by law, the following interrogatories and request for production of documents.

The within interrogatories and request for production of documents are continuing and require supplemental response upon the discovery of other or further information or documents pertinent thereto.

In answering the following interrogatories, the Defendant is required to give full and complete information based upon the knowledge, information and belief of all agents, employees, investigators, adjusters, attorneys and insurers of said Defendant.

1.

State the name and address of any person, including any party, who, to your knowledge, information or belief:

(a) Was an eyewitness to the incident complained of in this action;

(b) Has some knowledge of any fact or circumstance upon which your defense is based;

(c) Has conducted any investigation relating to the incident complained of or the background, employment, medical history or activities of the Plaintiff.

2.

To your knowledge, information or belief, has any person identified in answering the preceding interrogatory given any statement or report in connection with this action? If so, describe such statement or report and give the name and address of the person having custody and control thereof.

3.

Thirty days after service hereof, you are requested to produce for inspection and copying by the Plaintiff at the offices of *Law, LLC*, all such statements or reports. In lieu thereof, you may attach copies to your answers to these interrogatories.

4.

Please state the current address, employer's name and address, date of birth, Social Security number and driver's license number of the Defendant.

5.

To your knowledge, information or belief, are there any videotapes, photographs, plats or drawings of the scene of the incident referred to in the complaint, the vehicles or the Plaintiff? If so, please describe such videotapes, photographs, plats or drawings and give the name and address of the person having custody and control thereof.

6.

Thirty days after service hereof, you are requested to produce for inspection and copying by the Plaintiff at the offices of *Law, LLC*, all such videotapes, photographs, plats or drawings. In lieu thereof, you may attach copies to your answers to these interrogatories.

7.

Has any entity issued a policy of liability insurance to the Defendant? If so, state the names of all insurers providing liability insurance and give the limits of coverage of each such policy.

8.

Thirty days after service hereof, you are requested to produce for inspection and copying by the Plaintiff at the offices of *Law, LLC*, the policy of insurance identified in response to Interrogatory No. 7. In lieu of this, you may attach copies thereof to your answers to these interrogatories.

9.

Has any insurer referred to above denied coverage or reserved its right to later deny coverage under any such policy of liability insurance? If so, please explain.

10.

Do you contend that the Plaintiff caused or contributed to the incident in question? If so, state with particularity each and every contention made in this regard.

11.

If you intend to call any expert or technician as a witness at the trial of this action, state the subject matter on which he is expected to testify and state in detail the opinions held by each such expert or technician and give a complete summary of the grounds for each opinion held.

12.

Thirty days after service hereof, you are requested to produce for inspection and copying by the Plaintiff at the offices of *Law, LLC*, any videotape, photograph, report, data, memoranda, handwritten notes or other document reviewed by or generated by an individual identified in response to the preceding interrogatory. In lieu of this, you may attach copies thereof to your answers to these interrogatories.

13.

Thirty days after service hereof, you are requested to produce for inspection and copying by the Plaintiff at the offices of *Law, LLC*, any documents obtained through a request for production of documents or subpoena. In lieu of this, you may attach copies thereof to your answers to these interrogatories.

14.

In regard to any document that has not been produced on grounds of privilege, please state the following:

(a) The date each document was generated;

(b) The person generating each document;

(c) The present custodian of each document;

(d) A description of each document.

15.

Thirty days after service hereof, you are requested to produce for inspection and copying by the Plaintiff at the offices of *Law, LLC*, any medical records, videotapes, photographs, or other evidence concerning, referencing or depicting Plaintiff. In lieu of this, you may attach copies thereof to your answers to these interrogatories.

16.

Was the Defendant on the business of any individual or entity at the time of the accident? If so, please identify any such individual or entity including name, address and telephone number.

17.

State the point of origin, destination and reason for the trip being made by the Defendant at the time of the incident referred to in the complaint.

18.

Please identify all automobile accidents and moving violations for the Defendant prior to and subsequent to the incident referred to in the complaint, including the date of the event, the location, the jurisdiction and a description of the event.

19.

Thirty days after service hereof, you are requested to produce for inspection and copying by the Plaintiff at the offices of *Law, LLC*, a copy of the Defendant's driver's license. In lieu of this, you may attach copies thereof to your answers to these interrogatories.

20.

Please identify the cellphone number and service provider for all cellphones owned, used or operated by the Defendant on the date of the incident.

21.

Thirty days after service hereof, you are requested to produce for inspection and copying by the Plaintiff at the offices of *Law, LLC*, copies of cellphone records showing incoming and outgoing calls, texts and messages for the date of the incident. In lieu of this, you may attach copies thereof to your answers to these interrogatories.

22.

If the Defendant has ever been convicted of any crime, please identify the date of the offense, the jurisdiction and a description of the offense.

23.

Please state in detail the factual basis for each defense you have raised in your answer to the complaint.

This 1$^{th}$ day of January, 2021.

________________________

Attorney

# Offer of Settlement Template

***[BARE BONES OFFER OF SETTLEMENT TEMPLATE]***

**IN THE SUPERIOR COURT OF NEW TOWN COUNTY**
**STATE OF GEORGIA**

| | |
|---|---|
| EMILY ELIZABETH<br>Plaintiff,<br>v.<br>DAVID DING,<br>Defendant. | CIVIL ACTION<br>FILE NO.: SUCV20200202020 |

**PLAINTIFF'S OFFER OF SETTLEMENT PURSUANT TO O.C.G.A. § 9-11-68**

**VIA CERTIFIED MAIL, RETURN RECEIPT REQUESTED:**

TO: Attorneys for Defendant.
900 Circle 90 Parkway
Suite 1000
Atlanta, GA 30333

COMES NOW Plaintiff Emily Elizabeth and, pursuant to O.C.G.A. §9-11-68, hereby offers to settle the claims against Defendant David Ding.

1.

The offer to settle is for the payment of **$35,000.00** to the Plaintiff from the Defendant in exchange for the execution of a dismissal of this action **with prejudice** as to all of the Plaintiff's claims against the Defendant.

2.

As a condition to this offer, the Plaintiff is willing to execute a general release of all claims that the Plaintiff raised or which could have been raised in the instant civil action against the Defendant and his insurer(s).

3.

This offer includes amounts for any and all claims asserted by the Plaintiff in this tort action, including medical expenses, past and future loss of earnings, physical and mental pain and suffering, loss of services, society and consortium, emotional distress, and claim for attorneys' fees and/or expenses of litigation, and any future or other damages relating to the Plaintiff's claims against the Defendant and his insurer(s) and any and all claims that were or could have been raised in the instant lawsuit.

4.

The settlement in accordance with this offer is to be in full and final settlement of any and all claims (not limited to tort claims) by the Plaintiff against the Defendant.

5.

This offer of settlement is made solely for the purposes specified in O.C.G.A. §9-11-68 and is not to be construed either as an admission against interest or any limitation on the amount the Plaintiff can recover in this action.

6.

The offer includes zero dollars ($0.00) for punitive damages.

7.

This offer of settlement does not include an additional amount for the Plaintiff's reasonable and necessary costs and attorneys' fees.

8.

In accordance with O.C.G.A. §9-11-68, if this offer of settlement is not accepted by the Defendant within 30 days after service of the offer, the offer shall be deemed withdrawn, and any evidence of this offer will be inadmissible except in any proceeding to recover costs and attorneys' fees.

9.

In accordance with O.C.G.A. §9-11-68, if this offer of settlement is not accepted by the Defendant, and if the final judgment is obtained by the Plaintiff as provided by O.C.G.A. §9-11-68 (B), the Defendant must pay the reasonable attorneys' fees and expenses of litigation incurred by the Plaintiff or on the Plaintiff's behalf as allowed by law.

This 3rd day of September, 2020.

Respectfully submitted,

Attorney at Law

- 2 -

## APPENDIX F

# SETTLEMENT

# Settlement Statement Template

***[This is an actual closing statement with obvious redactions to maintain confidentiality for the client and some of the providers…]***

**CASE CLOSING SETTLEMENT STATEMENT FOR MANDY YYYYYYY**

**Gross Proceeds:** **$225,000.00**

$100,000 – State Farm Liability Payment
$25,000 – GEICO resident relative UIM
$100,000 – Country Financial Excess UIM

**Country Financial Medpay Offset:** **$ (5,000.00)**

**Out of Pocket Medical Expenses:** **$ (73,909.90)**
(see Medical Expense Summary Sheet for a detailed summary)

**Attorney's Fees:** **$ (60,000.00)**
(26.6% reduced from 33.3% per contingency agreement)

**Extraneous Case Expenses:**

| | |
|---|---|
| Postage | ($44.25) |
| Medical Records | ($196.70) |
| Extraneous expenses | ($300.00) |
| TOTAL EXPENSES | **($540.95)** |

------------- Total to Attorneys: **$60,540.95** -------------------------------

**NET TO CLIENT** **($85,549.15)**

I hereby certify that I have read the foregoing and accept the above figures as fair and accurate. I explicitly understand that I am responsible for any unpaid medical bills, or other expenses not listed above which were a result of this incident and were not paid out of the settlement proceeds. This obligation includes bills that are either known or unknown at this time. Likewise, I am responsible for any reimbursement or subrogation that is due to any medical insurance company that paid the medical expenses in this case.

I agree to indemnify and hold the firm of Law, LLC and its attorney harmless from any liability with this incident, including but not limited to, medical bills, medical liens, and any right to subrogation or reimbursement. If there are additional bills that we have not accounted for, Law, LLC will happily negotiate these bills lower, but CLIENT will be responsible for payment from settlement funds disbursed to him.

I understand that if I am currently receiving Supplemental Security Income benefits, Medicaid or any other government assistance, the acceptance of this settlement may affect my future eligibility for such assistance. If I receive Supplemental Security Income, Medicaid or a similar governmental benefit (for example, a benefit that I receive because of disability or low income), I should consult with an attorney who specializes in this area of Trusts regarding how receiving any money from this settlement may affect my entitlement to those benefits. I may be able to establish a Supplemental Needs Trust that could enable me to continue receiving Supplemental Security Income benefits, Medicaid, or other need-based governmental benefits which I may be receiving but may become ineligible for due to the settlement. The law firm of Law, LLC does not specialize in this field but strongly advises me to consult with an attorney who specializes in Trusts to assist me so that I can obtain advice on the benefits of establishing a trust that may help me to continue receiving these benefits.

The law firm of Law, LLC does not practice tax law nor does the firm have an attorney qualified to give tax advice. I should immediately consult with an accountant or tax advisor regarding my settlement proceeds to determine how much, if any, state and/or federal taxes I may own, and whether any tax forms need to be filed as a result of receiving my settlement proceeds.

I also expressly authorize my attorney to dispose of any portion of my file that the Georgia Bar does not require him to maintain. All portions of the file have been made available to me and I have received any and all parts of the file which I desire to keep for my benefit. Furthermore I recognize by acknowledging this statement, the attorney/client relationship has concluded for this case and that Law Firm, LLC no longer represents me.

I HAVE READ AND FULLY UNDERSTAND THE CONTENTS OF THIS CLOSING STATEMENT. MY ATTORNEY HAS PROVIDED A SIGNED COPY OF THIS DOCUMENT TO ME. Furthermore I recognize by acknowledging this statement, the attorney/client relationship has concluded for this case and that Law Firm, LLC no longer represents me

Read and approved the _ day of____________________, 20______.

//SIGNATURES//

SETTLEMENT EXPENSES COVERED ON NEXT PAGE →

Medical Expense Summary

| Provider | Date(s) of Treatment | Total Amount Billed | Out of Pocket Balance Remaining |
|---|---|---|---|
| Piedmont Regional Hospital | 12/14/VV | **$6,049.80** | $6,049.80 – Asked for 60% off via fax 5.8.WW – will hold funds in trust until response is received |
| Georgia Emergency Medicine Specialists | 12/14/VV | **$1,591.00** | $1,591.00 |
| Athens Radiology | 12/14/VV | **$318.00** | $318.00 |
| B. Orthopedics | 12/30/VV to 3/16/WW | **$75,281.97** | $30,000.00 per email 6.1.WW |
| American Health Imaging – c/o Pinnacle Healthcare LLC | 1/15/SS | **$2,225.00** | $1200 via email 5.8.WW |
| E. Sport and Personal Injury Centers (Neurology) – c/o Fortune Funding LLC | 1/8/VV | **$3,100.00** | $1,550.00 per email 5.8.WW |
| Benchmark Physical Therapy | 2/6/WW to 5/5/WW | **$8,002.75** | $3,201.10 per email |
| Omni Healthcare (covering surgery monitoring, Uber, medcard, surgery center) | various | **$63,391.94** | $30,000.00 per email |
| | | **$159,960.46** | **TOTAL: $73,909.90*** |

***53.8% medical expense reduction**

**CASE EXPENSES SUMMARY –**

**Medical Records – $196.70**
ITEMIZED EXPENSES BELOW
American Retrieval – $114.71
Chartswap – $35.88
Benchmark – $46.11

**Postage – $44.25**
ITEMIZED EXPENSES BELOW
$7.80 – Demand – State Farm $6.95 – LOR – Country FinancialDemand – GEICO

$7.80 – Demand – Co. Financial

$6.95 – LOR – GEICO
$6.95 – LOR – State Farm

**CHECK LEDGER SUMMARY – LAW, LLC**

CHECKS RECEIVED

| Received From | Date | Amount | Check No. |
|---|---|---|---|
| State Farm | | $100,000 | 8888 |
| GEICO | | $25,000 | 9999 |
| Country Financial | | $100,000 | 7777 |
| **TOTAL** | | **$225,000** | |

CHECKS DISTRIBUTED

| Written To | Date | Amount | Check No. |
|---|---|---|---|
| [Client] | | | 1111 |
| [Attorneys] | | | 2222 |
| Healthcare Provider A | | | 3333 |
| Healthcare Provider B | | | 4444 |
| Healthcare Provider C | | | 5555 |
| TOTAL | | $225,000* | |

*Distributions equal deposits. This case is balanced. GGG – 1/01/2020

# ACKNOWLEDGMENTS

When I started this personal injury journey years ago, it was a constant pattern of distributing my injury questions to five or six very qualified colleagues. I would spread them around because I didn't want to dry up that well of legal knowledge. I was literally begging for legal answers to whatever complex legal situation I had encountered with a client. I hope this book helps the reader pester their friends less than I had to.

This book began with a couple blogs I wrote explaining what I do for people. That evolved into a training manual for when I hired new employees that were new to personal injury. Then I heard Michael Mogill at Crisp Video talking about writing his book and how it forced him to dig so much deeper into what he does. In March, 2020 a pandemic hit all of us, and nobody was driving or getting injured. In coping with the silence of my phone not ringing, I ruminated on the idea of what if there was a playbook that spelled out the basics of everything a lawyer needs to know to get started in injury law. I was inspired to write and keep writing until this whole thing started to make sense.

Michael Goldberg and Joe Fried always inspire me with their generosity and gifts of legal expertise expecting nothing in return. I've done my best in this book to pay it forward. I tailored many of their forms and included them in this book. I've worked trucking cases with them, and cannot express enough gratitude towards their remarkable dedication to the craft.

Each lawyer that's active in GTLA at the seminars, CLE's, and the listserv has been a wealth of knowledge. Thank you to Tony Kalka and Bryan Baer for bringing me into this rabbit hole and always being a great resource. Jason Ferguson was my first and last law partner that I learned 80 percent of all this from and he somehow became like family to me. Alan Hamilton, Mike Neff, and all the other heavy hitters that always pick up the phone when I called - I look forward to working another case with you again soon.

A special thanks to my wife, Katie, who always supports whatever project I'm up to next. I will never be able to show enough appreciation towards her.

Justin Spizman is one of the hardest working, and most generous people I've ever met. A jack of all trades, he helped me to bring this book to life.

Alex Martinez wrote this with me, and I cannot thank him enough for his efforts and dedication. He loves our clients like family and always gives them 100 percent.

To all the other lawyers I have worked with over the years – you know who you are and I thank you. Most of all though, I'd like to thank my clients that trusted me after one second changed their life. Thank you for allowing me to play a small part in your recovery.

## ABOUT THE AUTHORS

**Jim Paisley** is a metro-Atlanta native from Marietta, Georgia. After studying Management at Georgia Tech and graduating with high honors, he briefly worked for the investment bank, INVESCO. Quickly realizing the stiffness and inauthenticity of corporate America, Jim decided it was time to get that law degree so he could realize his dream of providing people real-life benefits while getting to know them personally. Jim Paisley has a diverse experience in the law. Before finishing law school, he clerked for a public interest law firm that provided free representation of domestic violence victims that needed a legal strategy to escape their abusive partners. After finishing law school at Florida State University, Jim became a public defender and then a prosecutor in Orlando and Kissimmee, Florida. In 2010, Jim Paisley moved back up to Atlanta with his wife Katie to be closer to home and start a family. Today they have three children, James, Anna, and Jillian. After getting bored with the idea of working for someone else, Jim started Paisley Law, L.L.C. on April 1, 2010. Since then he takes immense pride that he has privilege of representing personal injury and wrongful death victims due to the negligence of others.

**Raphael "Alex" Martinez** grew up in rough areas of Los Angeles. He is a first generation American after his parents fled political instability in El Salvador. His older brother was going down the wrong path in L.A. and his parents started over again moving to metro-Atlanta in the late 90's. Alex has been the office manager and paralegal for Paisley Law, L.L.C since starting in 2013. He is now a top law student at Georgia State University. Alex personally wrote three chapters in this book. Alex has a great legal mind and I foresee a long and successful career in the law for him.